THE RESPONSE OF
THE ROYAL ARMY
TO THE FRENCH REVOLUTION

THE RESPONSE OF THE ROYAL ARMY TO THE FRENCH REVOLUTION

The Role and Development of the Line Army 1787–93

BY

SAMUEL F. SCOTT

1978

CLARENDON PRESS · OXFORD

Oxford University Press, Walton Street, Oxford, OX2 6DP

OXFORD LONDON GLASGOW NEW YORK
TORONTO MELBOURNE WELLINGTON CAPE TOWN
IBADAN NAIROBI DAR ES SALAAM LUSAKA
KUALA LUMPUR SINGAPORE JAKARTA HONG KONG TOKYO
DELHI BOMBAY CALCUTTA MADRAS KARACHI

© *Oxford University Press 1978*

British Library Cataloguing in Publication Data

Scott, Samuel F
    The response of the Royal Army to the French
Revolution
    1. France. Armée. – History 2. France – History –
Louis XVI, 1774–1793 3. France – Politics and
government – 1774–1793
    I. Title
    944.04   DC136.5   77–30117
    ISBN 0–19–822534–2

Printed in Great Britain by
William Clowes & Sons Ltd, London Beccles and Colchester

PREFACE

THIS STUDY developed out of an interest in the army as a social institution, and began with research on the changes in the composition of the Royal Army during the French Revolution. Early research brought to light a number of facts which had important implications for the development of the Revolution itself. For example, there was a disproportionately large number of soldiers from urban origins, especially among sergeants; a majority of the troops had been artisans before their enlistment; and excessive desertion rates coincided with political crises. Clearly, these factors might be closely related to the fact that the Revolution was to a large extent an urban phenomenon in which the artisan class played a very important part.

Other facts confirmed these early suspicions. Barricades, which had traditionally been a defence against repression and which were to be a hallmark of nineteenth-century revolutionary movements in France, were of little or no consequence in the Great Revolution of 1789. This implied a lack of concern for defence against the forces of repression, and in the eighteenth century necessarily implied that the army was not greatly feared. The attack on the Bastille, rightly considered as the beginning of the Revolution, was conducted, at least in its technical aspects, by professional soldiers. Thus, it became clear that not only had the Revolution drastically affected the army, but also that the army had had a very important part in the Revolution.

In order to accomplish the necessary research for this study, the assistance of a number of institutions and individuals was required; and these deserve recognition not only as a matter of courtesy, but also as a matter of justice. It is highly unlikely that this work could have been achieved without the financial and intellectual support of the Social Science Research Council. This organization, through the efforts of Rowland L. Mitchell, Jr. and Elbridge Sibley, provided me with the necessary preparation for this research under the auspices of a Research-Training Fellowship, and later continued their encouragement by means of a Faculty Research Grant. Wayne State University has generously given me a Research Grant-in-Aid and a

Faculty Research Award. And the American Philosophical Society, particularly George W. Corner, its Executive Officer, displayed an admirable patience towards a troublesome applicant and grantee.

French archival personnel have proven to me—and undoubtedly countless other scholars—the importance of the archivist's profession. The major portion of the research for this book was carried out at the Archives de la Guerre at Vincennes. M. Jean-Claude Devos and his entire staff have been not only helpful but also kind, despite the excessive burden which they have in this extraordinarily valuable repository. Although my contact with the staffs of the Archives nationales and Bibliothèque nationale was less personal, they were no less helpful. And the pleasant conditions of work provided by the personnel at the Archives départementales of the Bouches-du-Rhône, Isère, Bas-Rhin, Moselle, and Nord were enough to convince anyone to expend his efforts in local history.

Of the many people who helped me at various stages of this work, some deserve my special thanks. Donna Monacelli, Kathleen Taylor, Patrice Zemenick, Denise Di Mambro, and Kristen Juipe have all helped with the tiresome, essential task of typing and re-typing, without losing patience. Randolph Hennes, Charles Wrong, William Baldwin, and John Lynn have given me their own expert advice about different aspects of this study. My colleagues at Wayne State University, Christopher Johnson, Mel Small, and William Brazill have provided more general assistance and encouragement, as have Henry Hill, Morris Janowitz, and Gilbert Shapiro. John Shy, David Bien, André Corvisier, Albert Soboul, and the late Marcel Reinhard have shown interest and given suggestions when these were most needed. I shall never be able to determine how much of this work is mine and how much belongs to Jean-Paul Bertaud; along with his great help, he has shown me the meaning of *fraternité*. None of these people bear responsibility of this study; all of them have contributed to the results.

With the triteness that accompanies most verities, I do indeed owe most to my family. I only hope that they, especially my wife Denise, are not disappointed.

CONTENTS

INTRODUCTION

THE AIM of the following study is to describe and analyse the reaction of the line army in France to the revolutionary crisis of 1789–
93. It focuses upon the two essential aspects: on the army as a
peculiar institution that was deeply affected by the French Revolution, and the army in its relations to the larger society of which it
was a part and in which it assumed an influential role during an
especially critical time. Throughout this investigation the primary
emphasis will be upon unofficial developments and personal relations
both within the army and between soldiers and civilians. Although
they cannot be ignored, official policies and formalized relationships
often provide erroneous descriptions of historical reality, particularly during a period of political and social instability.

The first focus, which might best be summarized as the effects of
the Revolution upon the army, has been dealt with in previous
works. These have, however, largely neglected developments within
the regular army after 1789 and have devoted most of their attention
to the new armed forces, the levies of 'national volunteers', which
arose from the dual crisis of revolution and foreign war. When historians have dealt with the line army, their treatment has usually
been based upon preconceptions and inadequate research. One
example of this is the nearly complete ignorance of the remarkable
recovery that occurred in the line army in 1791 and 1792. Consequently, this book deals entirely with the regular army during the
early Revolution and uses information about the volunteers, available in scores of local and a few general studies, only for purposes
of comparison. Similarly, there is little discussion of the royal household troops, which, except for the two regiments of French and
Swiss Guards, had become exclusively ceremonial units by the late
eighteenth century. Finally, the militia, which was called upon only
during wartime and had last performed even limited active service
during the American War of Independence, did not form part of the
regular military establishment and will not be treated.

In order to evaluate the impact of the Revolution upon the army,
it has been necessary to compare that institution and its personnel
between two different dates. The years 1787–9 have been selected as a

basis for the comparisons used in this study. By then the reforms
initiated after the disaster of the Seven Years War had been implemented, and the new army was only beginning to be affected by the
events that led to revolution. The terminal date was pre-selected by
the development of the Revolution itself. In February 1793 the
National Convention decreed the amalgamation of the line army
with the units of volunteers summoned to active service since 1791.
Although the implementation of this policy took months and even
years, the official existence of the line army had come to an end and,
perhaps even more importantly, the line army had lost the distinctive
features which identified it as a separate, independent institution.

The second focus of this study is, in brief, the role of the line
army in the French Revolution. Few propositions enjoy such general
acceptance as the one that armed forces play a critical role in
revolutionary situations. Contemporary observations, subsequent
histories, and theoretical analyses of revolutions have made this a
truism. Despite the impressive consensus on the importance of this
phenomenon, however, historians—even those who recognize its
significance in general terms—have not devoted any substantial
research to this subject. Admittedly, it is difficult and sometimes
impossible to uncover other than circumstantial evidence about
the behaviour of armed forces in revolutionary situations. This is
especially true when one attempts to study the reaction of common
soldiers who are as anonymous as the mass of their civilian counterparts. Nevertheless, in the light of the crucial importance of the
army's reactions, a serious, well-substantiated investigation of the
military response to revolution will provide insight into the reasons
for the success (or failure) of the revolution, as well as into the
functioning of the very important social institution of the standing
army. It is the intention of this study to do this for the Royal Army
during the French Revolution.

The two main themes of this work are, in fact, separate and distinct only in a logical sense. One of the distinctive traits of the
modern state has been the monopolization of organized armed forces
by the government. In the event of widespread violent activity
against the established regime the army constitutes the ultimate
defence of the government and a hostile, or even neutral, reaction
on its part can turn revolt into revolution. At the same time, the
army, as a social institution, reflects and is affected by the society of
which it is an integral part. Hence, while the attitude of the armed

forces is decisive in a revolution, the revolution itself deeply influences the army's reactions.

In order to determine the response of the line army to the Revolution—both its influence upon the Revolution and the effects of the Revolution upon it—a broad investigation of the personnel who composed the army was made, including their civilian and military background, their relations among themselves, and their relationships with civilians. The nature of this study and the surviving documents both required an examination of general characteristics of large groups of military men. In all, for various purposes of this study the records of more than 20,000 individuals were investigated: almost 2,300 enlisted men for a general description of soldiers in 1789, over 2,800 for the same information in 1793, more than 5,000 troops for data on social origins, nearly 2,500 officers for a profile of the officer corps in 1793, over 6,500 soldiers involved in the crises of July and October 1789, more than 800 enlisted men promoted to officer, and approximately 100 nobles serving in the ranks. In addition, the inspection reports for scores of units containing thousands of men, the records of hundreds of courts martial, and accounts of scores of incidents of insubordination and police action by line troops contributed to the results of this study. Often, only limited information was obtained, e.g. the birthplace, age, rank, and length of service of the personnel involved or a brief description of an incident in which regular troops were employed to maintain order. From the mass of data collected, however, one can construct general but accurate descriptions of the personnel of the line army, how they functioned as members of this institution and as members of the larger society, how—and even to some degree, why—they reacted to the Revolution as they did, and the impact that the Revolution had upon them both as soldiers and as citizens. To my knowledge, no comparable study of an army involved in a major revolution has ever been made.

An obvious result of this approach is the prevalence of statistical evidence in the following text. Rather than interrupt the narrative or insert long notes, I have included a description of the bases for and uses of these statistics in Appendix I.

It is hoped that one result of this work will be to present a more complete and better substantiated view of the development of the French Revolution and, at the same time, some suggestions about the processes of revolutions in general.

CHAPTER I

THE FRENCH ARMY ON THE
EVE OF REVOLUTION

By THE late 1780s the French line army was on the verge of the most radical transformation in its history. The coming revolution would fundamentally alter its character within only a few years; but, unlike most institutions of the Old Regime, the Royal Army would also play a crucial role in affecting the outcome of the Revolution. The monarchy proved itself incapable of coping with the unprecedented challenge to its authority and a major factor in this failure was the collapse of discipline within the army. The insubordination of the soldiers towards their superiors—an insubordination for which officers had given the first example—deprived the government of its ability to enforce its will and forced it to accommodate the demands of the revolutionaries.

In order to explain how and why the army reacted to the Revolution as it did, it is necessary to analyse its composition, structure, and operation. The composition of the enlisted ranks will receive the first and most extensive treatment. Almost nothing is known of the anonymous soldiers who made up this force; most historians have concentrated on the officers, on military organization, or on government policy. Yet, during a period of revolution when traditional relationships are called into question, it is often the soldiers who determine its success or failure. Certainly, this was the case in 1789. The officers, who will be treated next, also occupied a critical position; they were intermediaries between the state and its troops. Unhappily for the monarchy, the officer corps by 1789 was divided into rival and hostile groups, many of whom blamed the monarchy for their frustrations. The government of Louis XVI, which inherited so many of its problems from its predecessor, had fallen heir to an uncompleted programme of military reform that had left most officers dissatisfied. As will be described in the third section, the King failed both to carry these reforms to their logical conclusion and to heal existing antagonisms between different groups of officers. Finally, the conditions of army life and the relationships of the soldiers will be examined. Most significant among these were the development of a cohesive society among the enlisted men, which was alien, if not hostile, to the officers, and extensive contacts between soldiers and civilians of similar background.

The combination of these elements boded ill for a regime that would soon be forced to rely upon armed force as the ultimate sanction to maintain the established order.

PROFILE OF THE TROOPS IN 1789

Despite the crucial importance of its reaction to the Revolution, the Royal Army of this period and, above all, its enlisted men have never been adequately studied. The primary reason for this neglect is the paucity of information on the men in the ranks of the French army (and indeed of all armies) in the eighteenth century.[1] This deficiency has not, however, prevented some historians from making gross generalizations about the subject. Almost alone, André Corvisier has provided a general but accurate view of French soldiers in the early eighteenth century by his extensive quantitative data on many of their characteristics.[2] The soldiers themselves, largely illiterate and totally incapable of conceiving of themselves as historical figures, have left little trace as individuals. Yet, it still remains possible, by following Corvisier's example, to describe in general terms the composition of the troops on the eve of the Revolution.[3]

The enlisted men of the line army in 1789 totalled approximately 156,000, over 8,000 less than its authorized strength.[4] The line

---

[1] David Ogg has remarked that the soldiers of eighteenth-century Europe are almost entirely unknown to historians; see *Europe of the Ancien Régime, 1715–1783* (New York, 1965), p. 160. The researches of John Shy on the British army in colonial America and of Lee Kennett on the French army in the Seven Years War confirm the view that the common soldier of the eighteenth century can be only very slightly known, and then only through his officers. See *Toward Lexington: The Role of the British Army in the Coming of the American Revolution* (Princeton, N.J., 1965), pp. 358–9 and *The French Armies in the Seven Years War: A Study in Military Organization and Administration* (Durham, N.C., 1967), p. 86.

[2] André Corvisier, *L'Armée française de la fin du XVIIᵉ siècle au ministère de Choiseul: Le Soldat*, 2 vols. (Paris, 1964). My own research owes a great deal to the example and guidance of M. Corvisier.

[3] A discussion of the sources and methods employed to determine the composition of the line army can be found in Appendix I; see the sections on 'Changes in Strength' and 'Background of the Soldiers'.

[4] This excludes the royal household units that comprised *c.* 7,200 men; the majority of these troops were in the two élite regiments of French and Swiss Guards which numbered approximately 3,600 and 2,300 men respectively. The militia, colonial troops, coast guards, and maréchaussée (a semi-military police force which operated in the countryside) are likewise excluded.

infantry included 79 French regiments, 11 Swiss, 8 German, 3 Irish, and a Liégeois regiment. On paper these units comprised over 116,000 men; in fact the line infantry was 4,000–5,000 men short of this number. Twelve light infantry battalions, formed in 1788, were 400–500 men short of their total complement of 5,000 enlisted men. The cavalry had been reorganized in 1788 into sixty-two regiments: two of carabiniers, twenty-four heavy cavalry regiments, eighteen of dragoons, twelve of chasseurs, and six of hussars. In 1789 this branch was at its authorized strength of approximately 33,000 men. The artillery was the most seriously understrength of the major branches. Although authorized almost 10,000 men in seven line regiments, artillery units mustered only *c.* 6,600 men.

The soldiers were recruited for eight years by voluntary enlistments, and received a bonus for each engagement. Since 1763, when recruitment had become a royal prerogative, each regiment regularly sent out a small number of sergeants and one or two officers, usually ex-rankers, to perform recruitment duties. In addition, following his 'semester' leave (an authorized, paid absence of seven and a half months due to officers every two years), each officer was expected to return to his regiment with at least two suitable recruits.[1] Civilian free enterprise also occupied an important place in recruitment; professional recruiters, *racoleurs*, were paid a bounty for each recruit they supplied. The bounty depended upon the need for recruits and their availability. The physical condition, particularly the height, and age of the recruit also affected the enlistment bonus paid. Although some recruiting went on continuously, the season of the most intense activity was between October and March.[2]

To induce enlistments in the line army, wine and false promises about pay, army food, advancement, the glories of military life, and the magnificence of the uniform were used freely. When all else failed, recruiters were not adverse to the use of force. Occasionally such fraud or violence was punished by officials, but hardly enough to curb the employment of these means.[3]

---

[1] The personnel and some of the practices used in recruitment can be determined by an investigation of the Archives de la Guerre (A.G.), X^b 13–106.

[2] One of the best accounts of recruitment under the Old Regime can be found in Corvisier, *L'Armée française*, I. 167–89 and 281–341.

[3] All authors appear to be in agreement about these methods of recruitment. Besides Corvisier, see Albert Babeau, *La Vie militaire sous l'ancien régime*, vol. I: *Les Soldats* (Paris, 1889), pp. 55–6; Richard Cobb, *The Police and the People: French Popular Protest, 1789–1820* (Oxford, 1970), p. 249; Jeffry Kaplow, *The Names of Kings: The Parisian Laboring Poor in the Eighteenth Century* (New York, 1972), pp. 102–3; and

However, for certain groups in French society the army could offer some real attractions. Potential social advancement lay in the possibility of becoming a non-commissioned officer, or even an officer. Escape from a dull village life or family restraints could provide sufficient motivation for some. Others might find haven in the *camaraderie* of the regiment. Nor can patriotism be neglected as a factor in some cases. Economic motivation was also undoubtedly very important to many recruits. Although, as indicated above, the market fluctuated according to the demand, some idea of the value of the enlistment bonus might be gained from the official bonuses: up to 100 *livres* in the infantry (depending on the regiment) and between 111 and 132 *livres* in the cavalry.[1] Sometimes, too, enlistment in the army was offered as an alternative to imprisonment to vagabonds, debtors, and criminals. The army could offer to many the way out of an intolerable situation, and to some the hope of fulfilling desires which would be doomed to frustration in civil society.

For the purposes of this study the results of recruitment are more important than the methods employed. What kind of men filled the ranks of the line army on the eve of the revolutionary upheaval which brought an end to the Old Regime?

The soldiers of the line army in 1789 were generally young men.[2] Excluding the N.C.O.s whose rank partly depended on length of service and age, almost exactly half of the soldiers were between the ages of 18 and 25; and another 5 per cent were younger than 18. 90 per cent of the soldiers in all the branches together were 35 years

Édouard Desbrière and Maurice Sautai, *La Cavalerie de 1740 à 1789* (Paris, 1906), p. 109.

[1] Charles-Louis Chassin, *L'Armée et la Révolution* (Paris, 1867), p. 18 and Desbrière and Sautai, *La Cavalerie, 1740–1789*, p. 109.

[2] The basis of these data is explained in Appendix I. Corvisier found a similar age structure in 1763: *c.* 45% of the soldiers were 25 or younger, and another 40% were between 25 and 35 (*L'Armée française*, II. 624–6). All information about the composition of the eleven Swiss regiments is based on data for 5,722 men in six regiments which can be found in inspection reports in A.G., Xᵍ 87–92. The inspection reports of 1788 and 1789 for the non-Swiss infantry and light infantry units as well as for the cavalry regiments show no major discrepancies from the proportions established by our sample, except that they indicate a somewhat higher proportion (7–10% higher) of men with less than four years' experience. This, however, is probably due to the fact that the categories in the reports overlap. All subsequent references to these inspection reports, unless otherwise indicated, are based on the reports in A.G., Xᵇ 14, 21, 22, 25, 26, 28, 29, 31, 33, 46, 49, 51, 62, 73, 74, 76, 81, and 103 for more than 19,800 men in eighteen infantry regiments; Xᵇ 124 for 1,769 men in five light infantry battalions; and Xᶜ 31, 33, 34, 40, 42, 45, 47, 50, 53, 64, 72, 76, 78, 79, 81, and 83 for more than 9,500 men in nineteen mounted regiments. No comparable data were available in A.G., Xᵈ for the artillery.

old or less. The youngest soldiers, those 15 years of age or under, who constituted less than 1 per cent of the total, were almost without exception *enfants de troupe*. These were the sons of soldiers or officers admitted to half pay from the age of six on; they usually served as drummer-boys until the age of 16 when they could enlist as ordinary soldiers.

Even the non-commissioned officers were comparatively young men. Except in the artillery, where N.C.O.s tended to be older, almost three-quarters of the corporals and more than half of the sergeants were 35 years old or younger. Less than 7 per cent of the N.C.O.s sampled were older than 50.

On the eve of the Revolution, therefore, the men in the ranks of the line army and their immediate superiors were young adults. Presumably, in light of their age and trade, they were reasonably vigorous. They were precisely the kind of men most able and most likely to be active in a revolutionary situation. What direction this activity would take, however, depended on other elements in their backgrounds.

Length of service in the army is the most simple, if not the most reliable, criterion for the professionalism of the soldiers of the line army in 1789. It is a measure of exposure to military principles and discipline, particularly for the majority of men who had enlisted as adolescents or young men. Also, it may be something of a measure of acceptance of military life, since possible alternatives existed, such as desertion or the purchase of a discharge. More than 60 per cent of the line troops in 1789 had served four years or longer in the army. Approximately one-fifth of the soldiers had ten years or more of military service. On the other hand, about one-eighth of the troops were recent recruits who had served less than one year. The lowest percentage of soldiers with four years' or more service was in the light infantry, an arm which had been separated from the cavalry the previous year and was still in the process of being organized and brought up to full strength.

Promotions normally required rather lengthy service, and fewer than 3 per cent of the N.C.O.s had less than four years of service. Corporals fell into three general categories: a minority of apparently talented soldiers who were promoted after four to six years' service; soldiers who followed a more common career pattern and were promoted around the time of the completion of their first-eight-year enlistment (sometimes as an inducement to re-enlist); and soldiers with long service, over ten years, who were promoted primarily on this basis. The cavalry and, especially, the artillery showed a greater reluctance to promote men with only a few years' experience than did the infantry. The more complicated skills required in these two branches, particularly the artillery, were undoubtedly the reasons for this. Generally, longer service was required for promotion to sergeant. It is, however, more difficult to establish neat career patterns for men of this rank. This is probably due to the importance of a less tangible element which does not appear in the records, namely ability; for it appears that talent, including both technical skill and general education, determined promotions to sergeant.[1]

Besides rather long service, a significant minority of the troops, between one-eighth and one-seventh of them, had combat experience. Because the most recent wars of France had been overseas expeditions, e.g. the War of American Independence and the suppression of rebellions in Corsica, there was a higher proportion of combat veterans in the infantry, about 15 per cent, than in the cavalry, about 5 per cent.[2]

The line army in 1789 might, then, be described as follows. A majority of the soldiers had enlisted in the army in their late teens and early twenties and had four years or more of military experience at the outbreak of the Revolution. A substantial core of veterans with combat service and a cadre of experienced N.C.O.s, mostly between 30 and 40 years old, provided the training and instruction, as well as leadership, for this majority and their less experienced comrades. Such an army one can readily call professional in a commonly accepted, if not very sophisticated, sense of the term.

As had been the case throughout the eighteenth century, the frontier provinces of the north and east, Flandre and Artois, Picardie, Champagne, Lorraine, Alsace, and Franche-Comté, continued to provide a disproportionately high number of men to the line army.[3] In 1789 these provinces contained approximately one-

---

[1] Lafayette claimed that in the late 1780s the N.C.O.s of the French army were superior to any in Europe. See Marquis de Lafayette, *Mémoires, correspondance et manuscrits du Général Lafayette, publiés par sa famille*, vol. I (Brussels, 1837), pp. 433-4. Although this may represent a biased view, the subsequent careers of hundreds of former N.C.O.s of the royal army indicate considerable military skill, despite an inability to grasp strategy. See, for example, Georges Six, *Les Généraux de la Révolution et de l'Empire* (Paris, 1947), pp. 49 and 53-6.

[2] Because information on combat experience was noted only sporadically in the troop registers, the source of these data is the inspection reports in A.G., X^b, X^c, and X^g.

[3] See Corvisier, *L'Armée française*, I. 427-9 and 439-41. The criterion used in this

fifth of the total population of France; yet about one-third of the infantry (except for the Swiss), one-half of the cavalry, and nearly three-quarters of the artillery were composed of men from these regions.[1] Some individual examples are even more extraordinary. Alsace, which contained about $2\frac{1}{2}$ per cent of the population of France, contributed more than 8 per cent of the men in the line army. Franche-Comté, with less than 3 per cent of the total population, contributed $3\frac{1}{2}$ per cent of the infantry and cavalry and nearly a quarter of the artillerymen. The populous provinces immediately to the rear of these frontier regions, Normandie, Île-de-France, and Bourgogne, also provided a large number of soldiers, although their contributions were less remarkable than those of the provinces on France's most dangerous frontiers.

This preponderance of soldiers from the north and east of France was due to a number of factors. Political geography and the mentality of a march people can provide useful suggestions as to why people in frontier regions are conscripted or enlist in the army.[2] Without doubt, the generally good communications in these provinces facilitated recruitment. However, the most elementary factor appears to be the most significant: most of the garrisons of the French army were in the north and east. There is, in fact, a correlation between the garrison-strength of a particular branch of the army in a certain region, and the proportion of natives of the region in that branch.

present study for regional origins was birthplace. Place of residence was rarely recorded in the troop registers. The standard used in the inspection reports was presumably the same, although this is not specifically indicated. In any case, domicile is difficult to determine since the duration of residence is an important factor which is never indicated. Furthermore, in c. 2,800 instances where both place of birth and domicile were indicated the region was the same in 80% of the cases. It should also be pointed out that, except coincidentally, the provincial names of the regiments (e.g. Provence, Normandie, Languedoc) bear no relationship to the regional origins of the men in them.

The estimates of the population of the provinces are based on Marcel Reinhard, *Étude de la population pendant la Révolution et l'Empire* (Gap, 1961), pp. 26–8. For this study, the departments have been converted into provincial designations.

[1] Discrepancies between the percentages in the sample used and in the inspection reports are comparatively minor, except in the case of the light infantry. The reports tend to increase the proportion of men from the frontier provinces. For example, where the sample indicates 33% of the line infantrymen were from the frontier provinces, the inspection reports indicate 38%. Inspection reports for the light infantry indicate almost 45% of the troops were from frontier regions; however, this is because the reports for two of the twelve battalions, the Royaux-Corses and Corses Light Infantry, both of which were recruited primarily from Corsica, Italy, and southern France, were unavailable. Hence, these groups are grossly under-represented.

[2] Corvisier in his explanation for the preponderance of soldiers from the north and east emphasizes the role of political geography: see *L'Armée française*, I. 439.

Half of the French infantry was garrisoned in the north and east, and one-third of the men in this branch came from these areas; three-quarters of the cavalry were stationed here, and over half the men were natives; six of seven artillery regiments were quartered in frontier provinces, and three quarters of the artillerymen came from the same regions. Clearly, many of the regimental recruiters found their task facilitated by recruiting in the areas near their garrisons among a population accustomed to military men and manners.

In contrast, regions of western and southern France provided fewer soldiers than their population warranted. The scarcity of garrisons, even along the Spanish frontier, together with the isolation imposed by poor communications helps to explain why comparatively few recruits came from these regions. Furthermore, provinces such as Bretagne, Poitou, Aunis, and Saintonge sent many of their young men into maritime service and so furnished fewer soldiers than might otherwise be expected. A strong traditional prejudice against military service was also a deterrent to successful recruitment in these areas, especially in the West.[1] Finally, a factor which limited the number of soldiers from southern France, or the Midi, was the height requirements in the army.

Height was an important consideration in the Royal Army. Tall recruits enhanced the prestige of a regiment and its colonel, and could command a higher enlistment bonus. Height was also the most common measure of strength and physical fitness. There were minimum height requirements in each branch and more demanding requirements for entry into élite companies, such as the grenadiers. In the infantry the minimum height requirement was 5 feet 6 inches (5 *pieds* 2 *pouces*); however, almost one-fifth of the men in the non-Swiss regiments were shorter than this, apparently because not enough recruits of the required height enlisted in the infantry.[2] Of the Swiss soldiers, whose conditions of employment were rigorously controlled by international agreements, less than 12 per cent were shorter than 5 feet 6 inches. The light infantry battalions contained

---

[1] See Joseph Dehergne, *Le Bas-Poitou à la veille de la Révolution* (Paris, 1963), pp. 179–80 and Jean-Paul Bertaud, 'Aperçus sur l'insoumission et la désertion à l'époque révolutionnaire: Étude de sources', *Bulletin d'histoire économique et sociale de la Révolution française: Année 1969* (Paris, 1970), p. 31.

[2] The discrepancies between the data on height in the sample and those in the inspection reports were negligible, usually 1% or 2% and never more than 5%. As with the other characteristics of the soldiers, the sole source on the Swiss was the inspection reports, and the only source for the artillery was the sample drawn from the registers.

the largest proportion, approximately a quarter, of men shorter than the official minimum.

In the cavalry and artillery the minimum height demanded was 5 feet 8 inches. Nearly two-thirds of the men in the cavalry met or exceeded this height; but shorter men were often accepted, especially in light cavalry regiments. Only a very few cavalrymen, 2–4 per cent of the branch's total strength, were shorter than 5 feet 6 inches, and these were either young recruits or specialists, such as saddlers, spur-makers, etc. The artillery contained the largest proportion of tall men in the line army; four-fifths of the men in this branch were 5 feet 8 inches or taller. The strenuous work required in the artillery, hauling heavy cannon, cutting trees, and building defensive works, necessitated big, robust soldiers.[1]

As we have seen, the shorter average height of southerners helps to explain why far fewer soldiers came from the Midi[2] than its population warranted. Southerners in the army served mostly in the infantry which had the least stringent height requirements. Conversely, the taller natives of northern and eastern France constituted a disproportionately high percentage of troops, especially in the cavalry and artillery.

In 1789 there were fewer foreign soldiers than one would expect in view of the high proportion of foreign regiments. Of ninety-one non-Swiss regiments in the line infantry, twelve were foreign regiments; yet less than 8 per cent of the men in these ninety-one regiments were in fact foreigners. In the eight German regiments nearly half of the soldiers were from Lorraine and, especially, Alsace. Most of the rest of the soldiers were from the galaxy of German states which were neighbours of France, although a few were from the Swiss cantons. The three Irish regiments were more thoroughly foreign, about three-quarters of their personnel being foreign born. Many of the soldiers in these regiments were also Germans; but the majority of the foreigners came from the Low Countries, and a small number were from the British Isles. The French subjects in the Irish regiments were from north-western

---

[1] For some of the duties of artillerymen and the type of men required for them, see Antoine-Augustin-Flavien Pion des Loches, *Mes campagnes, 1792–1815* (Paris, 1889), pp. 25–6. Pion des Loches served in the 5th Artillery Regiment from 1793.

[2] As with the provinces of the Old Regime, it is impossible to define the limits of the Midi precisely. As used here, it refers to that area of France south of a line drawn from the mouth of the Gironde to Savoy, but including all of Limousin, Auvergne, and Lyonnais.

France, particularly Flandre. About one-third of the foreigners in the line infantry were serving in French regiments.

The Swiss regiments had maintained the most exclusively foreign composition. Of all the units of the royal army, they were the most strictly controlled according to the *capitulations* between the King of France and the various cantons, and they enjoyed the greatest autonomy of all the regiments in the line army. About three-quarters of the soldiers in these regiments were Swiss and the rest of the men, except for two or three hundred French subjects spread through eleven regiments, were non-Swiss foreigners.

The proportion of foreigners in the light infantry was comparable to that in the line infantry (including the Swiss regiments), about one-seventh. The national origins of the foreigners in this arm were, however, quite different. Most of the foreigners in the light infantry were from the various Italian states, primarily in the northern half of the peninsula, and they were concentrated in two battalions, the Chasseurs Royaux-Corses and the Chasseurs Corses. Germans were much less numerous than in the line regiments; and there were a few Spaniards and Swiss. Although technically French, the Corsicans, who constituted about the same proportion of light infantrymen as did foreigners, were in the same two battalions as most of the Italian soldiers, and these units used Italian as the language of command.

Approximately 3 per cent of the men in cavalry regiments were foreigners, mostly Germans. Although there were some foreigners in almost every regiment of mounted troops, they were most common in certain foreign regiments, such as the Royal Allemand Cavalry, and, above all, in the hussar regiments where they constituted about 6 per cent of the troops. Even in the foreign regiments the vast majority of the soldiers were Alsacians and Lorrainers, whose native, and probably only language was German, the language of command in such units.

Of all the branches, the artillery had the lowest proportion of foreigners. Although the branch as a whole was short of approximately one-third of its authorized strength—and was to remain so until the outbreak of war in 1792—there had been no major recruitment movement which might have brought more foreigners into this branch. The French artillery, which enjoyed the reputation of being the best in Europe, remained very stable in strength in the years immediately preceding the Revolution, and seemed content to draw most of its recruits from the frontier provinces of northern and north-eastern France.[1]

More difficult than identifying the regional origins of the men of the line army is the problem of determining whether the soldiers came from a rural or an urban background. To begin with, eighteenth-century population statistics are not always reliable.[2] In addition, the definition of a city or town (*ville*) in eighteenth-century France included many traditional notions, such as juridical status, administrative role, economic activity, and even cultural significance.[3] For the purposes of this study, however, the only practical standard was population level. As a measure of urban, a population of 2,000 inhabitants, which was the most common contemporary norm, will be used.[4] Likewise the basic source used here for population figures, despite some inaccuracies, will be a contemporary document, *États de Population*, which was drawn up for establishing representation in the Estates General of 1789.[5]

Using this source and assuming a population of approximately 26 million inhabitants for France in 1789, one arrives at the following proportions of urban dwellers in the population. About 19 per cent of the French population lived in communities of 2,000 or more inhabitants.[6] More than half of these, approximately 10 per cent, were from cities of 10,000 or more; 4 per cent of the total population lived in cities of more than 50,000 inhabitants and half of these lived in Paris.

---

[1] Samuel F. Scott, 'The Regeneration of the Line Army during the French Revolution', *Journal of Modern History*, XLII (1970), 308–11.

[2] Besides Reinhard, *Étude de la population*, see O. Festy, 'Les mouvements de la population française du debut de la Révolution au Consulat et leur causes', *Annales historiques de la Révolution française*, XXVIII (1955), 37–8 and Paul Vincent, 'French Demography in the Eighteenth Century', *Population Studies*, I (1947), 45 and 56.

[3] For a good, but all too succinct, discussion of this problem, see Roger Mols, *Introduction à la démographie historique des villes d'Europe*, vol. I (Louvain, 1954), pp. xx–xxii.

[4] Marcel Reinhard, 'La Population des villes: Sa mésure sous la Révolution et l'Empire', *Population*, IX (1954), 279–88.

[5] Archives nationales (A.N.), Div ᵇⁱˢ 47. This valuable source was brought to my attention by Prof. Gilbert Shapiro. The statistics which it gives have been very commonly used in subsequent works, often without citation. During the July Monarchy it provided most of the figures for Ministère de Travaux Publics, de l'Agriculture et du Commerce, *Statistique de France* (Paris, 1837), pp. 267–79, which also contains a few cities not included in *États de Population*.

[6] This agrees with the estimate of one-fifth made by Arthur Young, quoted in Lucien Schöne, *Histoire de la population française* (Paris, 1893), p. 215, but is higher than the 15% estimate in Marcel Reinhard and André Armengaud, *Histoire générale de la population mondiale* (Paris, 1961), p. 196.

A significantly higher proportion of men in the line army were from urban centres than in the population as a whole.[1] The infantry was the most urban of the branches; approximately three-eighths of the enlisted men whose birthplace has been identified as rural or urban came from communities with 2,000 or more inhabitants. There was an even higher percentage of light infantrymen from urban backgrounds than of soldiers in the line, or heavy, infantry. A markedly lower proportion of men in the cavalry came from towns and cities, slightly more than one-quarter, although this was still higher than in the general population. Only in the artillery regiments was the proportion of 'urbans' closely approximate to that of the population at large. Big, strong country boys, particularly from eastern France, provided the majority of the soldiers in this branch.

Not only were infantrymen more urban in background than soldiers in the other two branches, but also infantry soldiers came from larger cities. Over 20 per cent of the infantrymen came from cities with 10,000 or more inhabitants. The comparable figure among cavalrymen was less than 13 per cent; while in the artillery less than one-tenth of the men came from cities with 10,000 inhabitants or more.

Usually there was a larger proportion of urban dwellers among the N.C.O.s, especially the sergeants, than in the ranks as a whole. In the line infantry regiments, 35 per cent of the soldiers were from localities with 2,000 or more inhabitants; but over 40 per cent of the corporals and more than half of the sergeants were from urban origins. In the cavalry, one-fifth of the soldiers, one-quarter of the corporals, and 45 per cent of the sergeants were from urban areas. In the light infantry battalions and artillery regiments, which together constituted about 7 per cent of the total strength of the line army, the same progression was not evidenced, although in both branches the sergeants were more urban in background than the corporals.

Although the precise reasons for the higher proportion of N.C.O.s from urban areas are not clear, literacy appears to be an important factor. Literacy had been a requirement demanded of sergeants

---

[1] The percentage of urban dwellers given here corresponds very closely to the situation in 1763; see Corvisier, *L'Armée française*, I. 408. Corvisier estimates that in 1763, 34·5% of the infantry and 25% of the cavalry and dragoons came from towns and cities. He gives no comparable data for the artillery. The inspection reports for 1788 and 1789 contain no information at all about the size of birthplace of soldiers.

since the ministry of Choiseul. Since men from towns were more likely to have some education, it is not surprising to find a high proportion of urban dwellers in the rank of sergeant. The rank of corporal on the other hand was both a stepping-stone to sergeant and a reward for loyal soldiers without much talent.[1] One could expect, therefore, to find a lower percentage of urban dwellers in this rank.

One of the most difficult, yet one of the most important, characteristics of line troops to be determined is the social origins of the soldiers. The most revealing indication of social origins in the troop registers of the period is the bald notation of civilian occupation, and even this is provided for only a small proportion of the soldiers. Beyond this problem, there exists the complex task of interpreting the social significance of hundreds of occupations in the highly localized society of eighteenth-century France.[2] Despite these difficulties, a general description of the social background of the soldiers is possible.

The work of Corvisier has already indicated several trends in the social composition of the line troops during the first two-thirds of the eighteenth century.[3] The proportion of soldiers in the ranks who came from the upper social strata—nobles, government officials, members of the liberal professions, merchants, *rentiers*, clerks, master artisans, and substantial farmers—declined progressively from 1716 to 1763. At the same time, however, the percentage of sergeants from these same groups increased. On the other hand, the lower classes—small shopkeepers, artisans, and agricultural and non-agricultural labourers—contributed a continually increasing proportion of soldiers. Between 1716 and 1763 artisans, both urban and rural, constituted 34–42 per cent of the troops, and peasants 35–48 per cent. The total percentage of peasants in the army increased during wartime; and throughout this period peasants tended to dominate the ranks of the cavalry, while artisans formed the single largest group among infantrymen.

The troop registers for 1789 contain the professions of slightly more than 1,500 soldiers who were serving in the line army on the

[1] Corvisier, *L'Armée française*, I. 409.
[2] For a more detailed account of the problems and methods involved in resolving this complicated subject, see my dissertation, 'The French Revolution and the Line Army, 1787–1793' (Univ. Wisconsin, 1968), pp. 192–243.
[3] See *L'Armée française*, I. 472–519.

eve of the Revolution;[1] this represents just under 1 per cent of the total strength of the army at that time. The regional and rural–urban origins of the men for whom this information was noted show a pattern similar to that which we have established for the line soldiers in general. They were, however, younger and had served a shorter period of time than the men in the general sample; and for this reason there were few N.C.O.s among them. A more serious limitation to the representativeness of the soldiers whose professions were noted is that a considerably higher percentage of men in the light infantry and artillery had such information indicated than did men in the line infantry and cavalry. Nevertheless, the data on professions in the troop registers provide important indications of the social origins of the line army in 1789.

The trend towards an increasingly larger proportion of soldiers from popular groups (artisans, small shopkeepers, and agricultural and non-agricultural labourers) which Corvisier noted earlier in the century continued until the Revolution. Between 85 and 90 per cent of the line troops in our sample for 1789 had practised these occupations in civilian life. Particularly outstanding was the proportion of artisans and shopkeepers, who constituted about three-fifths of all the soldiers in the sample.[2] Most numerous were the artisans in the clothing, building, textile, and metal trades who comprised about three-quarters of all the artisans and shopkeepers. Least common were the artisans in luxury trades. More than half the artisans were from urban areas.

Peasants, who constituted perhaps 80 per cent of the population of France, were grossly under-represented in the army. Many farm labourers listed their professions in a way which did not necessarily imply agricultural work, e.g. *sans profession*, *journalier*, and *manouvrier* or *manœuvre*; yet 75–80 per cent of the soldiers who

---

[1] This information came from examining all the available registers for information on the civilian occupations of soldiers serving in the Royal Army in 1789. Although a few such indications may have escaped detection, these could not possibly be numerous enough to substantially affect the general conclusions presented here.

[2] This percentage may be too high. As noted above, Corvisier has estimated that from 1716 to 1763 artisans composed between 34% and 42% of the soldiers (*L'Armée française*, I. 472). In 1793, as we shall see, artisans and shopkeepers accounted for just under half of the line troops. On the other hand, a report of the Military Committee of the National Assembly in late 1789 maintained that 'the major part of the recruits' were artisans and workers, and it estimated that nearly two-thirds of the army recruits came from *villes*. See 'Premier Rapport fait au nom du Comité Militaire à l'Assemblée Nationale par M. le Marquis de Bouthillier, le 19 Novembre 1789', Maclure Collection of French Revolutionary Materials (Univ. of Pennsylvania), vol. 848.

gave these occupations as their civilian status were from rural areas. Even when this is taken into consideration, only 20–25 per cent of the enlisted men in the sample for 1789 were peasants.[1] Difficulties of recruiting in the countryside and traditional peasant hostility toward military service made it impossible to exploit fully this vast reserve of manpower in the Old Regime.

The upper and intermediate social classes contributed few of their sons to service in the ranks of the army. Many young nobles, usually the poor *hobereaux* of the provinces, still found it necessary to serve in the ranks if they were to continue their traditional functions in the honourable profession of arms, albeit in an inferior position.[2] The number of such nobles had, however, decreased during the second half of the century to less than 2 nobles per 1,000 line soldiers. Whether this was due to an absolute decrease in the number of nobles actually serving in the ranks or to a growing reluctance on the part of such nobles to reveal their social status is an unresolved question.

The upper classes of non-noble society furnished more soldiers than did the nobility; but the number of such recruits remained small. Members of the business middle class sent very few of their sons into a military career which promised almost no hope of advancement or opportunity to merge with the established aristocracy. The more traditionalist segment of the middle class, composed of government officials, clerks, bourgeois who lived on their incomes, and, above all, members of the liberal professions, provided more soldiers to the line army. These men constituted only 6 or 7 per cent of the line army in 1789, but they became sergeants much more readily than their comrades of inferior social status. After the outbreak of the Revolution, these men, on the basis of their education and military experience, were to form the single most important nucleus of the new officer corps.

The number or proportion of vagabonds, beggars, and criminals who enlisted in the army cannot even be estimated. Traditionally it has been assumed that such men made up a substantial portion of

[1] This proportion seems to have been much higher in the Swiss regiments where, according to the inspection reports of 1788 and 1789, almost three-quarters of the soldiers were listed as 'Plowmen, pioneers, and other workers of the countryside'. See A.G., X^g 88, 89, 90, and 92.

[2] Information on these *soldats gentilshommes* is based on a study of 106 soldiers so identified in the registers of forty line regiments between 1787 and 1793. One can estimate that there were at least 450 such nobles in the entire army during this period.

soldiers in the eighteenth century.[1] While it is impossible to make a definitive judgement on this question because virtually no recruits indicated such a background, it seems unlikely that these elements constituted a significant number of troops.[2] It is more likely that claims about the number of beggars and criminals in the army are based partly on prejudice, both contemporary and subsequent, and partly on an identification of the unemployed members of the lower classes with social derelicts.

Such was the composition of the line army on the eve of the Revolution. The soldiers and their N.C.O.s were relatively young men. There was a disproportionately large number of men from urban areas, especially among the sergeants. Soldiers who had been artisans in civilian life constituted an absolute majority of the men in the ranks. Such characteristics could—in retrospect—portend unreliability, since the Revolution was so much the work of the urban lower middle classes.[3] On the other hand, a large proportion of the men were from areas of France where military service was a traditional occupation. More importantly, about two-thirds of the soldiers of the line army had served four years or more in the army. Thus, certain characteristics which could incline the soldiers of the line army to favour the Revolution, such as the youth of the troops and the significant proportion of men and N.C.O.s from urban lower-middle-class occupations, could be checked by the degree of professionalism which army life had inculcated in them.

THE OFFICER CORPS

Besides the soldiers, the other major component of the Royal Army was, of course, the officers. Their role and situation within the military were so completely different from those of the soldiers as to defy comparison, or even similar treatment.[4] The most striking characteristic of this group was the identification between noble and

[1] See, for example, Léon Mention, *L'Armée de l'ancien régime* (Paris, [1900]), pp. 11–14 and J. Revol, *Histoire de l'armée française* (Paris, 1929), p. 122.

[2] Of more than 17,000 beggars in the *dépôts de mendicité* of the generality of Paris between 1764 and 1773, only 88 entered the army, i.e. *c.* 0·5% (Kaplow, *Names of Kings*, p. 127). Unfortunately, there is no comparable information on criminal recruitment.

[3] See George Rudé, *The Crowd in the French Revolution* (Oxford, 1959) and Albert Soboul, *Les Sansculottes parisiens en l'an II* (Paris, 1958).

[4] Even the sources differ; registers on the officers are much less detailed and much more poorly maintained. In fact, it is impossible to make a study, based on the *contrôles*, of the officers at all comparable to that made of the soldiers. See A.G., *Contrôles des officiers. Révolution et Empire* (uncoded).

officer. Throughout the eighteenth century the French aristocracy dominated the officer corps of the Royal Army. From the middle of the century only 5–10 per cent of the officers directly commissioned in the army were non-nobles; and in the last years of the Old Regime even this small number was effectively eliminated.[1] Moreover, the French nobility exercised a psychological dominance over the officer corps; it was the nobles who set the standards for the attitudes and conduct of all officers, including commoners. Non-noble officers were seldom treated as equals and were sometimes subjected to mistreatment at the hands of their aristocratic comrades.[2]

One category of officers, however, was excluded from the situation described above; this was the *officiers de fortune*. These men had not been directly commissioned but rather by their exceptional ability or unusually good luck had risen from the ranks into the officer corps after many years, often decades, of service. Normally there were five or six such officers per regiment and altogether they comprised approximately one-tenth of all officers. Both in background and in function they resembled the sergeants from whose ranks they came. Of all officers they had the closest contact with the troops, being in daily supervision of their activities. In the eyes of their superiors they were little more than ranking non-commissioned officers.[3] In fact, the officers of fortune were so fully excluded from consideration that their fellow officers did not even regard them as a threat to noble dominance—until the Revolution.

Thus, from outward appearances the officer corps of the Royal Army seems to have been a highly homogeneous group. Yet, upon closer examination important differences and divisions become evident. Several factors were responsible for this, but the most important was the financial burden of a military career. Far from providing a livelihood, a military career in the Old Regime could represent a considerable expenditure for those who sought anything beyond the most limited and gradual advancement. Until the abolition of venality in 1776 the only positions that were officially recognized as venal were those of captain and colonel, which were conferred by the purchase of a company or a regiment. The price of

[1] See David D. Bien, 'La Réaction aristocratique avant 1789: l'exemple de l'armée', *Annales, Économies, Sociétés, Civilisations*, XXIX (1974), 29–36.

[2] Louis Tuetey, *Les Officiers sous l'ancien régime* (Paris, 1908), pp. 225–54 contains a discussion of this situation.

[3] Ibid., pp. 281–8.

these units varied considerably according to the prestige of the unit and the market for it. A company could cost between 6,000 and 14,000 *livres*; an infantry regiment from 25,000 to 75,000 *livres*; and a cavalry regiment from 22,500 to 120,000 *livres*. The other officer grades were ostensibly non-venal; however, colonels and captains frequently allotted these positions for financial considerations to recoup their own expenditures. In addition, when promotions were particularly restricted, the officers of a regiment would form a *concordat*, i.e. all would contribute to a fund that was given to a senior officer for his premature retirement which would then provide room for advancement within the regiment.[1]

Besides the cost of a commission and the expenses necessary for promotion, many officers, especially superior officers, had to use private resources in order to maintain themselves in the manner expected of them.[2] Even subaltern officers, of whom less was expected, frequently were hard pressed to meet their expenses without independent income. For example, Jean-Francois Le Parsonnier du Landey, a middle-aged captain in the regiment of La Marche during the 1740s and 1750s, was continually writing to his mother in Normandy for money to pay his expenses.[3] Later, in the 1770s and 1780s, the Chevalier de Mautort, a member of the *petite noblesse* of the provinces and a captain in the Austrasie Infantry, exemplified the typical problems of these officers by his concern over his expenditures for equipment, food, travel, etc.[4] Cavalry officers, who had to maintain horses and valets in addition to their other expenses, were even more pressed.

This situation had a number of unfortunate effects. It seriously hampered the development of professionalism among the officers by reinforcing the archaic notion of military service held by many nobles. For them, their duties as officers did not constitute a full-time occupation but were rather the traditional function and privi-

[1] Corvisier, *L'Armée française*, I. 130 and Tuetey, *Les Officiers*, pp. 134–7 and 153. Corvisier also provides an excellent example of this practice in 'Un officier normand de Louis XV: Le Lieutenant-colonel Jean-François Le Parsonnier du Landey d'après sa correspondance (1714–1785)', *Annales de Normandie*, IX (1959), especially 198–202.

[2] Louis Dussieux, *L'Armée en France: Histoire et organisation depuis les temps anciens jusqu'à nos jours*, vol. II (Versailles, 1884), pp. 301–4; Babeau, *Vie militaire*, II. 170–7; and Emile Léonard, *L'Armée et ses problèmes au XVIIIe siècle* (Paris, 1958), pp. 171–4.

[3] Corvisier, 'Un officier normand', pp. 196–208.

[4] Chevalier de Mautort, *Mémoires du chevalier de Mautort, Capitaine au régiment d'Austrasie, Chevalier de l'Ordre royal et militaire de Saint-Louis (1752–1802)* (Paris, 1895), *passim*.

lege of the warrior caste which should not interfere greatly with their other activities, such as supervising estates, family business, or even social obligations. Even officers with a more modern, careerist attitude needed frequent and extensive leaves to care for their personal affairs, since these provided the income necessary to maintain their military status. In addition, the expenditures required for advancement made it impossible to establish a hierarchy based on merit or accomplishment. Finally, the importance of wealth created a strong resentment on the part of the poorer, provincial nobility whose dedication and ability were, they felt, subordinated to the frivolous ambition of rich nobles and even commoners.

This last problem was exacerbated by the keen competition among nobles for officer vacancies. The impoverished nobility could still make a living in the army, if willing to resign themselves to subordinate grades and to exercise great care over their expenditures. Furthermore, many viewed the profession of arms as the only honourable occupation open to them. Consequently, there were usually more applicants than vacancies in the officer corps. In the latter part of the century many young nobles joined regiments as *volontaires* and served in these units, receiving neither pay nor lodging, until a vacancy among the junior officers provided them with a position and an opportunity to draw pay.[1] In a letter to the Minister of War in November 1786, Baron de Besenval noted that the frenzy (*fureur*) of the nobility for military service remained amazingly strong, although the chances of obtaining command of a regiment were less than one in hundred.[2] Increasing competition and declining opportunities for advancement served only to intensify rivalries among officers.

By the reign of Louis XVI a rather rigid hierarchy had become established in the officer corps, much to the disgust of many officers. The upper aristocracy dominated the highest ranks. A regulation of 17 April 1760 had distinguished the nobility presented at court from other nobles, and none but the *noblesse presentée* could advance beyond the grade of colonel.[3] This measure did little more than formalize the existing situation, but its very formalization un-

---

[1] For an example, see ibid., pp. 5–6 and 27.

[2] Pierre Victor, Baron de Besenval, *Mémoires du Baron de Besenval*, vol. II (Paris, 1821), p. 189.

[3] Arthur Chuquet, 'Roture et noblesse dans l'armée royale', *Séances et travaux de l'Académie des sciences morales et politiques*, CLXXV (1911), 237 and Henri Sée, *La France économique et sociale au XVIIIᵉ siècle*, 4th edn. (Paris, 1946), p. 77.

doubtedly made it more intolerable to the provincial nobility. At the end of the Old Regime, of the eleven marshals, five were dukes, four were marquis, one a prince, and one a count. Only nine of the 196 lieutenant-generals were non-titled. Of more than 950 other generals (770 *maréchaux de camp* and 182 *brigadiers*), only one-fifth were aristocrats without titles.[1]

Colonels too were almost entirely court aristocrats; of all the colonels in infantry regiments in 1789 (over 200), only six were non-titled nobles.[2] Usually the colonels were young men, in their twenties or thirties, whose wealth and influence guaranteed their rapid advancement to yet higher grades, despite the fact that they might have little taste and less talent for their military duties. Lieutenant-colonels and majors were mostly older men from the provincial nobility who had long service but whose ambitions for further advancement were limited by their financial resources. Captain was a rank dominated by the same group of petty nobility, most of whom would end their careers in this rank. In addition, a small minority of captains were officers of fortune who attained this grade before they were excluded from it in 1788. The ranks of lieutenant and second-lieutenant (*lieutenant en second* or more commonly *sous-lieutenant*) were shared by a number of different groups: they were held briefly by adolescents from the higher nobility, soon on their way to loftier grades; for much longer by lesser nobles who, after a number of years, could attain a captaincy; and until their retirement or death by the few commoners who had become officers of fortune.[3]

The most important result of this situation was the growing frustration of the provincial officers in the lower and middle ranks, who saw their personal ambitions and the welfare of the army being thwarted by a combination of wealth and court influence. This frustration, in turn, led to great fermentation and debate among officers throughout the last quarter-century of the Old Regime. The crushing and unexpected defeat of France in the Seven Years War compounded and served to justify this agitation.

[1] Albert Duruy, *L'Armée royale en 1789* (Paris, 1888), pp. 83–4.
[2] Ibid.
[3] This general description of the personnel in different officer grades is based on a number of sources: Capitaine Bacquet, *L'Infanterie au XVIIIᵉ siècle: L'Organisation*, p. 20; Léonard, *L'Armée et ses problèmes*, p. 64; Babeau, *Vie militaire*, II. 133 and 188; and the research of Charles Wrong and David D. Bien who have generously communicated their findings to me.

Within the officer corps during this period there was a growing tendency towards the adoption of more professional standards, a tendency which, however, always remained strongly coloured by noble prejudice. The intimate relationship between service as an officer and nobility continued to dominate ideas, even those of the reformers. This attitude was expressed by both positive and negative action. Positively, there was an increasing emphasis on education, particularly technical education, and dedication to service. On the negative side, there was a growing attempt to make the officer corps the exclusive reserve of those with an indisputably noble and military background. These ideals had been expressed as early as 1756 by the Chevalier d'Arc in his book, *La Noblesse militaire ou le patriote français*. D'Arc argued in favour of a distinct nobility of military service in which ability, including education, would be the criterion for advancement. Even commoners who proved their worth and dedication could be admitted; but, on the other hand, venality, which the Chevalier considered the source of evils in the army, would be completely abolished.[1]

Opportunities for a military education increased considerably in the second half of the eighteenth century. In 1751 the Comte d'Argenson had founded the École Militaire in Paris. This was open to boys between 8 and 11 years of age who could furnish proof of four generations of nobility and who were impoverished (*sans biens*).[2] In 1776 twelve new military schools were established in the provinces, which demanded the same requirements of their applicants. The school at Paris then became a superior military school for the graduates of the provincial *collèges*. The École Militaire was disestablished in 1787, but the provincial schools lasted into the Revolution. An alternative institution offering military preparation for noble aspirants to the officer corps was the *cadets-gentilshommes*. These noble cadets were attached to French regiments where they performed some of the duties of enlisted men and some of the functions of officers for approximately one year. This form of on-the-job training lasted, in one form or another, from 1776 to 1791. Finally, there were specialized schools for educating artillery and engineer officers.

While it is impossible to evaluate the full effects of these educa-

---

[1] The best discussion of this can be found in André Corvisier, 'Hiérarchie militaire et hiérarchie sociale à la veille de la Révolution', pp. 77–91.

[2] Léonard, *L'Armée et ses problèmes*, p. 178 and Tuetey, *Les Officiers*, pp. 37–8.

tional facilities on the quality of officers, it is safe to assume that there was some improvement, at least in technical training. This, however, satisfied only part of the aims of the provincial aristocracy. Besides improving military education, they also wanted to assure commitment to the profession of arms; and they used family background as the measure of this.[1] The supporters of military reform, largely but not exclusively provincial nobles, assumed that the tradition of military service over the course of generations was the surest guarantee of dedication. Intimately related to this criterion was the presumption that the older nobility, 'the nobility of the sword', almost alone was capable of providing the appropriate family background for future officers. The only exception which this attitude allowed was that some commoners, who would always constitute but a small minority, could achieve a similar preparation if military service had been a tradition in their families. This thinking underlay the military reforms of the late eighteenth century which most commonly required four generations of nobility on the part of the officer candidates, yet almost always exempted sons of *chevaliers de Saint-Louis* (who could be non-noble) from this requirement.

The primary objective of this attitude and of the reforms to which it gave birth was not the exclusion of commoners, who, at any rate, presented only a minor problem. It is, of course, entirely possible, and even likely, that commoners took offence at being excluded; and the complaints voiced shortly before the Revolution tend to indicate considerable non-noble resentment.[2] The major threat in the eyes of most nobles was the recently ennobled. Such persons seldom came from military families and, *not* coincidentally, they had usually achieved their new status as a result of their wealth, most often by the purchase of an office that conferred nobility. In the eyes of the provincial nobles, officers from this kind of background could not be committed to an army career and this lack of dedication was detrimental to the officer corps. At the same time, of course, their wealth would give the new nobles an undeniable advantage over the poorer officers in obtaining promotions.

---

[1] Recent research is providing considerable evidence for this. See Bien, 'Réaction aristocratique', pp. 522–4 and Roger Chartier, 'Un recrutement scolaire au XVIIIᵉ siècle: L'École royale du Génie de Mézières', *Revue d'histoire moderne et contemporaine*, XX (1973), 360–4. These articles provide the basis of the following discussion.

[2] Bien notes that there is little literary evidence of opposition to the Ségur decree until 1789, but then the complaints of commoners were voiced in pamphlets and in the *cahiers de doléances* of the Third Estate. See 'Réaction aristocratique', p. 27.

Thus, the thoroughly noble character of the Royal Army officer corps hid a number of very bitter divisions and resentments. A substantial majority of officers supported, actively or passively, major reforms. The government had to respond to this situation, but its response could not be a simple one; conflicting interests had to be satisfied. Over and above all this, the government had its own interests to protect. Military reform had become a necessity by 1763, but the precise form such change would take was a matter of considerable controversy.

REFORMS BY THE GOVERNMENT

Pressure from elements within the officer corps and, probably more importantly, the stunning defeat of France in the Seven Years War led the French monarchy to initiate a series of major military reforms during the last generation of the Old Regime. Some of the government programmes fostered the professionalism demanded by the provincial nobility, but this was only one part of a much larger process of modernization or bureaucratization of the army by the state; and many policies served merely to increase antagonisms among the officers. The most important aspects of the reform movement were a marked increase in government control over the army and more rational regulations and organization. The primary aim of the changes was greater efficiency. Although this process made substantial progress under the Old Regime, modernization of the army was not fully successful until the Revolution destroyed the social institutions that precluded its complete realization.

The ministry of Choiseul, which lasted from 1761 until his disgrace in 1770, began the reform era and inaugurated the most drastic changes. Choiseul's reforms, beginning with the ordinance of 10 December 1762, affected many levels and aspects of the military establishment. Prior to then the number of units in the army had fluctuated according to the requirements of war or peace. Choiseul fixed the number of units and planned simply to increase the number of men in each during wartime. In this way efficiency could be increased substantially, since it was much easier to induct men into established units with an existing apparatus to train and supply them than it was to create new units with new personnel. As a result of this measure, however, a large number of officers were retired, sometimes after long service, on meagre pensions. Their opposition was considerable and bitter.[1]

Probably the most significant of Choiseul's reforms was the transfer of recruitment from the competence of captains and colonels to that of royal agents. Henceforth, the soldiers took an oath of loyalty directly to the king. This was a major step towards centralized control of the army by the state; but it greatly increased the expenses and problems of the government which now had to provide directly for almost all the needs of its military personnel. It is likely that this one change doubled military expenditures. Furthermore, an entirely new machinery had to be established for recruitment.[2] At the same time this regulation weakened whatever solidarity there may have been between captains and the men in their companies who had often been personally recruited by their officers and who represented a personal financial investment.

Another reform in the direction of greater centralization gave the king the right to select the lieutenant-colonel and major of a regiment from any regiment in the royal army, rather than, as previously, from only that regiment in which the vacancy existed. This measure aroused considerable hostility among many officers since it gave 'outsiders' preference over the regiment's own officers. One notable example of this was the affair of the Royal-Comtois Infantry Regiment. After years of hostility and recriminations between many of the officers of the regiment and a lieutenant-colonel and a major who had been appointed from outside the regiment, a court martial held in July 1773 cashiered and imprisoned thirty-three officers for opposition to their superiors. In fact, even after the court martial, opposition to this prerogative continued to fester and the entire affair was reviewed in May 1791 by the National Assembly which condemned this act of 'ministerial injustice' and declared the sentence of 1773 void.[3]

Saint-Germain, Minister of War from 1775 to 1777, continued the reforms. The number of infantry companies per battalion was

---

[1] Albert Latreille, *L'Armée et la nation à la fin de l'ancien régime: Les Derniers Ministres de la guerre de la monarchie* (Paris, 1914), pp. 6–7.

[2] Robert Sars, *Le Recrutement de l'armée permanente sous l'ancien régime* (Paris, 1920), pp. 151–8. Sars estimates that at the time of the Treaty of Aix-la-Chapelle (1748) it had cost 112,000,000 *livres* to support an army of 402,000 men; in 1770, 94,000,000 *livres* for 203,000; and in 1786, 115,000,000 *livres* for 198,000 men.

[3] A full account can be found in 'Rapport fait à l'Assemblée Nationale, au nom du Comité Militaire, de l'affaire du régiment Royal Comtois, & de la sentence du conseil de guerre de 1773', Maclure Collection, vol. 831.

reduced from 17 (of 25 men each) to 6, thus reducing the excessively high proportion of officers to men. This measure turned most of the provincial nobles against Saint-Germain because the opportunities for promotion to captain were correspondingly reduced.[1] Towards the same end, increased efficiency, Saint-Germain cut the strength of the royal household by disbanding the Musketeers and Horse Grenadiers and reducing the number of Gendarmes and Light Horse. This, in turn, infuriated the great nobles whose sons traditionally began their military service in these units of great prestige.[2]

To end a long-standing abuse and to complete Choiseul's work of giving the king control over all ranks of the army, Saint-Germain suppressed venality of military offices in 1776. Henceforth, when a regiment or company lost its commander by death, resignation, or transfer, the price of the unit would be reduced by one-quarter. Thus, by the fourth change of commander all offices would be free and the government completely unrestricted in its appointments. This measure, of course, was implemented only over a period of time; however, by February 1790 when the National Assembly abolished venality, it had already virtually disappeared in the infantry and was confined to only sixteen regiments of cavalry.[3] The reform, while satisfying the complaints of the poorer nobility, alienated the wealthy aristocrats, often of recent vintage, and the few rich bourgeois who still saw the purchase of military office as a means of social advancement.[4]

Even in his attempts to reform conditions of life in the army Saint-Germain succeeded only in antagonizing other elements of the military. In eliminating some of the more barbaric military punishments, he introduced the Prussian practice of blows with the flat of a sabre. Although this punishment was no more cruel than most of those in use, its application was considered the epitome of degradation and complaints against it were strong until the National Assembly abolished the practice.[5]

Thus, although he initiated extensive reforms, most of which can be viewed as improvements, Saint-Germain aroused almost universal opposition to his legislation. The reforms which excited

[1] Louis-Auguste-Victor Susane, *Histoire de l'infanterie française*, I (Paris, 1876), 308.
[2] Latreille, *L'Armée et la nation à la fin de l'ancien régime*, p. 77.
[3] Henri Choppin, *Les Insurrections militaires en 1790* (Paris, 1903), pp. 34-5 and Duruy, *L'Armée royale en 1789*, p. 75.
[4] Léonard, *L'Armée et ses problèmes*, p. 249.
[5] Ibid., p. 250 and Latreille, *L'Armée et la nation à la fin de l'ancien régime*, p. 118.

little or no opposition, such as the establishment of the provincial military schools and the creation of a military health service, either were not immediately or widely effective, or were disregarded by his opponents. The lesser nobility saw its opportunities for employment and promotion substantially decreased; the court aristocracy resented the reduction in prestigious ceremonial units; men of wealth, both noble and non-noble, objected to being excluded from a traditional avenue of upward social mobility. Many noble officers from different groups saw—however vaguely—centralization and rationalization as threats to their control of the military. Even the nobles who were willing to accept more professional standards were unwilling to become mere employees of the state, subject to whatever demands or standards it might impose. The government, on the other hand, faced a serious dilemma: whether to reorganize the army along strictly rational lines or to maintain the aristocracy's traditional status of military leadership. The response was typically ambivalent, modernization of the organizational framework but maintenance of outmoded social patterns within this framework. As a result, no groups were satisfied and army reform remained incomplete.

After Saint-Germain's dismissal the supporters of military reform continued to press for change. This agitation culminated in the royal decision of 22 May 1781, most commonly known as the Ségur decree.[1] Essentially, this required four generations of nobility of anyone who wished to enter the army directly as an officer. Although at first it applied primarily to the French infantry, the provisions of the law were gradually extended so that by August 1784 almost all elements of the Royal Army were included. Even in branches where this decision was not directly implemented it had its effect. For example, although officers of engineers were not specifically included in the law, four generations of nobility were required for entry into the engineering school at Mézières, and this school produced all the officers in this branch. This measure simply

---

[1] Every history of the French army during this period has some, frequently erroneous, information on 'Ségur's decree'. The most comprehensive and useful discussions of the problem can be found in the following articles: Georges Six, 'Fallait-il quatre quartiers de noblesse pour être officier à la fin de l'ancien régime?', *Revue d'histoire moderne*, IV (1929), 47–56; Pierre Chalmin, 'La Formation des officiers des armes savantes sous l'Ancien Régime', *Actes du soixante-seizième congrès des sociétés savantes* (Paris, 1951), pp. 168–73; Corvisier, 'Hiérarchie militaire et hiérarchie sociale', p. 86; and Bien, 'Réaction aristocratique', pp. 36–41 and 515–30.

climaxed the trend which dated back at least as far as mid-century, and its primary novelty was, as Corvisier notes, 'its provoking effectiveness'.

The Ségur decree was above all a victory of the old, military nobility, largely provincial and comparatively poor, over commoners and especially nobles of recent origin, who seem to have been entering the officer corps in increasing numbers prior to 1781.[1] Yet, the victory was not complete. The proponents of this reform wanted to assure that only young men from a military background (who were, therefore, seriously devoted to an army career) could henceforth be commissioned into the army. Most of the petty nobles would have preferred both nobility *and* a military family to have been explicitly demanded; but practical considerations prohibited this. The influential court aristocracy and 'the nobility of the robe', whose status was based on civil not military office, would have been outraged at requiring military antecedents, and their opposition might have blocked the legislation entirely. Thus the decree was a compromise which still fell short of the desires of those officers who wanted to make the military nobility a completely distinct caste within aristocratic society.[2]

The ostensible impact of this legislation on commoners was extremely limited. To begin with, for decades there had been few commoners who were directly commissioned into the army. Furthermore, sons of men who had received the Cross of Saint Louis were specifically excluded from the provisions of the decree. However, it must be pointed out that this decoration was awarded only after twenty-six years of service for a captain and twenty-eight years for a lieutenant. Since enlisted service counted only for half of the service as an officer, very few sons of non-noble officers could have benefited from this exemption.[3] The only way most commoners could advance into the officer ranks after 1781 was by becoming officers of fortune. This required long and efficient service, performance of the most onerous officer duties (e.g. training and discipline), and the acceptance of a clearly subordinate role in the military hierarchy. Although the Ségur decree was primarily the result of inter-noble rivalry, its implications for non-nobles should not be ignored. The

[1] Although most authors present the decision of 1781 as a victory of the provincial nobility some—e.g. Henry Lachouque in *Aux armes, citoyens! Les Soldats de la Révolution* (Paris, 1969), p. 38—view it as a success of the upper aristocracy.

[2] Bien, 'Réaction aristocratique', pp. 517–28.

[3] Corvisier, 'Hiérarchie militaire et hiérarchie sociale', p. 90.

latent animosity of commoners toward noble dominance of the officer corps would, within a decade, be clearly expressed and would result in the purge of most of the noble officers; their replacements would be commoners whose frustrations had not even been considered during the debates about military reform.

The Ségur decree satisfied some, but by no means all, of the demands for reform in the Royal Army. The need for further military change led Louis XVI, on 9 October 1787, to convoke a council of war composed of leading generals and military theorists.[1] Besides a number of tactical and organizational reforms, e.g. the decision to use columns for movement and lines for combat and the reorganization of chasseur units, the council improved conditions of military service. A new pay-scale was established which raised the pay for all grades, but most of all for the officers. Annual pay was to vary from 4,000 *livres* for a colonel, to approximately 900 *livres* (depending on branch) for a lieutenant, to 114 *livres* for a common infantryman. Officers and N.C.O.s were forbidden to inflict any punishment except those authorized by regulations; they were likewise prohibited from mistreating their men and from using the second person singular form of address (*tutoyer*) with them, since it was degrading. Punishment by blows with a sabre flat was, however, maintained. Each regiment was required to establish a school for candidates to the N.C.O. ranks which would teach the men to read, write, and count.[2]

Other measures of the council of war in 1787 and 1788 continued the policies of rationalization and bureaucratization initiated by Choiseul. The royal bodyguard was further reduced and the Gendarmerie, approximately 1,000 men, was disbanded. The excessive number of general officers, around 1,200, was somewhat reduced and future limits were set. The use of attached officers and 'officers of replacement', who were on regimental rolls but who did not in fact serve, was abolished. Although the monopoly of the court aristocracy over the grades of colonel and general officer was maintained, longer service was required of these nobles before promotion to colonel; and, for the provincial nobility, it was decided that they

---

[1] The ordinances passed by this council, mostly in 1788, are treated in one way or another in every work dealing with the period. Two of the most useful discussions can be found in Jean Egret, *La Pré-Révolution française* (Paris, 1962), pp. 82–93 and Antoine Picq, *La Législation militaire de l'époque révolutionnaire: Introduction à l'étude de la législation militaire actuelle* (Paris, 1931), pp. 208–9, 225, and 295.

[2] Latreille, *L'Armée et la nation à la fin de l'ancien régime*, pp. 278–80.

would automatically be promoted to general (*maréchal de camp*) after twenty years' service as lieutenant-colonel.

By 1789 substantial reforms had been effected in the Royal Army; yet, because of the ambivalent attitude of the monarchy, these had resulted in exacerbating existing divisions and rivalries without accomplishing fundamental change. The court aristocracy was alienated by the reductions in royal household troops, the abolition of officers of replacement, and the opportunity for lieutenant-colonels to become generals, all of which were regarded as infringements on its prerogatives. At the same time, the provincial nobility resented the fact that the distinction between nobles presented at court and other nobles was maintained. Sincerely devoted to improvement of the officer corps (and to their own personal advantage), the provincial nobles were the major force behind the military reforms. Yet, they were determined 'to model the military hierarchy on a social hierarchy which was no longer that of the nation'.[1] Newly-created nobles and well-to-do commoners were frustrated by their nearly complete exclusion from the officers corps. Officers of fortune and ambitious N.C.O.s were relegated to subordinate ranks and functions with virtually no hope of advancement. All of these resentments and frustrations were blamed upon the government, which was at least partially responsible for the situation. The government, in its attempts to centralize and rationalize the administration and organization of the army, had failed to accept the full implications of this process and had provided only a semi-bureaucratic framework for what was still an institution based upon the estate system of the Old Regime. Thus, government policy contributed to the deterioration of morale within the Royal Army, especially among officers, which would seriously hamper the effectiveness of the army just at a time when it was the sole agency capable of protecting the regime against the coming revolution.

ARMY LIFE

Each of the elements discussed so far—the composition of the troops, the situation within the officer corps, and the policies of the government—affected the operation of the Royal Army. Of even greater importance in determining how the army would react to crisis was its day-to-day functioning. Certainly, relations between the government and many officers had been strained by the

[1] Corvisier, 'Hiérarchie militaire et hiérarchie sociale', p. 91.

monarchy's reforms; but the officer corps, like the nobility in general, would rally to the king when faced by a common revolutionary threat. What ultimately incapacitated the army and led directly to the collapse of both royal and noble authority was the breakdown of the discipline exercised by officers over their men. This failure arose primarily from the conditions of military life, particularly the relationship between soldiers and officers.

Most of the soldier's life was independent of interference from his officers; the only immediate superiors with whom he regularly had contact were corporals, sergeants, and officers of fortune. Since mid-century the nobles had made the officer corps a preserve of their own estate from which the overwhelming mass of the soldiers were completely excluded. In fact, military service meant something entirely different for the officers and for the soldiers. For the common soldier, a young man from the artisanate or peasantry, it meant hiring himself out for a period of eight years during which he was the king's man, completely subject to the superiors appointed over him. For the noble officer it meant a traditional service which was his birthright and in which only he and his peers were fit to establish the conditions of service. If the aristocracy were not members of a conqueror race, as Saint-Simon and others had claimed earlier in the century, the noble officer corps was certainly foreign to most of the soldiers in the ranks of the line army.

Extensive leaves were the officer's prerogative. Besides special leaves for emergencies, family business, etc., in alternate years every officer could expect seven and a half months of authorized absence from his duties, on full pay. A royal decision of 12 September 1788 slightly changed the dates, but not the duration, of this semester leave to the period beginning on 15 October and ending on 1 June of the following year; half of the officers in every regiment were eligible for this leave each year. This decision, however, made one major and significant change in policy: colour-bearers, supernumerary officers, and regimental quartermaster treasurers—all positions occupied almost exclusively by officers of fortune—were prohibited from taking these leaves.[1] Whatever illusions these commoners may have had about their status in the officer corps were destroyed. The only true officers were noble officers.

When the officers of a regiment were not on leave, they still had little to do with the men under their command. During peacetime

[1] A.G., *Ordonnances militaires*, vol. 64 (Juillet 1788 à Septembre 1788).

most of the soldiers' duty-time was taken up by training; but few officers participated in this basic military function. During the period 1788–9, of 1,013 men charged with training in eighteen infantry regiments, only 210, about one-fifth, were officers and most of these were lieutenants. In twenty cavalry regiments at the same period, only one-eighth of the personnel employed in training were officers, again mostly lieutenants.[1] Of those officers whose duties included training, most merely supervised and few, if any, conducted drill themselves. The social distance between nobles and commoners which civil society imposed was compounded in the army by the nearly complete separation of officers from men.

The non-commissioned officers, especially the sergeants, were the effective commanders of the men in the ranks. They lived among the soldiers, participated in the same duties, albeit in a supervisory capacity, and led basically the same type of life. At the same time, they were generally more urban, better educated, and of a higher social status than most of the soldiers.[2] For these reasons they were more likely to resent the privileges of their frequently less skilled superiors.[3] In the treatment of their inferiors, however, they could often be brutal both in their actions and in their words.[4]

A harsh but cohesive society developed among the enlisted men of the line army. The normal routine in garrison consisted of seven hours of sleep, two hours of rest, one hour eating, four hours of training, and ten hours of free time.[5] The training, conducted mostly by N.C.O.s, aimed not only at increasing technical competence but also at developing close co-operation among the men in a unit. In the cavalry where the soldier, the horse, and the two together had to be trained to manœuvre effectively as part of a unit, the training was

[1] These data were compiled from inspection reports in A.G., X^b 14, 21, 22, 25, 26, 28, 29, 31, 33, 46, 49, 53, 58, 62, 73, 74, and 81; X^c 31, 33, 34, 35, 40, 42, 45, 47, 50, 53, 64, 72, 76, 78, 79, 81, and 83; and X^g 89.

[2] For these characteristics of the N.C.O.s, see below, pp. 193–9. Although the N.C.O.s who gained promotion to officer during the Revolution represent only a part of the N.C.O.s of the Old Regime, they are representative of a common type which existed before the Revolution. Also see my essay, 'The French Revolution and the Professionalization of the French Officer Corps, 1789–1793', in Morris Janowitz and Jacques van Doorn, eds., *On Military Ideology* (Rotterdam, 1971), pp. 33–42.

[3] One of the most sympathetic descriptions of this frustration is in Hippolyte-Adolphe Taine, *The French Revolution*, trans. by John Durand, vol. 1 (Gloucester, Mass., 1962), p. 329.

[4] Marcel Reinhard, *L'Armée et la Révolution*, Fasicule 1 ([Paris], n.d.), p. 14.

[5] Corvisier, *L'Armée française*, II. 824.

more intense and longer than in the infantry. The training of an expert artilleryman required, for the scrupulous commander, the best part of an eight-year enlistment.[1] Besides the sharing of common duties, other intangible bonds evolved among soldiers: some sense of military honour, a feeling of distinctiveness from civilian society, and a real companionship based on sharing a difficult life. The regiment itself was often a focal point of great loyalty, and occasionally violent clashes occurred between men of different units when regimental honour was at stake.[2] These ties increased cohesion among the soldiers and between them and their immediate superiors, the N.C.O.s, but they did not extend, except in the rarest cases, to the officers.

Frequently the only time a soldier came into personal contact with his officers was when disciplinary action was taken against him. Some officers, whose notoriety probably far surpassed their numbers, discredited the officer corps by their brutality towards their men. The Duc de Châtelet, the commander of the regiment of the French Guards, was renowned for his frequent use of the cane and his constant harassment of the soldiers about their quarters, dress, and appearance.[3] The colonel of the La Fère Infantry Regiment was so excessive in his treatment of troops that he had to be dismissed in June 1788 for abusing his authority.[4] Such high-handed treatment of subordinates was even practised on officers by some colonels, such as the hot-headed Marquis d'Ambert of the Royal Marine

[1] General de Wimpffen maintained that an infantry recruit when incorporated into a unit with veterans could be trained to serve usefully in six weeks; but claimed that it took three or four years to train a cavalryman and seven or eight to train an artilleryman. See 'Discours de M. le Baron Félix de Wimpffen, Député de Caen, Prononcé dans la Séance de Mardi matin, 15 Décembre 1789, et imprimé par ordre de l'Assemblée Nationale', Maclure Collection, vol. 848. In a letter dated 15 March 1792, Lieutenant-Colonel Ratalier of the 2nd Artillery Regiment wrote to General de Rostaing complaining that the new four-year enlistment would not allow artillery recruits to learn their trade properly. See A.G., X^d 7. On cavalry training, see Desbrière and Sautai, *La Cavalerie de 1740 à 1789*, pp. 49–59 and 100–2.

[2] Léon Levy-Schneider, 'L'Armée et la Convention', in Émile Faguet, ed., *L'Oeuvre sociale de la Révolution française* (Paris, [1901]), p. 348 and Ernest d'Hauterive, *L'Armée sous la Révolution* (Paris, 1894), p. 13.

[3] Taine, *French Revolution*, I. 37 and [Henrietta-Lucy Dillon, Marquise de La Tour du Pin], *Memoirs of Madame de La Tour du Pin*, ed. and trans. by Felice Harcourt (New York, 1971), p. 53.

[4] Lieutenant G. Gerthoffer, 'Historique du 52e Régiment d'Infanterie, 1654–1888', pp. 58–68. This manuscript history was received at the Archives de la Guerre on 26 January 1889 and can be found in the series *Historiques des Régiments d'Infanterie* in the carton for the 52nd Infantry.

Infantry.[1] However, it was, above all, the enlisted men who suffered at the hands of such officers and even their less arbitrary colleagues.

Although there were some variations according to unit, military discipline and justice were generally very severe in the Old Regime. Corporal punishments were administered for virtually all breaches of discipline. More serious crimes, such as insubordination or striking a superior, carried a penalty of life imprisonment or death. Desertion was by far the most common offence tried by formal judicial procedures. Some general factors accounted for large numbers of desertions. War and the imminent threat of combat increased desertions considerably; towards the end of the Seven Years War deserters numbered c. 10,000 per year. Many soldiers deserted simply to enlist in a new regiment and thus draw the attractive bonus offered to recruits. The harsh conditions of a soldier's life convinced many that the dangers risked by desertion were preferable to remaining in the army. It was common for two or more soldiers from the same unit to desert at the same time, an indication that comradeship motivated some desertions. Homesickness or family crises prompted many soldiers to desert.[2] By the late 1780s there were approximately 3,000 desertions per year from the line army.[3] In more than 80 per cent of the trials involving a first desertion the punishment was for the convicted soldier to run a gauntlet composed of two files of 50 men each, ten times. The soldiers in these files beat their unfortunate comrade with their ramrods or rifle-straps. Following this punishment, the deserter was condemned to serve eight years beyond his original term of enlistment.

In certain circumstances the penalty was even harsher. Desertion while on guard-duty brought additional turns of the gauntlet, a longer extension of service, or, most commonly, condemnation to the galleys for a number of years, usually fifteen. If a soldier were

[1] For a full discussion of this affair, see A.G., YA 447. D'Ambert, in many ways a caricature of a haughty noble officer of the Old Regime, continued to disregard law, convention, and discretion even after the Revolution; see below, pp. 139–40.

[2] See Corvisier, *L'Armée française*, I. 724–5 and 736; II. 703–6; and Babeau, *La Vie militaire*, I. 324–6.

[3] The following discussion, unless otherwise indicated, is based upon an examination of A.G., *Archives justice militaire. Jugements. Ancien régime*, B[13] 56–67. Cartons 56–67 cover the period 1787–9. In most cases all that remains of the trials are the verdicts and sentences; but occasionally there are copies of the testimony presented. Supplementary sources which confirm the general conclusions and provide further examples are Archives départmentales (A.D.), Ille-et-Vilaine, C 1113 (*Jugements rendus par les Conseils de guerre assemblés, 1756–89*) and C 1115 (*Jugements rendus par les Conseils de guerre assemblés, 1784–9*).

unwise enough to desert more than once and unfortunate enough to be apprehended, he could not escape a long sentence to the galleys. If a soldier combined the crimes of desertion and theft, the almost inevitable penalty was branding and the galleys for life.

On the other hand, the punishment for desertion could be lighter than normal. A would-be deserter who changed his mind and returned voluntarily to his unit within a few days usually received a prolongation of his enlistment but no corporal punishment. In some instances mitigating circumstances were acknowledged and the punishment was either reduced or the accused exonerated. For example, Adrien-Jacques-François-Joseph Hullot of the Colonel Général Cavalry Regiment was tried for desertion when he did not return at the expiration of his leave in 1787; but he was exonerated upon the presentation of a surgeon's certificate that he had been ill at the time.[1] Armant Derbeck was found guilty of desertion at Perpignan on 19 August 1788, but absolved 'by reason of proofs of lunacy and imbecility which he has given for several years'.[2] The same excuse did not, however, succeed for Pierre Brunet, a member of the French Guards who had deserted in March 1789 after less than three months' service. Brunet claimed that at the time he deserted he was 'subject to an illness which deprived him of the use of his senses'. Brunet was found guilty and sentenced to ten turns of a gauntlet of 100 men and eight years' prolongation of service.[3]

Desertions frequently involved more than one soldier, and even in cases of individual desertion the deserter often revealed his plans in advance to some of his comrades; therefore, although they did not actually desert, other soldiers were sometimes implicated in a desertion plot. Such collusion was severely punished, when it could be proven; failure to inform one's superiors of a desertion plot was punished by fifty blows with a sabre flat and four years' prolongation of service. Yet this charge was rarely brought against soldiers; in 1,500 cases examined, there were only eight instances of this accusation.

Certainly, knowledge of a desertion plot was a difficult charge to bring and even more difficult to prove. However, the prosecuting officers had an extremely high conviction rate for desertion cases in general; of more than 1,500 cases, over 95 per cent resulted in findings of guilty. It seems certain that rather than the reluctance of the officers to accuse men of failure to reveal a plan to desert, it was the reluctance of the soldiers to betray their comrades which resulted

[1] A.G., B[13] 60.   [2] A.G., B[13] 58.   [3] A.G., B[13] 66.

in so few convictions for this offence. Some of the rare recorded testimonies which still exist support this contention. A trial which took place in Rocroy in September 1789 concerning a desertion plot in the regiment of Easterhazy Hussars provides examples of the comradeship among the soldiers which could sometimes foil their officers. One hussar in this regiment, Laurent Reiplinger, was asked why he did not inform his superiors about the planned desertion; he replied: 'I feared that I would be badly regarded by my comrades if I did.' Another soldier in the same circumstances, Philippe Klus, gave essentially the same response. Michel Husser when faced with the same question answered: 'I didn't want to cause anyone trouble.'[1] Attitudes like this prevailed despite the fact that co-operation with the authorities brought an immediate honourable discharge, and sometimes a cash reward, for the soldier who would expose his comrades.

The military authorities were thus frustrated by the *esprit de corps* among the men. Most factors of army life worked to establish a strong cohesiveness among the soldiers. They were recruited from similar social classes; many of them came from the same regions; they had served a substantial part of their adult life in the army; and they were all exposed to the same difficult conditions and harsh discipline. Military justice reinforced cohesion. No crimes were more intolerable or punished more harshly than those which were committed against the unit or its members. In 1788 Pierre Guadaux of the La Reine Infantry was sentenced to life in the galleys for stealing 'sheaves of straw in the company'.[2] Joseph Hellet of the Berry Cavalry, who was convicted 'of having stolen two handkerchiefs from one of his comrades of the barrack room', and François Cornibé of the Orléans Cavalry, who was convicted 'of having stolen and even sold some effects of his comrades', received the same punishment. In March 1789 François Michel of the Penthièvre Infantry was condemned to the galleys for life 'for having stolen a shirt apiece from two of his comrades', although his sentence was shortly afterwards commuted to three years because of his previous, irreproachable record. Hubert Gery, a corporal in the Maine Infantry, deserted with regimental funds and was sentenced to life in the galleys after being branded on both shoulders. Louis-François Chatelain of the Marine Infantry Regiment was sentenced to be strangled by hanging because he had seriously wounded one

[1] A.G., B¹³ 65.   [2] A.G., B¹³ 61.

of his comrades with a knife.[1] Later, in May 1790, when a soldier of
the Nancy garrison, named Roussière, admitted that he had pro-
voked quarrels between soldiers and civilians, he was discharged in a
formal ceremony and sent away wearing a cap inscribed 'Judas' for
his betrayal of his comrades.[2] Comradeship was not only natural but
also essential in the life of a soldier.

How harsh this life was can never be precisely measured. The
instances just related come from the records of courts martial, but
of the undoubtedly numerous instances of informal punishments
there is no record. There are, however, some hints. For example, in
the record of the trial of several members of the regiment of Esterhazy Hussars who had failed to report a desertion plot, two hussars,
Adam Hart and Laurent Reiplinger, when asked if they had any
complaints about their superiors, both complained of having been
caned by their sergeants.[3] Certainly, these were not isolated
instances, but it is impossible to say with any accuracy how common these informal punishments were.

Living-quarters for the soldiers were crowded, even in permanent
garrisons. Only privileged personnel, such as N.C.O.s and grenadiers, slept two to a bed; private soldiers slept three and four
together.[4] Food was supplied by private contractors and was often
insufficient in quantity and inferior in quality. This sometimes
affected the health of the men. In February 1788 the former surgeon-
general of the army of Marshal de Broglie wrote to the Council of
War that a large number of maladies in the army were directly due
to the defective nourishment of the soldier.[5] This situation, combined with the abysmal state of sanitation, made sicknesses and
epidemics, especially in winter quarters, more murderous than
combat. Hospital facilities were worse than inadequate. Indeed, the
constant notation in the troop registers. 'Died at the hospital', makes
it appear that being sent to an eighteenth-century military hospital
was tantamount to a condemnation to death.[6] It can be estimated

[1] A.G., B¹³ 58 and 59 and A.D., Ille-et-Vilaine, C 1113.
[2] William Clinton Baldwin, 'The Beginnings of the Revolution and the Mutiny of
the Royal Garrison in Nancy: L'Affaire de Nancy, 1790' (unpublished Ph.D. dissertation, Univ. of Michigan, 1973), p. 211.
[3] A.G., B¹³ 65.
[4] Mention, L'Armée de l'ancien régime, p. 272 and Duruy, L'Armée royale, p. 134.
[5] Desbrière and Sautai, La Cavalerie, 1740-1789, p. 112.
[6] One of the rare testimonies of a common soldier of the eighteenth century substantiates this evaluation. Speaking of a field hospital in Bavaria during the War of
Austrian Succession, Charles-Étienne Bernos wrote: 'Within three days of entering this

that in a peacetime year some 12 per cent of the troops entered the hospital; and of these only 2 out of 3 left it alive.[1] Only in 1788 was a military medical corps established with its own schools, hospitals, cadres, and hierarchy.

Quartering troops was a major problem for military and civil authorities. The provision of separate lodgings for soldiers, i.e. barracks or casernes, had made substantial progress during the eighteenth century.[2] The obligation of furnishing lodging for troops fell on the inhabitants; but they could fulfil this obligation by quartering soldiers in their own homes, by setting aside certain buildings for this purpose, or by constructing barracks for the soldiers. The latter two alternatives had become the most common method of liquidating this rather unpleasant and costly obligation in the course of the century. In their desire to keep the expenses of such a project to a minimum, civil officials or private entrepreneurs hired by them often provided facilities which were at best inadequate and at worst wretched.

In September 1788 the inspector-general of Provence, the Comte de Béthisy, complained that most of the housing and the furnishings provided for the troops by a civilian contractor were in poor condition. The count also observed that at Marseille a company of the Vexin Infantry was quartered near the latrines, and claimed that as a result almost every other man in the company had come down with scurvy; another company of the same regiment had to evacuate its quarters every time it rained. De Béthisy attributed such poor housing to the hostility of the Marseillais to the presence of troops. The colonels of the Royal Auvergne, Conti, and Dillon Infantry Regiments garrisoned at Calais in January 1789 claimed that the garrison's hospital was in such need of repair that the lives of the sick soldiers there were endangered. Colonel de Lostange of the Royal Picardie Cavalry requested that his regiment be moved from Angers in December 1788 because both the lodgings and the stables, some of which were in caves, were unhealthy.[3] Although all military

hospital three quarters of the sick perished . . .'. See 'Souvenirs de campagne d'un soldat du régiment de Limousin (1741–1748)', *Carnet de la Sabretache*, X (1902), p. 672.

[1] Colonel Henri-Joseph de Buttet, 'La Dépense du soldat en 1772', *Actes du quatre-vingt-dixième congrès des sociétés savantes*, vol. I (Paris, 1966), p. 141.

[2] The most comprehensive treatment of this subject is in André Eugène Navereau, *Le Logement et les ustensiles des gens de guerre de 1439 à 1789* (Poitiers, 1924), pp. 120–62 and 201–29.

[3] A.G., *Mémoires historiques et reconnaissances*, 1774: 'Casernement et garnisons, 1630–1791'.

quarters were not as bad as these examples indicate, the enormous cost of quartering even a small contingent of troops generally discouraged civilians from providing adequate facilities.

Apart from this general reluctance to spend large sums of money on military housing, civilian attitudes towards garrisons varied greatly according to local conditions. As just indicated, many of the inhabitants of Marseille opposed the presence of armed troops in their city, a hostility which later created a major crisis early in the Revolution. The presence of troops not only created a heavy financial burden but also threatened, at least potentially, the autonomy of cities. At Bordeaux in July 1788, for example, fifty men of the Champagne Infantry were allowed into the city to provide a guard at a funeral only after the consent of the municipal officers had been formally obtained.[1] Other cities and towns desired the presence of a garrison, primarily to assist the local economy. The municipal officers of Philippeville wrote to the Minister of War in March 1789 claiming that a garrison was necessary for the livelihood of the inhabitants. In January 1789 the city of Vendôme requested the Minister of War to order the Chartres Dragoons to return to this city because the area needed a garrison to consume its excess foodstuffs. The civil officials of Bergues in March 1789 claimed that this town 'could subsist only by means of the troops who are garrisoned there'.[2]

Regardless of whether a garrison was desired or only reluctantly accepted, the methods of lodging troops in the late eighteenth century made contacts between soldiers and civilians frequent. Troop movements which came as a result of changes in garrisons or movements to ports of embarkation necessitated quartering troops on the inhabitants of areas through which the soldiers passed. Permanent facilities could not be established in all such areas and so inevitably most of the troops on movement had to be housed and supplied by local inhabitants.[3] In localities where military quarters had been provided, the facilities were sometimes insufficient and a number of soldiers had to be lodged in private homes.[4] Even where

---

[1] Michel L'Heritier, *La Révolution à Bordeaux dans l'histoire de Révolution française*, vol. I: *La Fin de l'ancien Régime et la préparation des États généraux (1787–1789)* (Paris, 1942), p. 42.

[2] A.G., *Mémoires historiques et reconnaissances*, 1774.

[3] Général Navereau, 'Les Lignes d'étape', *Revue historique de l'armée*, 1962, No. 2, pp. 19–29.

[4] In the late 1780s this was true of such garrison towns as Colmar in Alsace, Aix in

adequate troop quarters existed the casernes were near the edge of a town, usually within the town boundaries, and the soldiers were not effectively isolated from the civilian populace except during training periods.

Civilian attitudes towards soldiers were not, of course, determined solely by the obligation of lodging troops, although this was an important factor. Soldiers occupied a peculiar status in eighteenth-century France, something between a trade and a separate estate in society. By enlistment a soldier made a contractual arrangement with the king which withdrew him from civil society for a number of years and thus deprived him of the protection afforded by the social groups to which he had previously belonged (family, parish, guild, etc.).[1] This made the soldier somewhat foreign to traditional French society. Futhermore, the presence of royal troops in an area, especially during wartime, could be no less ruinous to the inhabitants than occupation by foreign armies.[2] Finally, during the eighteenth century economists, moralists, and publicists attacked the warrior virtues of the past and the army in particular as unproductive, barbaric, and tools of despotism.[3] Towards the end of the Old Regime, however, this antipathy came to be directed more and more towards institutions rather than the soldiers themselves. Contemporary literature depicted the soldier in a more honourable and sympathetic light. There was increased concern for the condition of the soldier, and the vices of military life were attributed to the system of recruitment rather than to its victims.[4]

The most comprehensive plan for improving the lot of the soldier was offered by Joseph Servan, who later became Minister of War

Provence, and Sedan and Toul in Lorraine. See A.G., *Mémoires historiques et reconnaissances*, 1774. It is impossible even to estimate the number of troops quartered on civilians; not only are such records unavailable, but the continual variations from time to time and from region to region would make any estimate only the roughest approximation. All that can be said is that in periods of extensive troop movements, such as late 1788 and early 1789, a higher proportion of soldiers was quartered in civilian homes than in more quiet times.

[1] Corvisier, *L'Armée française*, I. 119–22 and Levy-Schneider, 'L'Armée et la Convention', pp. 346–50.

[2] Theodore Ropp, *War in the Modern World* (Durham, N.C., 1959), p. 40 and Jules Leverrier, *La Naissance de l'armée nationale, 1789–1794* (Paris, 1939), pp. 156–8.

[3] Corvisier, *L'Armée française*, II. 955; Hans Speier, *Social Order and the Risks of War* (New York, 1952), pp. 234 and 242; and John U. Nef, *War and Human Progress* (Cambridge, Mass., 1950), pp. 226 and 260–1.

[4] Charles Dejob, 'Le Soldat dans la littérature française au XVIIIᵉ siècle', *Revue politique et littéraire*, 4th Series, XII (7 Oct. 1899), 449–58.

twice in 1792. In a book published in Switzerland in 1780 Servan exposed many of the worst problems in the army: excessively harsh discipline, the large number of young and inexperienced officers appointed by court influence, the low pay, the poor quality of food, the wretched hospital conditions, and the dearth of educational facilities. Servan called for greater esteem for the military profession, and the abolition of fraud and abuses in recruitment. Above all, he argued: 'The soldier should, without doubt, be regarded as a citizen; he is the man of the nation, charged with the defence of our properties and our persons . . .'[1] Whether influenced by Servan or not, many line soldiers did, when the Revolution occurred, view themselves as citizens with legitimate grievances to be redressed, and many civilians were willing to accept them as such.

This sentiment was fostered by continuing contacts between soldiers and civilians in the latter part of the eighteenth century. Besides being lodged among civilians, troops frequently worked alongside civilians during their off-duty hours, a practice necessitated by the low pay in the army. Between 1759 and 1788 the daily pay of the average infantryman rose from 5 *sous* 8 *deniers* to 6 *sous* 8 *deniers*, despite the generally greater price increase during this period. Pay varied according to branch and rank, being higher in the cavalry and artillery and among the non-commissioned officers. Every soldier while in garrison was required to pay two *sous* for his daily ration of twenty-four ounces of bread. With the remainder of his pay he had to buy meat, vegetables, salt, and toilet accessories; to pay the barber and the laundress; and to provide his food on the thirty-first day of seven months each year, when he received neither pay nor bread.[2] At best the pay of most of the troops was barely sufficient, and in times of shortage and high prices it was inadequate for subsistence. According to a recent study, the average infantryman in 1772 needed 16 *livres* 18 *sous* 10 *deniers* (almost two months' pay) beyond what he received in order to purchase necessities.[3]

Despite the increase in pay decided upon by the council of war in

[1] [Joseph Servan], *Le Soldat citoyen, ou vues patriotiques sur la manière la plus avantageuse de pourvoir à la défense du royaume* ([Neufchâtel], 1780), pp. 33–6, 57–8, and 148–9. The quotation is from pp. 148–9.

[2] For information on pay, see Mention, *L'Armée de l'ancien régime*, pp. 265–6; Corvisier, *L'Armée française*, II. 822; Albert Soboul, *L'Armée nationale sous la Révolution* (Paris, 1945), p. 26; and Latreille, *L'Armée et la nation à la fin de l'ancien régime*. pp. 213–14.

[3] De Buttet, 'La dépense du soldat en 1772', pp. 141–9.

1788, the common soldier still found his army salary insufficient to support himself. The only means by which most soldiers could make up for this deficiency was to perform additional military duties, e.g. extra turns on guard-duty, or, more commonly, by taking some job in a nearby town. Many deplored this situation. In October 1789, the N.C.O.s of the garrison at Lille wrote to the new National Assembly and petitioned for higher wages and increased rations: 'That would give to soldiers the possibility of supporting themselves without being forced, as they are today, to double or triple their service or to work most often at vile and degrading jobs.'[1]

Soldiers also had the opportunity for close, personal contacts with civilians when they were fortunate enought to receive leave. As among the officers, a certain proportion of enlisted men were allowed to take semester leave each year; however, a smaller proportion of soldiers could take this leave and its duration was one month shorter than that of the officers. Approximately one-fifth of the enlisted men in each regiment were eligible for six and a half months' leave, from October to April or May, each year.[2] While on such leave the soldiers received only half-pay (the rest going into the regimental funds), and they were required to return with certificates of good conduct signed by the local constabulary.[3] In addition, special limited periods of leave, whose duration was subtracted from the service of the soldier and so had to be made up, were authorized in particular circumstances. Some soldiers, around fifty per regiment, were allowed to return home in the summer and work in the fields, if they could prove that this was necessary to their family.[4] Finally, those men sent out to recruit new soldiers were technically on leave, although they were still performing military duties.

In sum, numerous and frequent contacts with civilians, usually

[1] Quoted in Desbrière and Sautai, *La Cavalerie, 1740–1789*, p. 113. Other evidence of the employment of soldiers in civilian occupations can be found in A.D., Bouches-du-Rhône, L 3245 and A.G., YA 447, which indicate that this practice continued into the Revolution.

[2] For the regulations governing this leave, see A.G., *Ordonnances militaires*, vol. 55 (janvier 1777 à mai 1778) and vol. 64 (juillet 1788 à septembre 1788). The pertinent regulations are dated 18 Oct. 1777 and 12 Sept. 1788.

[3] Lieutenant-Colonel Belhomme, *Histoire de l'infanterie en France*, vol. III (Paris, 1896), p. 351 and A.G. *Ordonnances militaires*, vol. 55.

[4] Corvisier, *L'Armée française*, I. 100 and II. 831. Such periods of leave, however, were almost never recorded (I have seen evidence of only *one* such leave), and no estimate can be made of their frequency.

from the same social background, were a common part of military life for most soldiers. While not always cordial, these contacts did increase familiarity and possibly fostered better understanding between soldiers and civilians. At the same time, the soldiers had developed a peculiar cohesiveness of their own. The officers, however, were mostly removed from this cohesive society both by their social status and by their personal conduct; apart from being members of the same institution, they had almost nothing in common with the soldiers. Within the officer corps serious divisions and rivalries existed which governmental reforms, despite their administrative and organizational improvements, had exacerbated. All of these circumstances constituted serious problems for the Royal Army on the eve of the French Revolution, although their implications could not even be guessed at the time. Under ordinary conditions none of these problems, individually or collectively, would have destroyed the effectiveness of the army. But, in the extraordinary stress created by the coming revolution they would lead to the collapse of the army and of the entire regime of which it was the ultimate defence.

CHAPTER II

THE CRISIS OF 1789

DURING THE year prior to July 1789 the Royal Army was subjected to a series of pressures that severely strained the structural weaknesses described in the previous chapter. These pressures originated in the political and economic problems of civil society, but had an immediate impact upon the army. From mid-1788 political disturbances and food riots required the extensive employment of line units in a police role. These functions led to increased disaffection on the part of some officers and growing suspicions about the reliability of soldiers employed in such duties. How widespread and how strong these sentiments were, however, remained uncertain. A decisive test seemed to be in the offing when the king determined to break the deadlock between him and the self-styled National Assembly by an appeal to force; but a violent confrontation did not occur. Instead, upon the advice of officers, who themselves knew little of the men under their orders, Louis XVI refused to employ his troops against rebellious Parisians. This decision, coupled with increasing exposure of the soldiers to revolutionary ideas and activities destroyed both the King's authority over his army and that of the officers over their men.

THE ARMY AND INTERNAL DISORDER

The Royal Army had traditionally performed police functions during the Old Regime; indeed, military power had been a major instrument in the consolidation of the monarchy. In the face of widespread disorders in 1788 the government naturally turned again to the line army. The army itself had, in the past generation, been substantially reformed; yet, simultaneously, it was experiencing many of the divisions and hostilities that existed in society at large. Now it was exposed to a challenge which would determine whether its external framework and organization could compensate for the serious problems which existed in its internal operation and composition.

In mid-1788 the long political struggle between the monarchy and the *parlements* was reaching a climax. In early May a number of royal orders issued through the influence of Lamoignon, the Keeper of the Seals, severely restricted the powers of the parlements. The reaction of the *parlementaires* in parts of France was rebellion; they refused to accept the legality of such 'tyrannical' legislation. Ostensibly, the parlements were defending liberties against royal absolutism, and in some cities there was widespread popular support for them. Certainly, the parlements were defending traditional privileges against state authority; and many nobles, including army officers, approved of their reaction.

The parlement of Rennes refused to register the new edicts in defiance of the King and his ministry; and on 9 May a popular demonstration supported this position. The next day the provincial intendant and the military commander of the region, accompanied by a detachment from the Rohan Infantry Regiment which was stationed in Rennes, forced the registration of the Lamoignon edicts and arrested some of the officers of the parlement. Upon emerging from the hall, the royal officials and the troops were attacked by a crowd and pelted with stones, bottles, and pieces of wood. More serious violence was avoided because Lt. Blondel de Nouainvelle, a noble officer of the Rohan Infantry, ordered his men not to fire on the people. The commander of the province, the Comte de Thiard, subsequently called for reinforcements, and by the end of the month the regiment of Penthièvre Infantry and detachments of the Forez Infantry and Orléans Dragoons arrived in the city. The inhabitants responded by refusing to lodge the troops and by holding another demonstration in support of the parlement on 2 June.

Meanwhile, signs of disaffection began to appear among the troops and especially among the officers. A number of officers from the newly arrived units assured the first president of the parlement that they had no intention of mixing in the political quarrel. More significantly, a Breton noble and captain in the Penthièvre Infantry, Bonin de la Ville-Bouquais, resigned his commission on 1 June after twenty-four years of service on the grounds that he could not associate himself with any armed repression of Bretons. Other Breton officers in the same regiment also announced their intention to resign; and the colonel warned Thiard that his soldiers could not be depended on if they were ordered to march against the Rennais. Thiard then separated all Bretons from the regiment and sent them back to their previous garrison at Dinan.[1]

[1] The most complete description of these events at Rennes can be found in Barthélemy Pocquet du Haut-Jussé, *Les Origines de la Révoltuion en Bretagne*, vol. I (Paris, 1885),

Even before order had been fully restored at Rennes another major disturbance had taken place at Grenoble. A riot in support of the local parlement in this city broke out in early June 1788. Two infantry regiments garrisoned there, the Austrasie and Royal Marine Infantry, were called out to maintain order; and both were attacked by a rock-throwing crowd. The Royal Marine, under its intrepid Colonel D'Ambert, performed loyally by firing on the demonstrators. The regiment of Austrasie Infantry on the contrary, showed the same disturbing reluctance to shoot at crowds as had the officers and men at Rennes. The lieutenant-colonel of this regiment, Boissieux, forbade his soldiers to fire on the crowd, even though he himself had been struck on the face by a stone or tile.[1] When riot turned into revolution such reluctance to use force would lead to the collapse of the regime.

Elsewhere in mid-1788 there were examples of officers and men objecting to their police role. At Toulouse an officer instructed to conduct a parlementary official to prison resigned from the army rather than perform such a distasteful duty. In Béarn some troops, following the lead of their noble officers, refused to suppress antigovernment demonstrations. Later, in March 1789 when crowds attacked the homes of members of the parlement of Besançon, the garrison commander, the Marquis de Langeron, refused to deploy his forces, claiming that the army was to be used against the enemies of the state, not its citizens.[2]

While these incidents did not constitute conclusive proof of widespread disaffection within the army, they were ominous warnings for the future. Officers who refused to execute government orders, even by the passive device of resignation, had given an example of disobedience which helped to undermine their own authority over their subordinates. In only a few months hundreds of soldiers would respond to unpopular orders with their own form of passive disobedience, mass desertion.

The repression of political disturbances was the most striking of the police duties of the army in 1788–9; however, it constituted only a minor portion of military activities at the time. Much more com-

---

pp. 75–253. Also see Jacques Godechot, *Les Institutions de la France sous la Révolution et l'Empire*, 2nd edn. (Paris, 1968), p. 122 and L. Hartmann, *Les Officiers de l'armée royale et la Révolution* (Paris, 1910), pp. 56–7.

[1] For a first-hand account of this episode, see Mautort, *Mémoires*, pp. 363–6.

[2] Albert Mathiez, *The French Revolution*, trans. by Catherine Allison Phillips (New York, 1964), p. 33.

mon was the repression of riots whose origins were economic. The harvest of 1788 had been the worst in decades, and in a country where most of the inhabitants lived on a subsistence economy this was a major disaster. The full impact of this crisis came in the spring of 1789, when the meagre reserves of the previous harvest had been used up before the new harvest was in. At this point the policing of food riots became the most important function of the French army.

On 7 March 1789 there were grain riots at Vendôme, and 150 men of the Royal Comtois Infantry were summoned to re-establish order. On 23 March flour storehouses at Nancy were pillaged, and cavalry detachments from Lunéville and Pont-à-Mousson had to be called in. In late April a grain riot at Amiens forced the municipal officials to request the Diesbach Swiss Infantry and the cavalry regiment of Cuirassiers to assist the constabulary in preventing attacks on the houses of local merchants. In the small town of Bray-sur-Seine in Île-de-France a detachment of twenty troopers of the Royal Cravattes Cavalry had to be present each market-day to prevent disturbances. At Rennes early in May the same officials who had only a few months before objected to the very presence of soldiers were not reluctant to call in numerous troop detachments to repress a riot over the price of bread 'among the workers and day labourers [ouvriers et manœuvres]'. Even the presence of two infantry regiments and four squadrons of cavalry could not prevent the grain riot which broke out on 6 May in Cambrai. At the end of the same month detachments of the Royal Lorraine Cavalry and Schomberg Dragoons had to be summoned to Bourges because of disorders connected with the price of grain. On 27 June 1789 there was a riot by the *menu peuple* of Quimperlé when they saw grain necessary to their survival being loaded on boats for exportation; a company of the Bassigny Infantry was insufficient to control this disturbance. A detachment of the Auvergne Light Infantry was summoned to Issoire on 3 July to establish order in that town after yet another grain riot. Such examples could be multiplied many times over; but these should suffice to indicate that a large part of the line army was being employed continually in early 1789 to police disturbances over the price and availability of food.[1]

[1] A.N., H^{1453} and BB^{30} 87 contain these and many more examples of the use of the line army to control food riots. Louis Gottschalk maintains that there were more than 300 riots in the spring of 1789, many of them due to hunger; see *The Era of the French Revolution* (Cambridge, Mass., 1957), p. 131. The most comprehensive treatment of this phenomenon remains Georges Lefebvre, *La Grande Peur de 1789* (Paris, 1932).

Some authorities were convinced that the soldiers found these missions highly distasteful. In June 1789 a civilian official in Poitou complained that '. . . the soldiers, when they are not commanded [by officers], have always exhibited repugnance for forcibly opposing popular disturbances whose cause is the dearness of grain.'[1] In July the military commander of Picardie described the attitude of the soldiers in his command to the minister of war: 'I can not hide the fact that the troops have shown little will or firmness.'[2] Regardless of the general validity of these observations, the repressive activities of the army in 1788 and 1789 certainly had debilitating effects on the troops. Regiments were seldom employed as units but were usually broken up into small detachments, sometimes of less than company strength. As a result, unity of command and discipline suffered as exposure to rebellious activity, and sometimes propaganda, increased. Moreover, the continual marching and counter-marching and the frequent inadequacy of quarters and supplies weakened large segments of the army physically.[3]

Disturbances in the provinces, however—no matter what their origins, scope, or results—could not decisively affect the country at large or the army as a whole. Only developments in the capital could have such an impact; and it was here in the summer of 1789 that the monarchy and the Royal Army were subjected to their most critical test.

The dismal state of French finances had forced Louis XVI to capitulate to the political demands of the aristocracy and to summon the Estates General to meet in May 1789 at Versailles: this, in turn, gave rise to expectations of the most extensive and diverse reforms which were expressed in the *cahiers de doléances*, drawn up for the deputies of the three estates, and in the countless political pamphlets that flooded the capital and the rest of the country. After the first sessions of the Estates General the representatives of the Third Estate demanded a full share in governing the nation. This threat to the established political and social system led the nobility to rally, somewhat belatedly, to the crown in order to thwart the revolutionary demands of the commoners. Simultaneously, as the economic situation worsened, the urban and rural masses of France also looked

---

[1] Letter of M. de Nanteuil, dated 17 June 1789, in A.N., H¹⁴⁵³.

[2] Lefebvre, *Grande Peur*, p. 30.

[3] Jacques Godechot, *The Taking of the Bastille : July 14, 1789*, trans. by Jean Stewart (London, 1970), p. 131.

to the capital for the alleviation of their plight. Political and economic crises converged and the situation in and around Paris became highly explosive.

Since April 1789 the military commandant of Paris and its vicinity, the Baron de Besenval, had been increasing the strength of his command by ordering detachments of line troops from provincial garrisons to the Paris region. The normal police force of the city numbered only about 1,500 men and was inadequate to handle any but routine matters. The regiments of French and Swiss Guards, nearly 6,000 men in all, were also available for police duty; but in light of the situation, Besenval felt that even more troops were necessary to keep order. In late April the Réveillon riot in Paris required the employment of detachments of the French Guards and the Royal Cravattes Cavalry to restore peace.[1] Between 13 April and 1 May Besenval ordered detachments from six cavalry regiments, some 1,500 men in all, and the Swiss regiment of Salis-Samade, about 900 strong, to towns near Paris and Versailles. During the first three weeks of June an additional 500–600 cavalrymen and another Swiss regiment were summoned to the region around the capital. By late June nearly 4,000 line troops, over 2,600 of whom were in foreign-speaking units (four hussar detachments and two Swiss regiments) had been stationed around Paris.[2]

These troop movements caused consternation in the city; and the size of the military build-up was greatly exaggerated. The semi-official United States representative, Gouverneur Morris, was convinced that by 17 April the government was assembling 'ten thousand troops in the vicinity of Paris'. By late May, Morris had been informed that this force had been ordered to the area to prevent trouble in the event of the dissolution of the Estates General.[3] By late June one observer estimated that there were 4,000 troops around Paris and Versailles; and 'the city of Paris was alarmed.'[4] This

[1] Rudé, *Crowd in the French Revolution*, p. 98.
[2] This information is in a document prepared by the Minister of War and entitled 'Mouvements de Troupes qui ont eu lieu dans la Généralité de Paris depuis le premier Mars 1789 jusqu'au quinze Juillet suivant', in A.N., BB[30] 161.
[3] Gouverneur Morris, *Journal de Gouverneur Morris, Ministre plénipotentiaire des États-Unis en France de 1792 à 1794, pendant les années 1789, 1790, 1791 et 1792*, trans. by E. Pariset (Paris, 1901), pp. 15 and 39–40.
[4] Bibliothèque nationale (B.N.), *Manuscrits français (Ancien supplément français)* 13713: *Journal des évenements survenus à Paris du 2 avril au 8 octobre 1789 ; analyse des comptes rendus des séances de l'Assemblée nationale, etc., par un clerc de procureur au Châtelet*, feuillet 20.

worry was exacerbated by the predominance of foreign units who, it was feared, had been ordered to slaughter the people.[1]

Despite such concerns, it appears that the government's claim that these troops had been assembled merely to preserve order was sincere—at least until the last week in June. The crisis which began on 20 June with the 'lock-out' of the deputies and their subsequent oath to establish a constitution, and which terminated in the King's apparent capitulation to the National Assembly on 27 June, radically changed the character of the military deployment. The King's message at the royal session of 23 June explicitly, as well as implicitly, rejected many of the demands for reform, e.g. equality of opportunity for employment in government positions. More decisively, on 26 June the government ordered a military build-up in the vicinity of Paris of such strength that it was clear that the King and his advisers had decided to dismiss the National Assembly, by force if necessary.[2]

On 26 June marching orders were given to three cavalry and three infantry regiments, two of which were German regiments. These orders increased the number of troops in the Parisian region by 4,800 men and more than doubled the strength of line units there. On 1 July 11,500 more troops were summoned to Paris and its vicinity.[3] Thus in less than one week the strength of line units called to Paris increased from fewer than 4,000 to more than 20,000 men. It was impossible to doubt any longer the government's intention.

Fear in Paris grew to panic proportions. Both the numbers and mission of the recently summoned troops continued to be exaggerated. Gouverneur Morris said that there would be 25,000 troops in the Paris area by 11 July; and he was virtually certain that the Estates General would be dissolved.[4] Lafayette claimed that there were 30,000 soldiers in the area by early July, for the same purpose.[5] A minor official of the Châtelet estimated that there were 36,000

[1] Lefebvre, *Grande Peur*, pp. 69–70.

[2] Despite more recent work, the best discussion of this event remains Pierre Caron, 'La Tentative de contre-révolution de juin-juillet 1789', *Revue d'histoire moderne*, VIII (1906–7), 5–34 and 649–78.

[3] These units included five Swiss regiments (Castella, Vigier, Châteauvieux, Diesbach, and Courten), five French infantry regiments (Bourbonnais, Dauphin, Vintimille, Hainaut, and Saintonge), a detachment of 300 men from the Flandre Chasseurs, and one battalion each of the Besançon and Toul Artillery Regiments. See A.N., BB³⁰ 161.

[4] Morris, *Journal*, p. 53.

[5] Lafayette, *Mémoires*, I. 434.

troops by 8 July and claimed that each day brought a new regiment.[1]
The more poorly informed public probably exaggerated the exag-
gerations. In addition the purpose of these troops, especially the
foreign units, was the subject of wild speculation which was often
taken for certainty. It was generally 'known' that the King was going
to use force of arms to disperse the National Assembly. It was also
believed that Montmartre would be bombarded and the Palais Royal
sacked.[2] A major in the Versailles National Guard later testified that
the city of Versailles (with almost 45,000 inhabitants) was to be
given over to the Berchény Hussars to pillage for a period of three
days.[3] The royal display of armed force had clearly frightened the
populace; but, unfortunately for the government, it had not sufficiently intimidated them. The people of Paris and the surrounding
areas had come to suspect that many of the soldiers recently
assembled to suppress them would not, in fact, carry out such
orders.

Doubts about the reliability of the soldiers had begun as early as
February 1789. In that month the Controller-General of Finances,
Necker, had told Malouet: 'We are not even sure of the troops.'
Shortly after the opening of the Estates General, Necker expressed
this same fear to the King.[4] By the end of June, Gouverneur Morris
believed that the troops in the Paris area could not be depended on
to obey their officers.[5] The Saxon ambassador was sure that even
some of the foreign soldiers would not march against civilians if so
ordered.[6] Such opinions had also percolated down to average
civilians. On 30 June at Nangis, near Paris, the servant who dressed
his wig told Arthur Young '. . . be assured as we are, that the French
soldiers will never fire on the people. . . .'[7]

The bases for such opinions are, unfortunately, unknown; but it
seems likely that those expressed in late June and early July were at
least partially affected by the example of the French Guards. By the
third week of June many men of this regiment, who were quartered
in Paris and worked at various trades there during off-duty hours,

[1] B.N., *Manuscrits français*, 13713, feuillets 27-8.
[2] Lefebvre, *Grande Peur*, pp. 93 and 71.
[3] A.N., BB30 161.
[4] Caron, 'Tentative de contre-révolution', p. 655.
[5] Ibid.
[6] Albert Mathiez, *La Victoire en l'an II* (Paris, 1916), p. 37.
[7] Arthur Young, *Travels in France during the Years 1787, 1788, and 1789*, ed. by
Jeffery Kaplow (Garden City, N.J., 1969), p. 136.

were fraternizing with the crowds and agitators at the Palais Royal.[1] Discipline in this élite unit deteriorated rapidly. From 23 June soldiers began to refuse to perform police duties; on 27 June five companies deserted and went to the Palais Royal; on 30 June ten French Guards imprisoned in the Abbaye for insubordination were forcibly freed by a crowd of 4,000 Parisians who hailed them as brothers and protectors. By this date many, including the Duc de Châtelet who commanded the regiment, were convinced that the French Guards were completely unreliable as police. Subsequent events confirmed this evaluation. On 6 July men of this regiment stationed at Versailles engaged in a violent quarrel with German-speaking hussars, in the course of which townspeople aided the French Guards. Six days later in Paris French Guardsmen helped to defend civilians against an attack by elements of the Royal Allemand Cavalry that had been ordered to clear the area around the Place Louis XV. By 14 July five of the six battalions of the regiment defected; and French Guards were numerous and prominent in organizing the attack on the Bastille.[2] In early July, however, it still remained to be seen whether the soldiers of the other units, who did not have such close ties with the local populace, were equally disaffected.

During the first week in July the military cordon around Paris and Versailles was drawn tighter. Units which had at first taken up positions on the outskirts of the capital were moved in closer. The regiments of Nassau and Bouillon Infantry were brought into Versailles and quartered on the palace grounds. Part of the large force summoned from provincial garrisons on 1 July was stationed in Saint-Denis, close to Paris, and in the faubourgs of the city itself.[3]

[1] E.g., Hoche, then a sergeant in the French Guards and a few years later one of the Revolution's greatest generals, worked manufacturing caps; and Lefebvre, who served in the same regiment and later became a Marshal of the Empire, gave German and Latin lessons to the petty bourgeois of Paris. See P. Chalmin, 'La Désintégration de l'armée royal en France à la fin du XVIIIᵉ siècle', *Revue historique de l'armée*, 1964, No. 1, p. 85.

[2] On the role of the French Guards, see Jules Michelet, *Histoire de la Révolution française*, vol. I (Paris, 1868), pp. 136 and 146–7; Mathiez, *French Revolution*, p. 46; Caron, 'Tentative de contre-révolution', pp. 653–4; Godechot, *Taking of the Bastille*, pp. 183 and 189; Jean Mérilys, 'La Propagande révolutionnaire dans l'armée en 1789', *Revue hebdomadaire*, 22 May 1937, pp. 482–3; Young, *Travels in France*, p. 192; and B.N., *Manuscrits français*, 13713, feuillet 20.

[3] For details on the location of the various units, see Caron, 'Tentative de contre-révolution', pp. 12–16 and Godechot, *Taking of the Bastille*, pp. 26 and 179–80. The basic primary source is A.N., BB³⁰ 161.

This concentration of such a large number of men created new problems. The alarming food crisis in Paris was worsened by the arrival of each contingent of soldiers.[1] Upon arrival the troops who had been on the march for days and who had been engaged in maintaining order found the preparations made to receive them inadequate. Food was scarce and very expensive; and the soldier's pay was insufficient. No suitable quarters could be prepared for so many men in such a short time. Clothing and equipment were worn and damaged after strenuous activity by both men and animals; and no replacements were available. Even some of the officers complained about the miserable conditions which they faced.[2]

These troop movements not only resulted in physical discomfort for the soldiers but also increased their contacts with civilians and their exposure to revolutionary propaganda. Certainly, the soldiers were at least vaguely aware of demands for military reforms contained in the *cahiers* (e.g. that military grades be open to all without distinction of class, that the harsh disciplinary system be ameliorated, that soldiers retain all the rights of other citizens)[3] and could not but sympathize with those who supported such changes. In Paris the troops came into personal contact with proponents of revolutionary change. According to the Marquis de Maleissye, a lieutenant in the French Guards and an eyewitness to the events of July, as each unit arrived in the capital it encountered 'the agents of the Duc d'Orléans' and was immediately demoralized.[4] The journalist Montjoye concurred: 'All the troops that passed through Paris disbanded as soon as they came into the city and the soldiers rushed off to the Palais Royal.'[5] On 11 July a battalion of the Toul Artillery, many of whose cannoneers had fraternized with the crowds at the Palais Royal, was, in fact, withdrawn from Paris to Jouy-en-Josas.[6]

---

[1] See the report of M. Garran de Coulon in A.N., BB³⁰ 161.

[2] See the correspondence in A.N., BB³⁰ 161.

[3] Examples of demands for military reforms in the *cahiers* can be found in François Furet and Denis Richet, *The French Revolution*, trans. by Stephen Hardman (London, 1970), p. 66; M. Chaulanges, A. C. Manry, and R. Sève, *Textes Historiques, 1789–1799: L'Époque de la Révolution* (Paris, 1970), p. 11; Pierre Goubert and Michel Denis, *1789: Les Français ont la parole* (Paris, 1964), pp. 209–11 and 213; *Archives parlementaires de 1787 à 1860*, vol. III (Paris, 1879), pp. 218 and 476.

[4] Caron, 'Tentative de contre-révolution', p. 654.

[5] Godechot, *Taking of the Bastille*, p. 183.

[6] Caron, 'Tentative de contre-révolution', p. 654 and Mérilys, 'Propagande révolutionnaire dans l'armée', p. 484.

Although it is impossible to evaluate fully the content and measure the quantity of propaganda distributed among the soldiers, since such activity is by nature surreptitious and transient, some evidence remains. An officer of the Mestre-de-Camp Général Cavalry wrote to the colonel commanding the Colonel-Général Hussars that as soon as his detachment had arrived at Château-Thierry on 11 July, '. . . our cavalrymen began to be inundated by seditious pamphlets [*imprimés*] and advice to abandon us and go to Paris.'[1] The situation in Paris was the same. One particularly well-documented case can serve as an example of what was probably a rather common phenomenon.

On 8 July 1789 one Jean-Claude Monnet, aged 46 and a native of Franche-Comté, was arraigned before the court of the Châtelet in Paris.[2] Monnet, a pedlar of lottery-tickets who resided in central Paris, was charged with distributing 'various printed leaflets of suspect works, tending to incite sedition' the previous day. The court was especially concerned that he had distributed these writings among soldiers on the Champ de Mars, a charge which Monnet denied although he had been arrested by two officers of the Swiss regiment of Diesbach which was camped there. One of the pamphlets found in Monnet's possession was *Avis aux Grenadiers et Soldats du Tiers-État par un ancien Camarade du Régiment des Gardes Françoises*. This pamphlet not only presented typical complaints of soldiers (low pay, harsh and degrading discipline, exclusion from most honours and promotions), but also urged the troops not to be passively obedient to their noble officers and not to fire on fellow citizens. It argued: '. . . we are Citizens before being Soldiers . . . we are in short Frenchmen and not slaves.' If necessary, it advised resistance to officers' orders with force, arguing convincingly that '. . . if they have swords, have you not sabres? If they are a hundred, are you not a thousand?' The pamphlet concluded with the appeal: 'Children of the Fatherland, generous defenders of France, brave citizens of the Third Estate, let us embrace, let us unite!'

The situation led contemporaries to conclude by 14 July that the recently arrived troops were unreliable. Gouverneur Morris wrote

[1] Quoted in Henri Choppin, *Les Hussards: les vieux régiments, 1692–1792* (Paris, 1899), p. 245.
[2] The proceedings of this arraignment can be found in A.N., Y 9999 or in Y 13,818, which is a duplicate record. The anonymous pamphlet is in the Bibliothèque nationale (8° Lb39 1867).

to the United States ambassador to Spain that: 'It is believed certain that the French troops would refuse to serve against their fellow citizens. . . .'[1] The Marquis de Clermont-Gallerande claimed that the French regiments of Provence and Vintimille Infantry as well as the battalions of Besançon and Toul Artillery had been lost to the royal cause well before 14 July.[2] Montjoye asserted, 'The general officers themselves said that if the king should try to interfere with the slightest action of the National Assembly, he would be unable to count on the loyalty of a single regiment.'[3] On 13 July the commanding officer of the detachment of Royal Cravattes Cavalry informed his superior that 'he was no longer sure of his detachment'.[4] By this date even Besenval was convinced that he could no longer depend on the loyalty of his forces, and before evening had begun to withdraw all regular troops from Paris; this evaluation was confirmed by his subordinate commanders at a council of war held at the École Militaire early the next morning.[5]

Circumstances in and around the capital—the inadequacy of preparations to receive the troops, fraternization between soldiers and civilians, and efforts to sow disaffection—certainly tended to support suspicions about the unreliability of the soldiers. Furthermore, some incidents provided indisputable evidence of a breakdown of discipline. The defection of the French Guards had badly shaken confidence in the troops. During the second week of July some dragoons told one of their officers that if he ordered them to fire on their fellow citizens they would shoot him.[6] Some of the French regiments had also begun to suffer excessive desertions. The Provence Infantry lost 90 deserters in 1789 prior to 14 July, 79 during the first two weeks of that month alone; and the Vintimille Infantry had 43 desertions before 14 July, 29 of which occurred in the first half of that month.[7] Even foreign units exhibited disturbing sentiments. The Swiss regiment of Châteauvieux 'declared that it

---

[1] Morris, *Journal*, p. 339.
[2] Caron, 'Tentative de contre-révolution', p. 655n.
[3] Godechot, *Taking of the Bastille*, p. 184.
[4] Marc Bouloiseau, 'Une Source ignorée de l'histoire de la Contre-Révolution: *Les Archives françaises*: Le Royal-Allemand Cavalerie en juillet 1789', *Actes du quatre-vingt-douzième congrès national des sociétés savantes: Strasbourg et Colmar 1967. Section d'histoire moderne et contemporaine*, vol. III (Paris, 1970), p. 406.
[5] Ibid., pp. 406–7; Godechot, *Taking of the Bastille*, pp. 191 and 216; and Caron, 'Tentative de contre-révolution', pp. 663–4.
[6] Mérilys, 'Propagande révolutionnaire dans l'armée', pp. 484–5.
[7] See A.G., Y 14° 5 and Y 14° 71.

would never fire on the people'.[1] Although quartered in the Oran-
gerie at Versailles and fêted by the court aristocracy, the German
regiments of Bouillon and Nassau Infantry, a majority of whose
soldiers were German-speaking French subjects, indicated that they
'did not wish to serve against their country'.[2]

All of this contributed to the conviction that the line troops would
not obey orders to repress the Parisians, with whom many soldiers
shared a similar social background, or the National Assembly, many
of whose deputies were attempting to abolish inequities that
victimized the soldiers. Yet there were other strong indications that
many of the line units in the Paris area were dependable as late as
14 July. One unit, the Royal Allemand Cavalry, clashed with a
crowd on the Place Louis XV in Paris on 12 July. Early that evening
a detachment of this regiment was ordered from the north of Paris
to disperse a crowd that had gathered around the Place Vendôme
and the Tuileries. These soldiers, whom some Parisians had
attempted to win over earlier the same day, were greeted by insults,
rocks, and finally bullets. Some French Guards joined the crowd
and the detachment was ordered to charge. When the more numerous
civilians retreated to high ground in the Tuileries, the result was a
stalemate and the cavalrymen were pulled back.[3] The action of this
regiment was striking evidence that discipline had not totally disintegrated in all regular units. Of greater and broader significance
was the fact that, despite the alarming desertion rate in the Provence
and Vintimille Regiments, the number of deserters in all other line
units stationed around the capital was not significantly greater before
14 July than it had normally been in the previous two years.[4]

What had in fact failed was the confidence of the officers in their
ability to command obedience from their men. Like other observers,
the officers concluded, on the basis of largely circumstantial evidence, that discipline had been severely undermined. Many noble
officers had by now forgotten their past grievances against the
government, in face of the common danger posed to both monarchy

---

[1] Michelet, *Révolution française*, II. 29.

[2] See Caron, 'Tentative de contre-révolution', p. 676; Comte Miot de Melito,
Mémoires du Comte de Miot de Melito, vol. I (Paris, 1858) p. 13; and Morris, *Journal*,
p. 62.

[3] Bouloiseau, 'Royal-Allemand Cavalerie', pp. 405–6.

[4] This information is from the troop registers of the units in question for all but the
Swiss regiments. For the Swiss, whose registers are not at the Archives de la Guerre,
inspection reports for 1788 and 1789 were used. See also my article on the 'Regeneration
of the Line Army', pp. 311–14.

and aristocracy; they could not so readily overcome their ignorance of and disregard for the conditions of their soldiers. Differences in social status and in conditions of military service had been compounded by limited personal contact and abusive treatment; and no amount of concern on the part of the officers during the crisis of 1789 could compensate for years of neglect and alienation. As a group, the officers either were ignorant of the cohesiveness, discipline, and professionalism developed among the troops by years of training and service or were unwilling to put these intangible but important qualities to a test. Of course, it is possible that had the officers maintained self-confidence and used their troops against the people on 14 July the results would have been wholesale desertion and insubordination. The fact remains that the soldiers were not employed, and it was the advice of the officers, along with the King's indecision, that was responsible for this. After 14 July any chance of halting or controlling the revolutionary movement by the use of the Royal Army was lost.

THE REVOLUTION OF THE SOLDIERS

By 14 July *c.* 17,000 regular troops had arrived in the Paris-Versailles area and 3,000 more were due to arrive within four days. These forces included 3,400 cavalrymen, 12,600 infantry, and about 900 artillerymen. Of these, approximately 5,800 were foreigners.[1] None of these units played an active role in the events of 14 July; they had all been withdrawn from the area of conflict. Individual soldiers who had left their units and joined Parisian civilians did, however, actively participate in the attack on the Bastille. Besides sixty-four soldiers of the French Guards who helped to direct the operations against the fortress, seven men from the line regiments in and around Paris were subsequently recognized officially as 'Conquerors of the Bastille', along with forty-seven soldiers from other line units.[2] There were undoubtedly other soldiers who participated in the attack but whose efforts did not receive formal recognition.[3] A few

[1] Unless otherwise noted all the following data on the soldiers, except the Swiss, is based on the *contrôles de troupes*; the only source available for the Swiss units was the inspection reports.

[2] Joseph Durieux, *Les Vainqueurs de la Bastille* (Paris, 1911), pp. 13–217, *passim* and 247–9.

[3] E.g., one of the civilian attackers, J.-B. Humbert, saw the body of a soldier in the uniform of the Vintimille Infantry during the struggle, although no member of this regiment was recognized as a *Vainqueur*. See Godechot, *Taking of the Bastille*, Appendix I.

soldiers received notoriety. The most outstanding example is Jacques-Job Elie, a colour-bearer in the regiment of the La Reine Infantry, who was in Paris on leave from his regiment. Elie, the son of an officer of fortune from Alsace, had served in the army since 1765, had participated in four campaigns, including the siege of Savannah during the War of American Independence, and had been wounded once. In 1787 he had applied for a commission as second-lieutenant but had been rejected. Four years after his contribution to the fall of the Bastille, in July 1793, Elie became a general![1]

For most of the line soldiers their primary contribution to the events of 14 July was the lack of confidence which they inspired in their officers. Theirs was a completely passive role, but no less important for that. On 15 July Marshal de Broglie, Besenval's superior, felt forced to admit that the soldiers could not be used against civilians. During the morning of 16 July Louis XVI held a council of war and Broglie repeated that the attitude of the troops precluded any hope of military operations against Paris. When a suggestion was made that the King depart to some provincial fortress, Broglie '. . . declared that he could not guarantee the safe passage of the royal family through a country the whole of which was in a state of insurgency, escorted by troops that were ready to side with the rioters'. Resignedly, the King then ordered the line regiments to return to their garrisons.[2]

As already indicated, not all of the troops were unreliable, and not all of the officers had lost confidence in them. The Royal Allemand Cavalry, condemned to eternal damnation in public opinion for its attack on the people on 12 July, had remained loyal and hopeful that the King would put himself at the head of his troops and crush the rebels.[3] But Louis XVI was an indecisive man with little talent and less interest in the military; he also wanted to avoid civil war; and, he had been advised against relying on his troops. This estimate which most officers had made about the unreliability of their men, regardless of its untested validity before 14 July, was becoming a self-fulfilling prophecy.

Of the nearly 17,000 line troops that had arrived in the vicinity of Paris by 14 July, about 760 men deserted in the course of that month, all but 185 *after* the fourteenth. By the end of the year there

---

[1] Durieux, *Vainqueurs de la Bastille*, pp. 73 and 76.
[2] Godechot, *Taking of the Bastille*, pp. 253-8.
[3] Bouloiseau, 'Royal-Allemand-Cavalerie', pp. 407-8.

were well over 1,600 desertions in these same units, almost three and a half times as many desertions as had occurred in the course of the previous year. Some units suffered extremely severe losses. The Provence Infantry lost 118 deserters in July 1789 and 137 during the year. The Vintimille Infantry lost 246 deserters in 1789, over one-fifth of its enlisted personnel; 71 men deserted in July, 100 in August, and 47 in October. The Royal Bourgogne Cavalry lost 95 deserters in 1789, 41 in the second half of July, and 82 in the last six months of the year. The Royal Dragoons had 96 desertions during the year, all but five of them between 15 and 31 July. Even the foreign regiments were not immune. The Swiss regiment of Diesbach suffered 135 desertions between October 1788 and September 1789, of whom 113 stayed in Paris after the regiment had been ordered back to its garrison in Arras on 16 July. Another Swiss regiment in Paris, the Salis-Samade Infantry, lost nearly 80 deserters between 15 and 25 July. Even the German regiment of Bouillon Infantry, which had been confined to the grounds at Versailles where it had been wooed by the court, lost 61 deserters in 1789, 42 of them after 14 July. The Toul Artillery, some of whose men had been very close to the people in the Palais Royal during their sojourn in Paris, suffered 109 desertions during the year, all but twelve after the attack on the Bastille.

On the other hand, some of the units ordered to Paris in the summer of 1789 suffered minor, even negligible, losses from desertion. The Royal Allemand Cavalry lost only 15 deserters during 1789, three of them in July. A major factor in limiting the number of desertions in this regiment was the great popular hostility which existed towards it after 12 July. Almost every Frenchman showed nothing but animosity towards the men of this unit from then until the regiment was virtually 'hounded' into emigration three years later. Such an attitude, rather than encouraging desertion, forcibly increased cohesion within the regiment. Also, this was a German-speaking regiment composed almost exclusively of Alsatians, Germans, and men from 'German' Lorraine. This certainly hindered close relations between the unit and the civilian populace.

Difference in language also seems to have been a factor in the ability of other foreign units to resist civilian propaganda. The detachments from the three hussar regiments which served in the Paris area in the summer of 1789 suffered only 5 desertions in July of that year. Over 90 per cent of the men in these units were from Alsace,

Lorraine, and Germany; and German was their language of command. Three of the Swiss regiments in Paris in July, the Castella, Châteauvieux, and Reinach Infantry, composed almost exclusively of foreigners, suffered between them less than 90 desertions between September 1788 and September 1789. And the German regiment of Nassau Infantry had only 15 men desert in 1789.

Although difference in language certainly hampered communication between the soldiers and civilians in Paris in 1789 and thus helped to maintain military discipline, this was not the decisive factor. The excessive desertion rate in the Swiss regiments of Salis-Samade and Diesbach in July 1789 and the abnormally high number of deserters in the German regiment of Bouillon Infantry during that year show that this difference did not automatically ensure the maintenance of military authority. On the other hand, soldiers in French units sometimes were more disciplined than their foreign comrades-in-arms. The French regiments of Bourbonnais and Saintonge Infantry lost only 29 deserters between them in 1789, although all but two of these desertions came in the second half of the year. The regiments of Mestre-de-Camp Général and Comissaire-Général Cavalry and the Dauphin Dragoons, which sent detachments to the Paris-Versailles area in mid-1789, suffered no more desertions that year than they had in 1788 or 1787.

On the whole, French units suffered more from desertions than did foreign regiments, but the nationality or, more exactly, the native language of the soldiers did not alone determine the reaction of the troops to a revolutionary situation. The foreigners and non-French-speaking subjects of the King had developed the essential means of communication during their long and varied service in France.[1] And, even native Frenchmen could remain essentially untouched by the entreaties of their countrymen under the most trying circumstances. Factors besides a common language must be sought to explain the defection of the troops in July of 1789 and after.

Examination of the individual characteristics of deserters and comparison with the characteristics of all the men in their units can help to describe the type of men who deserted in 1789 and can provide some indications of the reasons for desertion. To examine the background of all the 17,000 men in Paris in July 1789 would be a

[1] For a clear example of the ability of foreign troops in the French service to understand French, see Marc Bouloiseau, 'Deux relations de l'arrestation du Roi à Varennes', *Annales historiques de la Révolution française*, XLIV (1972), 444.

task beyond the scope of this study. Furthermore, it is impossible to identify with certainty all of the cavalry troops who served in Paris during the uprising. The cavalry units sent to the capital were detachments, usually squadrons, and it is impossible to find out which specific squadrons were sent in all of the detachments. The absence of the troop registers of the Swiss regiments also makes it impossible to study the men of these units in detail. Therefore, what I have done is to select certain regiments which sent troops to Paris; to examine the background of all the men serving in them as of 14 July; and to compare this with the background of all deserters from these regiments during 1789.[1]

The regiments studied include three of the twelve infantry regiments in the Paris area on 14 July: the regiments of Provence and Vintimille, which suffered many desertions in 1789, and the regiment of Saintonge, which lost no more men in that year than in the previous two years. Four cavalry regiments among the thirteen which sent contingents to Paris were also selected: the Royal Dragoons which sent 300 men, the Lorraine Chasseurs which furnished 400, the Royal Cravattes Cavalry which sent 100, and the Royal Allemand Cavalry which furnished 400 men. The first three of these cavalry units lost numerous deserters in 1789, while the last suffered very few desertions. These regiments represent a total of 5,453 men, of whom 669 deserted during 1789.

First, let us examine some general characteristics of the deserters. Of the 669 deserters in these seven regiments, few had had previous difficulties with military discipline. Only sixteen had prior desertion records and only twenty-one had been reduced in rank before 14 July 1789. Less than 6 per cent of these deserters, then, could even possibly be considered chronic offenders against military discipline.

Soldiers from Île-de-France, where Paris was located, and the provinces contiguous to it (Normandie, Picardie, Champagne, and Orléanais) were more likely to desert during the crisis of 1789 than were soldiers from other regions. In the seven units studied, men from these five provinces constituted 26·9 per cent of the total strength; yet, 35·7 per cent of the deserters were natives of these areas. In the same way, the Parisians in these regiments were more likely to desert than soldiers from other regions. Of 128 Parisians in

[1] One potentially very important factor, social origins, cannot, unfortunately, be studied. The troop registers do not provide this information for the units in question and the data in the inspection reports are too broad to be of any real use.

the seven units, 28 deserted in 1789; all but three of these desertions came during the events of July and their immediate aftermath. Soldiers from urban areas were somewhat more likely to desert than men from the countryside. Men from towns of 2,000 or more inhabitants made up 36 per cent of the total strength in the regiments under examination, but 39·5 per cent of the deserters had urban origins.

The case of the Vintimille Infantry provides more striking, but somewhat extreme, evidence of these tendencies. Of all the units called to the Paris area in mid-1789, this regiment suffered most heavily from desertions. Nearly half (49·2 per cent) of the men in this regiment were from Île-de-France and the surrounding provinces; and 54·5 per cent of the deserters came from this region. More than half (51·1 per cent) of this regiment came from an urban background; and 55·6 per cent of the deserters came from towns with a population of more than 2,000. The regiment also contained a large number of Parisians, 44, of whom 15 deserted in 1789. Thus, there was a tendency for men from regions around Paris and from urban backgrounds to desert more readily than their fellow soldiers.

Another significant factor in desertion was age. Of all the soldiers in the regiments studied, 54·2 per cent were between the ages of 21 and 30; yet 69·1 per cent of the deserters from these units were in this age-group. Similarly, 92·6 per cent of the deserters were 18–35 years old; while 82·1 per cent of all the personnel were between these ages. As might be expected, young men, generally beyond adolescence, constituted most of the deserters.

Quite contrary to what one might expect, however, was the length of service of the deserters. Of 669 deserters in the seven regiments, 452 (or 67·6 per cent) had served in the army for four years or more. This was almost exactly the same proportion as existed among all the soldiers in these units, 68 per cent. A much smaller proportion of men with ten years' or more service deserted than the proportion of all the soldiers under discussion, 17·8 per cent as compared with 27·5 per cent. And few N.C.O.s deserted; there were only 10 sergeants and 25 corporals among the 669 deserters in 1789, a proportion markedly below the ratio of N.C.O.s to soldiers. Men who had already invested a large portion of their life in a military career were, understandably, reluctant to sacrifice this investment by deserting. It remains true, however, that more than two-thirds of the total number of deserters were soldiers who had spent a good portion of their adult life in the army and who, on this basis, might be expected to have maintained a tighter discipline.

While the large number of deserters among the units called to the Paris area in the spring and summer of 1789 indicates a major breakdown in discipline, the pattern of desertion shows a high degree of cohesion among the enlisted men. In those regiments where numerous desertions took place in 1789 the incidence of desertion was concentrated during brief time-periods and in certain units. The regiment of Provence Infantry, for example, arrived at Saint-Denis on 8 July; within one week 108 soldiers of this regiment had deserted, 38 on 14 July alone. Of the 137 desertions from this regiment in 1789, 113 occurred in five of its ten companies; three companies, Le Bel, Chasseurs, and Grenadiers, alone lost 78 deserters in the year, almost all of them between 8 and 14 July. Particularly remarkable was the case of the grenadiers. This élite company, commanded by officers who had been promoted from the ranks, lost one-fifth of its complement during the first five days it was in Paris. Although only four corporals deserted the regiment in July, it is inconceivable that many N.C.O.s, especially in companies with high desertion rates, were not aware of their subordinates' decision to desert; indeed, it is probable that some tacitly concurred, although they did not participate, in the desertions. The same hypothesis can be applied to the officers of fortune. Their stake in a military career, even greater than that of the N.C.O.s, prohibited them from deserting themselves; but at the same time their frustrations in this career may well have inclined them to countenance desertions which could contribute to the overthrow of the regime which was responsible for these frustrations. The later activity of these ex-rankers against their superior officers and royal authority tends to confirm such a view.

The regiment of Vintimille Infantry had a similar experience. Between 10 July, when it arrived in the vicinity of Paris, and 13 July, 41 men deserted, all but three on 13 July. 100 soldiers deserted this regiment in August, 84 of them between 10 and 17 August. All but two of the 47 desertions in October occurred between the nineteenth and twenty-ninth of that month. All the companies in this regiment suffered heavily from desertions, but certain companies were particularly hard hit. The company of chasseurs, which the Marquis de Maleissye had observed mixing with a crowd of 'rioters' on 13 July,[1] lost over one-third of its strength, including a sergeant, during its first four days in Paris. The company of grenadiers lost a quarter of its men during the same period.

In the Royal Cravattes Cavalry, which had been stationed in the Paris area since December 1788, all but 8 of the 69 desertions in 1789 came between 14 July and 14 August; and 35 occurred in one of the regiment's three squadrons. The regiment of Royal Dragoons lost 91 deserters in the last two weeks of July, 79, including four corporals, on 15 July alone. 72 of the 96 deserters during the year came from the two squadrons which had been ordered to the Paris area in April 1789. Of the 85 deserters from the Lorraine Chasseurs, 62 deserted in July; and 54 of these deserted between 14 and 23 July. 41 of these desertions occurred in one of the four squadrons of the regiment, while another squadron, presumably the one not sent to Île-de-France in early May, lost only 7 deserters during 1789.

Cohesion developed among the soldiers of a unit during years of military service could, and often did, lead to mass desertions of men when the authority of the officers had disintegrated. On the other hand, it could serve as a force in maintaining discipline. The Royal Allemand Cavalry was the most homogeneous of the seven regiments studied in detail. Over half the soldiers in this regiment were Alsatians and almost all of the rest were from Lorraine or one of the German states; German was the native tongue of these men and the language of command. More than 80 per cent of the men whose birthplace was identified as rural or urban came from villages with less than 2,000 inhabitants. More than three-quarters of the men (76 per cent) had served for four years or more in the army, a significantly higher proportion than the average among the regiments studied. Finally, the great public hostility towards this regiment strongly reinforced the factors which naturally tended towards cohesiveness among the troops.

The case of the Saintonge Infantry Regiment, which lost only 21 deserters during 1789, is more difficult to explain. In their age, length of service, and rural–urban origins the soldiers of this unit were comparable to the men in the other two French infantry regiments studied. Fewer men of the Saintonge Infantry (21·8 per cent) came from Île-de-France and neighbouring provinces than in the other regiments, but this fact alone appears insufficient to explain the maintenance of discipline in this unit. The decisive factor in the

[1] Mérilys, 'Propagande révolutionnaire dans l'armée', p. 484.

low desertion rate of this regiment seems to have been that the officers were able to preserve their authority over the soldiers. The regiment was withdrawn from Paris in good order on 17 July, although it lost 8 deserters that month and the same number in August. In late October the officers of this regiment purged a large number of potential troublemakers; during the last week in October 68 soldiers were summarily dismissed. Unlike the officers in other regiments, the officers of the Saintonge Infantry retained control of their subordinates during this crisis; and the cohesion which existed among the soldiers worked to their advantage.

One final aspect of these desertions which has been mentioned by some historians, assumed by others, and proven by none is the 'patriotism' of the soldiers and their commitment to the new Revolution. The line troops recognized as 'Conquerors of the Bastille' actively participated in the revolutionary events of July. Certainly many other soldiers who deserted their regiment and remained in Paris were at least passive participants in these events; their number and role can, however, never be evaluated. One other gauge of the support of the soldiers for the Revolution is enlistment in the Paris National Guard.

On 13 July the municipal officials of Paris had ordered the creation of a citizen militia both to counter the military preparations of Versailles and to preserve order in the city. Although barely organized before the attack on the Bastille, it enjoyed phenomenal growth shortly thereafter.[1] By the beginning of August the municipality had decided that in each of the sixty battalions there would be a 'centre company' of 100 men. These companies would be paid and permanently available for service in the capital. The daily pay in these units was set at 20 *sous*,[2] about two and a half times the pay of a private in the line infantry. From their inception these companies recruited their strength primarily from former line troops, many of whom were recent deserters.

Within only a few days of the fall of the Bastille large numbers of soldiers from the French Guards, the Swiss Guards, and the line units in and around Paris tried to enter the paid National Guard companies. Soon deserters from line regiments outside the Paris

[1] The most recent and one of the most comprehensive discussions of the Paris National Guard is in Louis Gottschalk and Margaret Maddox, *Lafayette in The French Revolution, Through the October Days* (Chicago, 1969), *passim*.

[2] The information on the pay of the centre companies was generously furnished to me by Louis Gottschalk.

region made their way to the capital for the same purpose.[1] Surely the motivation of many of these soldiers included the higher pay offered in the National Guard. Just as surely many of the soldiers who enlisted in the National Guard were motivated by a desire to serve the Nation and the Revolution. Probably in most cases one motive complemented the other by a coincidence which was very attractive to many line troops. By early 1790 most of the centre companies had reached their full strength.

Although complete records were unavailable and are probably lost, the troop registers for three of the six divisions of the paid Parisian National Guard are available and provide an invaluable source for the activities of hundreds of line soldiers in the early Revolution.[2] This source is incomplete not only because it covers only half of the paid companies, but also because of the incompleteness of many of the entries. At best one can present only approximate figures, but even these are very revealing.

Between August 1789 and August 1791, when the paid National Guard of Paris was incorporated into newly formed line units, over 4,000 men served in these thirty paid companies, and probably double that number in all sixty companies. At least 1,100 of these 4,000 paid National Guardsmen were soldiers from line regiments, and a minimum of 950 were former French Guards.[3] Once again, for all the paid companies of Paris these figures should probably be doubled. Of the line troops who joined the thirty paid companies for which we have records, more than 240 were from the regiments and detachments which had been summoned to police the city in July 1789; thus, in all likelihood, approximately 500 of the paid soldiers in the Paris National Guard formerly served in these units.

It is not possible to estimate accurately the total number of deserters from each of the units in the Paris area who subsequently joined the National Guard. Although records are available for half the paid companies, the simple method of doubling the numbers given in the

---

[1] Gottschalk and Maddox, *Lafayette Through the October Days*, pp. 120–1 and 139.

[2] This source on the 3rd, 4th, and 5th Divisions of the paid National Guard of Paris is at the Archives de la Guerre. It is, however, uncoded, uncatalogued, and almost entirely unknown. It is shelved with the troop registers of the battalions of National Volunteers. It is due only to the knowledge and kindness of my very good friend and colleague, Jean-Paul Bertaud, that I became aware of its existence.

[3] These and other figures can be only approximate and are almost certainly minimum estimates. Prior military service is not indicated in each case or, if noted, the indication is often very vague. Likewise, the fact that a man had no previous military experience is made explicit in only some instances.

existing records, valid when dealing with large numbers of only broadly differentiated groups, would almost certainly be misleading when applied to deserters from a single regiment or detachment. The reason for this is simple but instructive; just as the soldiers from units called in for the planned *coup* in July 1789 deserted in groups, so too they enlisted in the National Guard in groups. The deserters from specific regiments tended to enlist in the same company or division of the National Guard. For example, while no deserters from the Royal Cravattes Cavalry enlisted in the third division and only one enlisted in the fourth division, twenty-six joined the fifth division. The cohesion developed among soldiers during the rigorous military life of the Old Regime continued even in the new, more liberal atmosphere of the Revolution.

Despite the impossibility of determining the total number of deserters from a given regiment who joined the paid units of the National Guard, a few examples can shed light on the motives and subsequent fate of some of the soldiers who deserted from the units ordered to the Paris area in mid-1789. 53 men from the regiment of Dauphin Infantry, which lost 129 deserters in 1789 and 96 in July alone, joined the three divisions of the Paris National Guard for which records are available. More than a quarter of the deserters from the Vintimille Infantry, 64 soldiers in all, enlisted in these divisions. And, as already indicated, 27 of the 65 deserters from the Royal Cravattes Cavalry subsequently joined these units.

It was not merely the higher pay which motivated line soldiers to join these companies; at the time of their desertion and enlistment in the National Guard these men could not presume to anticipate the course of the revolution to which they had made such a crucial commitment. Their support of this revolution was unequivocal, although few contemporaries realized this. Even such a sympathetic noble officer as Lafayette was later surprised during the October crisis when the paid National Guardsmen took the lead in demanding a march on Versailles.[1]

In July 1789 the internal problems of the Royal Army decisively undermined the ability of the Old Regime to survive intact. First, the officers lost confidence in their ability to command obedience; then as they and the king acknowledged this loss of authority, large numbers of soldiers transferred their allegiance to new, revolu-

---

[1] Jean Egret, *La Révolution des Notables: Mounier et les Monarchiens, 1789* (Paris, 1950), p. 187.

tionary authorities. These circumstances contributed to the early success of the Revolution and led to important repercussions in the army and the country as a whole.

THE AFTERMATH OF 14 JULY

While it would be erroneous to view revolutionary developments elsewhere in France as mere reflections of events in Paris, there can be no doubt that the example of the capital was of paramount importance in spreading the Revolution. The crisis of July had not only forced the King to share power with the Assembly and destroyed discipline among many of the line troops in the capital, it also encouraged and even sanctioned challenges to established civil and military authorities throughout the provinces. These developments involved thousands more soldiers directly in the great political upheaval that was taking place and increased their contacts with pro-revolutionary elements in the civilian population.

On 16 July news of Necker's dismissal reached Rennes and soon crowds gathered in the streets and searched for arms, as had their counterparts in Paris.[1] The next day, when people began to seize weapons from the municipal armoury, the military commander of the city, the Marquis de Langeron, called out the regiments of Artois and Lorraine Infantry and the Orléans Dragoons and ordered them to fire on the crowds. The response of the troops was to turn down their muskets and shout: 'Long live the Third Estate!' Subsequently, 800 men of the garrison joined the inhabitants of Rennes and promised to show no mercy to anyone who threatened the life or liberty of these citizens. After considering calling reinforcements, Langeron reluctantly resigned himself to accepting the collapse of his authority.

Similarly, on 19 July soldiers of the regiment of La Fère Artillery disobeyed orders to fire on a crowd at Auxonne.[2] At Strasbourg not only did line troops refuse to attack a crowd which was plundering the town hall during the night of 21 July, but some soldiers joined the crowd 'even in sight of the officers of the detachment'.[3] In August at Nancy men of the King's Own (Du Roi) Infantry joined demonstrations in support of the commoner deputies in the National

---

[1] Anon., *Relation de ce qui s'est passé à Rennes en Bretagne, lors de la nouvelle du renvoi de M. Necker* ([Paris], n.d.) contains a contemporary, but somewhat prejudiced account of this episode.

[2] Hartmann, *Les Officiers de l'armée royale*, p. 131.

[3] Young, *Travels in France*, pp. 152–4.

Assembly.[1] At Thionville soldiers of the Brie and Bretagne Infantry Regiments likewise joined in demonstrations against royal authority.[2] At Bordeaux the citadel had to be handed over to insurgents when troops called out to police a crowd joined it instead.[3]

At Caen an incident occurred which points out dramatically the impact of civil–military relations upon the conduct of the troops.[4] In April 1789 Major de Belsunce, an arrogant and outspoken court noble, was assigned to the regiment of Bourbon Infantry in garrison at Caen. Shortly after joining the regiment Belsunce took charge of repressing a grain riot, thereby arousing the enmity of many of the inhabitants against him. In July he commanded a detachment of his regiment which dispersed a demonstration in support of Necker; and this confirmed his public image as the representative of re-pression and hostility to the Revolution, a judgement in which his whole regiment was implicated. A few weeks later, on 11 August, some men of the Bourbon Infantry were drinking in a cabaret with two soldiers of the Artois Infantry who had recently come from Rennes. The latter, who had already shown their patriotic tendencies in July, toasted Necker and the Nation. Fighting broke out between the two groups of soldiers. A crowd soon gathered and by evening had surrounded the barracks of the Bourbon Infantry, demanding that Belsunce be handed over. The Major had become the symbol of counter-revolution and was held responsible for the events earlier in the day, although he had no direct part in them. Later that night, 11–12 August, Belsunce surrendered himself and was charged with disturbing the peace, arming troops against citizens, and encouraging the insults offered to the soldiers of the Artois Infantry.

This did not, however, end the tumult. The crowd remained around the barracks of the Bourbon Infantry and demanded its departure from the city. A few soldiers left their quarters and joined the people. Apparently, these men carried stories about the plots of some of their officers, including Belsunce. One such story was that the officers planned to pillage Caen and set fire to the faubourg of Vaucelles. As the hostility of the people increased, the regiment, after its ammunition had been taken away, was escorted out of the

---

[1] Choppin, Less Hussards, p. 246.

[2] Hartmann, Les Officiers de l'armée royale, p. 131.

[3] Norman Hampson, A Social History of the French Revolution (Toronto, 1966), p. 77.

[4] A full account of this episode is contained in Eugène de Beaurepaire, 'L'Assassinat du Major de Belsunce (Caen, 12 août 1789)', Revue de la Révolution, III (Jan.–June 1884), 409–29 and IV (July–Dec. 1884), 26–47.

city by the National Guard. Shortly afterwards, Belsunce, who was being transferred to prison, was attacked by a crowd, shot some fifty times, and decapitated.

By September 1789 the regiment of Forez Infantry, which had sent one battalion to police Rennes in the previous year, found itself rent by insubordination. As in other regiments, the grenadier company, commanded by officers of fortune, had initiated much of the trouble. In his report the inspecting general, the Comte de Murinais, attributed the problem to the service of the regiment at Rennes. He attempted to restore discipline by discharging many of the trouble-makers, including six grenadiers.[1] Throughout the autumn of 1789 insubordination continued to spread among the line troops. Even isolated units became affected. The regiment of Austrasie Infantry was stationed at Briançon in the Alps, far removed from the centres of revolutionary activity. Furthermore, the officers of this regiment took it upon themselves to censor the mail, destroying all revolutionary material addressed to the soldiers. All of these precautions, however, were insufficient. As soldiers returned from periods of leave which had taken them away from their isolated garrison, they began to spread news of what was happening in France and in the rest of the army. Increased surveillance became necessary.[2]

These examples of military insubordination reflected the general fragmentation of authority which had developed after 14 July. The power of traditional authorities had been destroyed, but not entirely; and it still remained to be determined how political power was to be redistributed. Regardless of the ultimate decisions on this crucial question, however, no government could allow its control over the armed forces to lapse; and both the King and the Assembly attempted to assert authority over the Royal Army in the months immediately following the events of mid-July.

One pressing problem was the treatment of the soldiers who had deserted their regiments to join the Paris National Guard. These men, who were regarded by many as national heroes, could not be harshly punished, but at the same time the wave of desertions had to be stopped before the entire army disintegrated. On 21 July the King informed Lafayette, the recently appointed commander of the Paris National Guard, that at his discretion he could enrol all line soldiers who attempted to enlist up to that date, or he could send

---

[1] See the inspection report for 20 Sept. 1789 in A.G., X^b 26.
[2] Mautort, *Mémoires*, p. 389.

them back to their regiments with a note explaining their absence. In the latter case, the soldiers were to be accepted back into their units without punishment.[1] This decision, however, failed to end the wave of desertions, and on 14 August the King declared that the regiments of his army would take back, without prejudice, all deserters since 1 June who returned by 10 October. The municipal government of Paris, flooded by volunteers from line units, supported this policy and offered to provide a travel allowance and passport to all soldiers who had arrived in the city since 22 July, if they left within twenty-four hours.[2] This decision appears to have been implemented in the regiments, although many of the deserters who returned received a prolongation of service, usually for one year.[3] The French Guards, who had given their allegiance to the Revolution at an early stage, were allowed to retain their flags, insignia, and regimental property after the formal dissolution of the regiment on 1 September; and most of the sergeants were promoted to lieutenants in the paid companies of the Paris National Guard.[4]

The King also attempted to gain popular support for his position as commander-in-chief of the army by the appointment of La Tour du Pin as Minister of War on 4 August. La Tour du Pin was an experienced military man who had a reputation as a liberal noble since he had been among the first deputies of the Second Estate to join the commoners in June.[5]

At the same time, the National Assembly attempted to assert civil authority over the army. During the second week of August it decreed that all officers, at the head of their troops and in the presence of civilian officials, must take an oath of loyalty to 'the nation, the king and the law'. The officers were also required to swear that they would not employ their troops against civilians except on the order of civil authorities.[6] In order to strengthen their position with the soldiers, the national deputies appointed a Military Committee on 1 October. The primary task of this committee,

---

[1] Lafayette, *Mémoires*, I. 257.
[2] Gottschalk and Maddox, *Lafayette Through the October Days*, pp. 205–10.
[3] A.G., B¹³ 64.
[4] Gottschalk and Maddox, *Lafayette Through the October Days*, pp. 180–4.
[5] The most complete study of La Tour du Pin's ministry is Lucien de Chilly, *Le Premier Ministre constitutionnel de la guerre, La Tour du Pin: Les Origines de l'armée nouvelle sous la Constituante* (Paris, 1909). The author, himself an army officer and a warm admirer of Taine, is sympathetic to the minister.
[6] Hartmann, *Les Officiers de l'armée royale*, p. 101.

which included Mirabeau and Dubois-Crancé, was the proposal of military reforms.

None of the measures halted the desertions in the summer and early autumn of 1789. In fact, in a typically ill-advised move the King contributed to this military problem. In mid-September Louis XVI, apparently no wiser after his experience two months earlier, again ordered the movement of troops to Versailles. The reasons for this action are unclear. Perhaps it was the first stage of another attempt to crush the Revolution by military force. As was later revealed, the King had accepted none of the revolutionary changes, his public statements notwithstanding. There is, however, no evidence of a military build-up on the order of June and July. Perhaps the King feared that the unrest in Paris would lead to precisely the kind of events that actually did take place on 5–6 October. On 17 September Lafayette warned the ministry of the possibility of a march on Versailles by hungry and irate Parisians; and this warning was used as a pretext for the summoning of the Flandre Infantry Regiment, although this regiment had already been ordered to Versailles from its garrison in Douai on the previous day.[1] Whatever its purpose—and probably the King himself had not made any final plans—the arrival of the Flandre Infantry in Versailles on 23 September inflamed the suspicions of the Parisians.

The regiment of Flandre Infantry, stationed at Douai since March 1788, had generally maintained good discipline during the first three months of the Revolution. It had suffered 23 desertions in the third week of August during disorders in Douai; but in his inspection report of 3 September, the Duc d'Ayen had nothing but praise for the soldiers of this regiment.[2] Its colonel, the Marquis de Lusignan, originally a deputy of the Second Estate, sat on the left of the National Assembly and so appeared reliable to the liberals. It was for its discipline and the reputation of its commander that the Minister of War had recommended it to the King.[3]

When it arrived in Versailles the regiment contained slightly less than 1,100 soldiers. Almost half of these men (48 per cent) were from Île-de-France and the neighbouring provinces; and 2 out of every 7 soldiers were from Île-de-France alone. Although 70 per cent of the enlisted men were from rural backgrounds, more than 5 per

---

[1] Gottschalk, *Lafayette Through the October Days*, pp. 292–4.
[2] A.G., X^b 31.
[3] Chilly, *La Tour du Pin*, p. 67.

cent were from the city of Paris, including 15 N.C.O.s. Nearly three-quarters of the soldiers had been in the army for at least four years.[1]

Upon its arrival the regiment took the new civic oath and handed over to the municipal authorities the two cannons it had brought from Douai, along with some munitions.[2] Thus some of the fears of the civil officials were quieted. On the evening of 1 October the officers of the royal bodyguard gave a dinner for the officers of the Flandre regiment. During the festivities both the King and Queen visited the officers and even presented the young Dauphin to them; the royal family received an enthusiastic reception. In the course of the subsequent celebrations the tricolour cockade, the symbol of the new Revolution, was trampled upon. When news of these happenings reached Paris two days later old fears and animosities were rejuvenated and a new crisis appeared closer.

Meanwhile, like their predecessors in July, the soldiers of the regiment of Flandre had begun to associate closely with the local citizens. Officers soon saw their men frequenting the cabarets of Versailles where, it was alleged, they were amply supplied with money and women. On the night of 4 October a major in the regiment, Montmorin, arrested two sergeants in one such establishment for drunkenness and being out of their quarters after retreat. This caused a crowd of between 150 and 200 persons, some in the uniform of the Paris National Guard, to berate and verbally assault this officer.[3]

The following day the situation reached a climax. A crowd of 6,000 people, mostly women, started out from Paris before noon on 5 October to present their demands concerning unemployment and the price of bread to the King. By about 4 p.m. this crowd began to pour onto the palace grounds. The regiment of Flandre was called out and drawn up in formation. The women began to mix with them and some of the soldiers handed over their cartridges to members of the Versailles National Guard. The officers tried to maintain discipline by passing among the soldiers and using advice, reprimands, and threats. Nevertheless, some of the soldiers placed ramrods in the barrels of their muskets and proclaimed that they too were members of the Nation.[4]

---

[1] These data and subsequent information on the soldiers of the regiment are based on an analysis of its troop register.

[2] Chilly, *La Tour du Pin*, p. 69.

[3] Ibid., pp. 69 and 74.

[4] Ibid., pp. 76–7 and Michelet, *Révolution française*, I. 321–2.

Lafayette, in an attempt to control the crisis or avoid a greater one, departed from Paris with a large contingent of the National Guard late in the afternoon. At the Pont de Sèvres, about halfway to Versailles, he received word that the soldiers of the Flandre Infantry, but not their officers, requested his orders. Lafayette told them to stay in their barracks, an order which was apparently followed.[1] The regiment took no part in the bloody struggle between members of the royal bodyguard and some of the people early in the morning of 6 October. This fighting decided the affair. Shortly afterwards, the King capitulated to the demands of the people and agreed to return to Paris. Preparation began for the transfer of the royal residence to the Tuileries.

During the morning of 6 October the soldiers of the Flandre Infantry left their quarters and mixed with some of the soldiers of the National Guard, many of whom were from the paid units. When the royal family and its entourage began their journey to Paris, Major de Montmorin, the son of the Foreign Minister and an officer in the regiment, collected a contingent of 300 men to escort the King from Versailles, along with his 'subjects' and the Paris National Guard.[2] On this day, 106 men of the Flandre Infantry deserted, many of whom subsequently joined the paid companies of the National Guard of Paris.[3] Three-quarters of these deserters came from five of the regiment's ten companies; and the grenadier company, officered almost exclusively by men promoted from the ranks, suffered more heavily from desertions than any other company in the regiment.

These incidents of insubordination culminating in the crisis of October gave further evidence of what the events of July had indicated: the soldiers of the line army generally could not be depended upon to obey their officers and defend the established regime against the Revolution. The men in the ranks were too close to the people in the streets and too alienated from their superiors to be expected to repress a movement from which they could gain so much. Furthermore, traditional lines of authority had been challenged beyond recovery.

During the crisis in July the collapse of discipline among the line

[1] Gottschalk and Maddox, *Lafayette Through the October Days*, p. 343.

[2] Chilly, *La Tour du Pin*, pp. 82–3.

[3] Chilly claims that only eighty of the three hundred man escort came back to Versailles (ibid., p. 83). Thirty men of the Flandre Infantry joined the three divisions of the paid National Guard for which records are available.

troops (at first suspected by their officers, and proven after 14 July) had been a decisive factor in the royal government's acceptance of revolutionary demands. Insubordination among the soldiers had subsequently increased dramatically: in 1788 there had been instances of insubordination among only about 3 per cent of the line units, but in 1789 this figure rose to over 20 per cent.[1] In the instances studied, insubordination during 1789 took a distinct form, one that indicated the peculiar situation of the soldiers. By far the most common expression of insubordination was large-scale desertion, a passive rejection of the authority of military and civil officers.[2] Among seventy-three units investigated there were 16 cases of insubordination in 1789, of which 12 consisted of an excessive desertion rate, i.e. 10 per cent or more of the unit's total strength. The government's lenient treatment of deserters provided some legitimization for this insubordination. In two other instances, demonstrations by the regiments of Brie Infantry at Thionville and Dauphiné Infantry at Toulon, insubordination took the form of support for the new regime,[3] behaviour which also derived legitimacy from the situation after 14 July. Furthermore, in half of the cases of insubordination close links between soldiers and civilians (e.g. assurances by the troops that they would not fire on the people, numerous enlistments by line soldiers in the National Guard, and joint demonstrations by troops and citizens) were established so that the soldiers had strong informal support, if not legal sanction, for their behaviour.

[1] For an explanation of the sources and method used to establish patterns of insubordination, see the section on the 'Incidence of Insubordination' in Appendix I. When all of the units for which I have accumulated data for 1789 (a total of 94) are considered, the proportions given change somewhat but the pattern remains the same. Of these 94 units, 31 experienced instances of insubordination (33%); but this high proportion is probably due to the special attention given to events in and around Paris in July. In 19 units insubordination took the form of excessive desertion; in 8 units it consisted of support for the Revolution or hostility to the Old Regime; and in 4 regiments it represented open defiance of the officers. In 17 of these 31 examples of insubordination (54·8%) the units in question had close relations with the civilian populace.

[2] Richard Cobb, in discussing desertion later in the Revolution (after 1794) and during the last years of the Empire, sees desertion as an important form of popular protest by common people against 'a regime which had repressed and impoverished them in a heartless and systematic manner'. See *Police and People*, pp. 95–7 and 104. The same judgement is equally applicable in 1789.

[3] For the Brie Infantry, see Hartmann, *Les Officiers de l'armée royale*, p. 131. For the Dauphiné Infantry, see Capitaine D'Izarny-Gargas, *38ᵐᵉ Régiment d'Infanterie: Historique des corps qui ont porté le numero 38* (Saint-Étienne, 1889), pp. 105–7 and Chilly, *La Tour du Pin*, pp. 54–5.

In only two of the seventy-three regiments studied did soldiers directly defy their officers, and in at least one of these cases the troops were apparently encouraged by civilians. The Forez Infantry, which had sent a detachment to maintain order in Rennes during the troubles there in 1788, displayed in 1789 what the Inspector-General called 'une indiscipline très marquée' which he found particularly strong in the grenadier company.[1] In July 1789 a quarrel between the fusiliers and grenadiers of the Auvergne Infantry broke into violence which the officers of the regiment were powerless to halt and which was blamed on the influence of the populace of Maubeuge where the unit was stationed.[2]

Instances of open defiance of officers by soldiers were rare in 1789. The bonds of discipline in many units had been severely strained—indeed, beyond repair—but they had not yet been entirely destroyed. Generally, the soldiers expressed their insubordination passively, by desertion, and they required reinforcement both from their comrades and from sources outside the army. The general uncertainty and ambivalence prevalent in the early stages of revolution were particularly poignant for the soldiers of the line army who had been subjected to a rigorous discipline, who were more readily identified than civilian rebels, and who risked swifter and probably harsher punishment. Despite the largely passive role of the line troops in the early Revolution, their reaction to the events of 1789 was no less decisive than that of their more active civilian counterparts, since it deprived the monarchy of its most substantial defence.

Whatever form insubordination among the soldiers took in 1789, it was frequently related to the police functions that they were called upon to perform.[3] The incidence of insubordination was strikingly high among those units that were expressly ordered to maintain or restore order among civilians. Of 83 instances of line troops serving as police in 1789, insubordination resulted in 21 cases, a quarter of the total. This insubordination followed the pattern indicated above: in sixteen units it consisted of excessive desertions; in three

---

[1] See the inspection report for this regiment, dated Saint-Servan, 20 Sept. 1789, in A.G., X^b 26.

[2] Capitaine Pagès-Xatart, 'Auvergne—17eme Régiment d'Infanterie de Ligne 1597–1893: Historique', pp. 195–205. This manuscript was received at the Archives de la Guerre on 3 Oct. 1894 and can be found in the carton for the 17th Infantry in the series *Historiques des Régiments d'Infanterie*.

[3] For an explanation of the basis for the conclusions about the police role of the line army see Appendix I, the section on 'Police Functions of the Army'.

cases the soldiers broke discipline in order to join civilian demonstrations; and in only two units did soldiers openly and without
civilian support defy the authority of their superiors.[1]

The circumstances in which insubordination was expressed are
informative. Although more than 50 per cent of the incidents in
which line troops were employed as police involved disturbances
that were primarily political in nature, all but one of the twenty-one
cases of insubordination connected with police functions occurred
during political disturbances. This tendency was to remain strong
throughout the early Revolution. Line units were normally dependable in protecting food supplies, in repressing brigandage, in
restraining anti-feudal disturbances, in the general maintenance of
law and order, during religious disputes, and even when serving as
military police against other soldiers, but political quarrels tended
to divide the army as deeply and as severely as they did society at
large.[2] Certainly, political divisions frequently cloaked other issues,
but even these were usually translated into terms of political loyalty.
One had to be for or against the Revolution; all else followed.

One other important factor affecting the police function of the
army was violence. In 12 of the 83 incidents studied for 1789 there
were violent confrontations between soldiers and civilians. However,
none of the twenty-one units that displayed insubordinate conduct
in the course of their police duties had perpetrated violence or been
the victim of violence during or immediately prior to the disturbances.[3] This too was to remain a general pattern until 1793.

[1] These last two incidents involved the Orléans Dragoons and the La Fère Artillery
at Rennes and Auxonne respectively. Men from both regiments refused to fire upon
disorderly crowds shortly after 14 July. See Hartmann, Les Officiers de l'armée royale,
p. 131.

[2] I have broken down the types of disturbances in which line troops were used as
police into the seven general categories indicated here. Naturally, not all those involved
in the disturbances were so single-minded as individuals or united as a group as to have
but one aim. Most frequently, however, there was a dominant complaint or primary
objective which justified assigning the disturbances to one particular category. The
large proportion of political disturbances in 1789 is due in part to the emphasis upon the
crisis in and around Paris in July, which has received so much attention by contemporaries and historians (including the present writer). Almost certainly, disturbances over
food in 1789 have been under-estimated in this study. Nevertheless, there can be little
doubt that line troops were much more likely to become insubordinate when ordered
to repress political disturbances than when called on to police other kinds of disorders.

[3] It might be noted that a detachment of the Royal Cravattes Cavalry had assisted in
the repression of the Réveillon riots in Paris in April. The regiment was involved in no
further violence after then, however; and 63 of the regiment's 65 desertions in 1789
dated from July on.

Violence on either side during civil-military confrontations generally hardened attitudes on both sides: when committed against the soldiers, it tended to increase cohesion among them and alienation from civilians; when the soldiers committed violence, it usually created such hostility among civilians that they abandoned all attempts to win over the troops. The fighting between Parisians and a detachment of the Royal Allemand Cavalry on 12 July was simply one, outstanding, example of this kind of situation. The regiment of Bourbon Infantry, which in July had helped to disperse demonstrations by the people of Caen protesting against the recall of Necker, less than a month later was besieged in its own quarters by the same irate citizens and forced to leave the city.[1] The regiment maintained exemplary discipline through 1789 and lost only 12 deserters during that year. One can barely refrain from speculating what might have been the effects on the Royal Army and the entire Revolution if self-confident officers had marched their troops to a violent confrontation with hostile Parisians on 14 July.

In the first months of the Revolution the factors which would dominate the development of the Royal Army for the remaining years of its existence had been clearly evidenced. Many of the subsequent changes in the army would take place because of circumstances within this institution, most importantly the alienation between officers and men. These developments would also have an important impact outside the army. On the other hand, the army was deeply affected by developments in civil society—particularly during a period of revolution. Both government policy and informal civil-military relations would continue to influence the attitudes and actions of officers and soldiers. Whatever else it entailed, the Revolution constituted a major transfer of political power; the fate of the line army, as the primary instrument for exercising political authority on a national basis, was intimately related to the fate of the Revolution.

[1] See Beaurepaire, 'L'Assassinat du Major de Belsunce'.

CHAPTER III

TURMOIL WITHIN THE ARMY, 1790–2

FROM 1789 to 1793 both the Royal Army and the Revolution itself underwent startling metamorphoses whose stages were closely related. Like other French institutions, the regular army was deeply affected by changes in the course of the Revolution. Yet at the same time, developments within the army also reflected its internal problems. Those two factors will be the subject of the following two chapters. The present chapter will concentrate upon the internal situation of the army from late 1789 to the autumn of 1792, a period marked by bitter conflicts between hostile segments of the army which contributed to the transformation of the military. The following chapter will deal with civil–military relations during the same period, the formal and informal, friendly and hostile intercourse between soldiers and civilians and the mutual effects of these contacts.

THE SOLDIERS' MUTINIES OF 1790

Rendered ineffective by the collapse of discipline in the summer and autumn of 1789, military authorities responded to the spread of insubordination by initiating two policies: the discharge of actual or potential troublemakers and the restriction of enlistments. The regiment of Saintonge Infantry, which had maintained firm discipline even in Paris during the turmoil of July, was purged of almost seventy soldiers in the month of October.[1] During the general inspections which were conducted in the autumn of 1789 many other soldiers suspected of being bad influences were discharged. General de Murinais attempted to restore discipline in the Forez Infantry by dismissing some sixty soldiers.[2] Likewise, General D'Herliot who inspected the regiment of Metz Artillery in September noted that discipline in this unit was improved by the discharge of 'mauvais sujets'.[3] Three soldiers of the regiment of Evêchés Chasseurs, Pierre Chabot, Louis André, and Louis Simon, were discharged on 26 October 'for having spread seditious talk tending to rebellion and

---

[1] See the troop register of this regiment, A.G., Y 14ᶜ 119.
[2] A.G., Xᵇ 26.
[3] A.G., Xᵈ 7.

for having tried to stir up the troops'.[1] Discharges such as these became a common phenomenon in late 1789 and in 1790.

Besides the liberal use of dishonourable discharges, military commanders attempted to curtail drastically enlistments which might bring into the army factious recruits. The Inspector-General of the Bourgogne Infantry recommended that 'officers and non-commissioned officers charged with recruitment concern themselves with a very high quality of men and not with quantity'.[2] And on the advice of the Comte de Gomer, an Inspector-General of artillery, the Minister of War approved of recruiting only 'sure men' in October 1789.[3]

As a result, the total number of men discharged from the line army for disciplinary reasons was between four and five times as great in 1790 as it had been before the Revolution. At the same time, enlistments in 1790 were only one-half to one-third as many as they had been in the previous two years. Although such policies were followed in all the major branches, cavalry officers were especially quick and thorough in applying them.[4] The situation thus created alarmed some members of the Assembly. By August 1790, Dubois-Crancé charged that 10,000 soldiers (a rhetorical figure) had been discharged for insubordination, many of them unjustly, and that this together with the serious lag in recruitment, was endangering France's frontiers. He further claimed that during the same period not a single officer had been dismissed for lack of patriotism.[5]

These policies compounded rather than alleviated the single greatest problem in the Royal Army, the alienation between soldiers and officers. Indeed, in their arrogance and ignorance most officers continued to disassociate themselves from their men. Despite conclusive evidence of a serious breakdown of discipline among the troops, nearly half of the officers of the line army took their regular semester leave between October 1789 and the end of May 1790.[6] Sometimes this was done even in direct contradiction to the recom-

---

[1] See the uncoded troop register for this regiment at the Archives de la Guerre.

[2] A.G., X^b 73.

[3] A.G., X^d 7.

[4] Scott, 'Regeneration of the Line Army', pp. 315-16.

[5] Théodore Jung, L'Armée et la Révolution: Dubois-Crancé (Edmond-Alexis-Louis), mousquetaire, constituant, conventionnel, général de division, ministre de la Guerre (1747-1814), vol. I (Paris, 1884), pp. 149-50.

[6] This and the following estimates on the proportion of officers on leave are based on the inspection reports in A.G., X^b, X^c, and X^d for 22 infantry regiments, 11 cavalry regiments, and 1 artillery regiment.

mendations of superiors. The Inspector-General of La Couronne Infantry Regiment, who strongly criticized the officers of this regiment in his inspection report of 25 August 1789, recommended that no officer be allowed leave 'who had not acquired the training and style of command which might be lacking in him'. Despite this warning, thirty-five of the regiment's sixty-eight officers took their leave in October.[1]

The proportion of officers on semester leave was highest in the infantry (49 per cent), and somewhat lower in the cavalry and artillery (43 and 40 per cent respectively). Broadly speaking, there was a direct relationship between these proportions and the amount of trouble that each of these branches suffered in 1790. The total number of officers absent from their regiments was even higher than this because many officers were on special leaves. For example, a number of superior officers, especially colonels, had been selected as deputies to the Estates General and continued to sit in the National Assembly.

Not only were about half of the officers of the line army away from their regiments during this crucial period, but also there was an important distinction between those who left and those who stayed with their units. Probably, most colonels were absent between the autumn of 1789 and the spring of 1790.[2] Since officers of fortune had been denied the right of semester leave, these officers, whose careers could only benefit from revolutionary changes, were present with their men throughout this time. This group included the chief administrative officer of the regiment, the quartermaster-treasurer, who exercised effective authority out of all proportion to his rank (either lieutenant or captain). Most of the remaining officers were members of the provincial nobility who, although opposed to many principles of the Revolution, could also benefit from extensive changes in the military. During a period when discipline was rapidly disintegrating, those officers most interested in maintaining it were away from the men under their command; and those left behind in charge were often the least likely to take drastic measures to preserve a hierarchy which had long been prejudiced against them.

[1] A.G., X^b 58.
[2] It is impossible to estimate this accurately because the reports on the officers on leave and those remaining with the regiment very frequently make no mention of the colonel in either category. Because of both semester leaves and special leaves and because of the greater freedom which colonels exercised, it is virtually certain that a substantial majority of colonels were absent during all or part of this time.

Had it not been for the blindness of so many noble officers, ingrained by generations of disdain for their men and by their social and physical distance from them, it would have been much less of a surprise to them to find many of the soldiers in open revolt against their authority. Indeed, had most of the officers been closer to their subordinates, they might have been able to avoid, or at least alleviate many of the crises of 1790. For in this year the line army clearly bifurcated into hostile factions.

In March the Military Commander of Douai, the Chevalier Defrédy, was deeply worried about the 'intimacy' which existed between the troops of his garrison, which included the Vintimille Infantry,[1] and the local National Guard. In fact, Defrédy claimed that he felt it 'indispensable to break this intimacy by transferring the two infantry regiments here that are too intimately linked with the bourgeois . . .'. Defrédy and the officers of the garrison were also upset about a patriotic play, 'Charles IX', being performed in the city; and they forbade the soldiers to attend it, although many did so anyway. Defrédy's superior, the Marquis de Livarot, had to inform the general that he and the officers had no right to censor what the soldiers did while off duty; and he advised the officers that they should beware of separating themselves from their men, a warning which was obviously too late.[2]

More serious trouble erupted in Lille early the next month.[3] Two infantry regiments stationed there, the Royal Vaisseaux and La Couronne Infantry, had become very friendly with the National Guard and many of the inhabitants, and correspondingly alienated from their officers. In the latter regiment this alienation had been developing for some time. The general who had inspected the regiment of La Couronne seven months before had complained of the lack of discipline in this unit and had censured the officers for this state of affairs. Furthermore, not a single officer in the regiment was employed in training the soldiers. In spite of all this more than half the officers went on leave in the autumn of 1789 and most were absent in April.[4]

[1] This is the same regiment which had suffered so heavily from desertions during and after its stay in Paris in July 1789.

[2] This correspondence can be found in A.G., YA 447.

[3] The most complete account of these events can be found in Charles Poisson, *L'Armée et la Garde Nationale*, vol. I (Paris, 1858), pp. 215-17. See also, Capitaine Veslay, *Historique du 45me Régiment de Ligne (1643-1898)* (Laon, 1899), pp. 74-80 and Lieutenant-Colonel Le Moine de Margon, *Historique du 11e Régiment de Chasseurs* (Vesoul, 1896), p. 10.

[4] A.G., X^b 58. The officers of the Royal Vaisseaux Infantry were little better. During

At the beginning of that month a duel took place between a grenadier of the Royal Vaiseaux and a private of La Couronne on one side and two troopers of the Normandie Chasseurs on the other. Both infantrymen were killed. Whatever the basis for the duel, the affair soon became a major political quarrel which pitted the soldiers of the two pro-revolutionary infantry regiments, supported by the National Guard and the bulk of Lillois, against the 'aristocratic' regiment of chasseurs. A veritable pitched battle took place between these opponents which the officers of the three regiments were powerless to stop. When the men of the Normandie Chasseurs were besieged in the citadel of the city, the regiment of Colonel-Général Cavalry, also stationed in Lille, came to their assistance and the fighting escalated. Even the lieutenant-general commanding the province, the Marquis de Livarot, was unable to restore order. The fighting ceased after nine days only on an order signed by the King himself. The King and his ministry subsequently found the two infantry regiments at fault and ordered them to leave the city; but the populace demanded that the cavalry regiments also depart. In the end, all four regiments were withdrawn from Lille.

Another major mutiny broke out in Hesdin in the same month among the soldiers of the Royal Champagne Cavalry Regiment.[1] This regiment was commanded by its lieutenant-colonel, the Marquis de Broc, since the colonel, the Marquis de Fournes, was on leave as a deputy to the National Assembly. On 20 April a *fédération* ceremony which the regiment attended took place in the nearby village of Grigny. At a dance held that evening a quarrel developed between Second-Lieutenant de Fumel and a simple soldier named Furet, both of the Royal Champagne Cavalry. The disagreement, over the favour of a local girl, led to the soldier's arrest. A year before such an incident would have been easily settled by the severe punishment of the enlisted man; in the spring of 1790 it was immediately transformed into a crisis.

Second-Lieutenant Louis-Nicolas Davout, a young noble

the manœuvres of 1788 many officers refused to attend drills and objected to demonstrating the new tactics. When informed of this situation by the Colonel of the regiment (whom his own officers refused to see socially), the Prince de Condé threatened to arrest the officers and only in this way restored some semblance of authority in the regiment. Despite this restoration of discipline, the Colonel, La Tour du Pin, did not hesitate to leave his regiment *without permission* in order to return to Versailles during the crisis of July 1789. See Mme de la Tour du Pin, *Memoirs*, pp. 90–1 and 111.

[1] See Chilly, *La Tour du Pin*, pp. 89–107 and Choppin, *Insurrections militaires*, pp. 152–202.

educated at the École Militaire in Paris, was the commanding officer of Furet's company in the absence of his superiors who were on leave. Davout had warmly welcomed the Revolution, much to the chagrin of most of his fellow officers. He immediately ordered the release of Furet, but his order was countermanded by Lieutenant-Colonel Broc. Davout organized the N.C.O.s and soldiers of the regiment against what he considered an injustice. On 22 April the men of the regiment, supported by many of the townspeople of Hesdin, forcibly released Furet from prison. The Commander of the local National Guard, Varlet, a former officer of engineers, gave his complete support to the soldiers. On 27 April a *fédération* between the men of the Royal Champagne Cavalry and the National Guard of Hesdin took place, a report of which was sent to the National Assembly. On 7 May the Assembly voiced its satisfaction at the *fédération*.

Strengthened by what they viewed as an official endorsement of their actions, the soldiers of the regiment increased their activity against their officers. They demanded the expulsion of certain officers whom they found particularly objectionable and forbade other officers from entering the enlisted men's quarters. The soldiers also refused to care for the horses belonging to officers. One sergeant demanded that Lieutenant-Colonel Broc hand over to the soldiers the regimental funds, but Broc refused on the grounds that this money belonged to the unit and not to individual members of it. Broc and the other officers became the object of frequent insults by their men. The municipal officials, disturbed by the state of affairs, could do nothing since the National Guard supported the soldiers.

On 15 May the regiment was ordered by the Minister of War to leave Hesdin for Normandy. But the soldiers claimed that this would allow the officers to reassert their tyranny over them and invoked the example of the French Guards to justify their mutiny. The soldiers sent representatives, including Davout, to the National Assembly and to the military commander of the province, but to no avail. When the soldiers still refused to leave Hesdin, the National Assembly ordered the municipal officials and National Guard to enforce the order to withdraw. In the face of the persistent refusal of the troops, no one, including the Minister of War, was prepared to force the issue, and for two months more the regiment remained at Hesdin in an atmosphere of uneasy peace.

At the beginning of August new violence broke out when Sergeant

Odille, who had supported the officers, was promoted to second-lieutenant, an event which the officers celebrated by a banquet and a ball. Once again the soldiers insulted and threatened their officers. By 21 August, however, the officers of the regiment, reinforced by those back from leave, felt strong enought to act. Moderate politicians in the Assembly, frightened by the spectre of revolution in the army, had come to support firm repression by the officers. On 21 August thirty-six enlisted men who had been leaders in the mutiny were arrested and later discharged. Davout, who had been unable to sway the National Assembly, was imprisoned for six weeks, but upon his resignation he was released. One year later he was elected lieutenant-colonel in the Third Battalion of National Volunteers of the Department of the Yonne. By the time he was 34 he had become a Marshal of the Empire.

In Perpignan also there were close relations between the National Guard and many of the soldiers of the regiment of Touraine Infantry. On 19 May the grenadiers of the regiment joined the local National Guard in a parade, against the orders of the military commander of Perpignan. When some officers ordered the regimental adjutant to arrest and punish the leaders of this demonstration, the soldiers protested and drove off the adjutant and three of their officers. The men then proceeded to select a sergeant to replace the adjutant. Temporarily things settled down.

On 8 June the colonel of the Touraine Infantry, the Vicomte de Mirabeau, the brother of the great orator and a deputy of the nobility of Limoges, returned from his duties in the National Assembly. The Colonel, a proud and quick-tempered man, ordered the soldiers to accept back the adjutant and the three officers whom they had chased away. A majority of the soldiers refused. Angered at such insubordination, Mirabeau drew his sword and attacked some of the disobedient soldiers. The enlisted men began to take arms and prepare for combat with the supporters of the colonel. At this point, the Mayor of Perpignan called out another regiment stationed there, the Vermandois Infantry, to maintain order while he attempted to arbitrate the quarrel in the Touraine Infantry.[1]

---

[1] Accounts of this incident can be found in Poisson, *L'Armée et la Garde Nationale*, I. 227–9 and Chilly, *La Tour du Pin*, pp. 132–7. Mirabeau's side of the case can be found in A.N., 119 AP, a letter from Mirabeau to La Tour du Pin dated 14 June 1790. The soldiers presented their case in 'Exposé justificatif de la conduite du Régiment de Touraine depuis le 19 Mai jusqu'au 11 Juin 1790' in the Maclure Collection, vol. 831. And the position of the National Guard of Perpignan is in 'Discours prononcé à l'Assemblée

The Colonel and representatives of the rebel soldiers could not, however, come to an agreement about the reinstatement of the officers. Furthermore, many citizens of Perpignan, including the National Guard, supported the soldiers; and the men of the Vermandois Infantry would not use force against their comrades of the Touraine Infantry. Frustrated, Colonel Mirabeau took the regimental colours and fled from Perpignan.[1] He apparently hoped to rally around him the soldiers of the regiment, perhaps some 300 men, who still supported him and the other officers. Infuriated by Mirabeau's action, most of the soldiers put pressure on the municipal government to order his arrest, and the Colonel was apprehended at Castelnaudary.

The conflict was soon placed before the National Assembly. Colonel Mirabeau was released by virtue of his inviolability as a deputy. Representatives of the soldiers testified that Mirabeau had attempted to win back their loyalty by offering them a bribe and claimed that this was part of an aristocratic plot to seduce the army. A deputy from the Perpignan National Guard testified to the good conduct, patriotism, and civil and military virtues of the soldiers. He went on to say they had witnessed attacks on patriots and the National Assembly by some of their officers for a year. Who, he asked, could blame these soldiers for choosing loyalty to the fatherland over subordination? Two months later, the Committee of Reports of the Assembly charged Mirabeau with being responsible for the insurrection; he resigned and by 18 August had joined the *émigré* army of Condé. Thus, the claims of the soldiers were vindicated.

Confrontations between officers and men increased in number during the summer of 1790; in July and August mutinies occurred among line units at Saint-Servan, Epinal, Stenay, Brest, Longwy, Metz, Sarrelouis, Compiègne, and Hesdin.[2] A prominent complaint of the soldiers in many of these incidents concerned unit finances; 30 per cent of all instances of insubordination in 1790 involved this issue.[3]

Nationale par M. Siau, Médecin, Député de la Garde Nationale de Perpignan, dans la Séance du 26 Juin 1790', Maclure Collection, vol. 874.

[1] The flags of a regiment had great symbolic value and also practical significance. The presence of the colours meant the presence of the regiment or at least of the authority of the regiment. Any soldier away from the regimental colours without permission was liable to a charge of desertion.

[2] See Hartmann, *Les Officiers de l'armée royale*, pp. 156-7.

[3] Among the units studied during the period 1788-92, 28% of the cases of insubordination in 1790 began over unit funds; of the units investigated for 1790 only, 42% of the examples of insubordination involved this issue.

Certain sums were allotted to the regiments for each soldier to cover such expenses as wood, lighting, hospital care, and replacement of uniforms and equipment. Many soldiers felt that these funds rightly belonged to them, and that the officers were cheating them of this money by fraudulent deductions from their pay, by collusion with contractors, and by keeping back the pay of soldiers who were on leave.[1] The fact that many soldiers had not yet received a pay increase recently voted by the National Assembly exacerbated the situation.

Shortly after mid-July the soldiers of the Poitou Infantry, garrisoned at Hesdin, demanded an accounting of the unit funds and forced their colonel to hand over 40,000 *livres* to them.[2] On 30 July the men of La Reine Cavalry revolted against their officers. The citizens of Stenay, where the regiment was stationed, took the side of the soldiers, who demanded an audit of unit funds and charged the officers with mishandling them.[3] A similar incident involving the German regiment of Salm-Salm Infantry took place at the same time in Metz. These soldiers also demanded that regimental funds be turned over to them, and persisted in their demands even when upbraided personally by General de Bouillé. As in other instances, the townspeople supported the soldiers. When Bouillé called upon the regiment of Condé Dragoons to disperse the mutinous soldiers, the dragoons would not mount their horses and the other units of the garrison likewise refused to take action against their comrades. The officers were powerless; and it was the mayor of the city who ultimately convinced the soldiers to return peacefully to their quarters.[4] In the course of 1790 the Salm-Salm Infantry lost 198 deserters, 83 of them in July and 35 in August.

In the spring of 1790 when their regiment was stationed in Metz, soldiers of the Picardie Infantry revolted against their officers and joined some of the inhabitants in excessive drinking. After being reprimanded by General de Bouillé, the soldiers returned to order.[5] In the next three months twenty-nine members of the regiment were dishonourably discharged. On 2 August, however, the soldiers

[1] Chilly, *La Tour du Pin*, p. 122 and Belhomme, *Histoire de l'infanterie*, III. 437.

[2] Hartmann, *Les Officiers de l'armée royale*, pp. 156–7 and Poisson, *L'Armée et la Garde Nationale*, I. 247.

[3] For more details, see Choppin, *Insurrections militaires*, pp. 206–28.

[4] François-Claude-Amour, Marquis de Bouillé, *Mémoires du Marquis de Bouillé* (Paris, 1821), pp. 133–5.

[5] Ibid., pp. 110–11.

demanded the sum of 27,495 *livres* 9 *sous* 7 *deniers*, money of which, they claimed, the officers of the regiment had cheated them. They were given this sum, but on 7 August the regiment was transferred to Sarrelouis. Within four days of arriving at this new garrison, the soldiers demanded an additional 23,836 *livres*, based on claims which dated from the War of American Independence. The municipal officials, fearing violence, raised the money by loans from individual citizens and paid this to the troops on 13 August. The soldiers expressed their satisfaction, promised that there would be no further claims, and swore to maintain perfect discipline henceforth. The officials of Sarrelouis later testified that during the incident the soldiers' conduct had been above reproach.[1]

In some of the other numerous instances like those above, while discipline was shaken, it was not destroyed. In late August 1790 soldiers of the Forez Infantry charged that regimental funds had been misused and demanded reimbursement. The demand, which forced the regiment's quartermaster-treasurer to retire after thirty-four years of service, was decided in favour of the soldiers. In December, however, the soldiers publicly repented of their action and agreed to have 1 *sou* withheld from their daily pay for a period of one year.[2] When the men of the Royal Cavalry presented their complaints to the officers of the regiment, their superiors investigated each complaint and attempted to satisfy those which they felt were just. In the end the soldiers announced that they were gratified by the results.[3] Many regiments, like the Castella Swiss Infantry, made no complaints at all against their officers during this period.[4]

The disputes that were not amicably settled and that resulted in mutiny or insubordination seriously alarmed the National Assembly. Reports from irate officers and frightened local officials led the government to seek solutions to the problem. Some hoped to end the disorders by improving the soldiers' morale. Emmery, one of the members of the Military Committee of the Assembly, perceptively argued that the personal bonds between officers and men must be strengthened and suggested that captains should recruit men for their companies in regions where they themselves lived, as one

---

[1] See the documents on this affair in A.G., X^b 14.

[2] A.G., X^b 26.

[3] Anon., *Relation de ce qui s'est passé au Régiment de Royal-Cavalerie du 27 juin jusqu' au 11 juillet 1790* (Strasbourg, 1790).

[4] See the statement of the enlisted men of this regiment in A.G., X^g 88.

means of accomplishing this. He further urged that veterans be awarded larger pensions and be given preference for certain public offices after their discharge.[1] Others wanted harsher policies to restore discipline. On 6 August the Assembly outlawed deliberating associations or clubs within the regiments, since many considered these the prime instigators of disorder. Shortly afterwards, General de Bouillé's command was extended to include all of Lorraine, Alsace, and Franche-Comté thus putting under his orders nearly half of the entire army. Bouillé himself was sceptical about the about the amount of confidence he could put in these troops; he estimated that of the ninety infantry battalions in his command he could depend on twenty, all German or Swiss, and of 104 cavalry squadrons he could count on sixty, twenty-seven of which were German-speaking hussar units.[2] Bouillé was the most competent general officer in the army at the time; and, as was well known, he was anxious to restore rigid discipline among the troops.

Apart from these firm measures, the Assembly attempted to be conciliatory towards the complaints of the soldiers. In the same decree that abolished deliberating associations of soldiers, the Assembly required an accounting of all unit funds. Commissioners were to be sent to each regimental headquarters to audit the regiment's account. Upon arrival the commissioner was to read the law to the assembled regiment. Then he was to proceed to the verification of the accounts in the presence of a committee composed of the commanding officer of the regiment, a captain, a lieutenant, a second-lieutenant, two sergeants, two corporals, and four soldiers, selected by lot from the soldiers who could read and write and had served at least two years.[3]

All of these developments—increasing tension between officers and men, civilian support for the soldiers' complaints, distrust about the use of unit funds, and Bouillé's new appointment—prepared the way for the greatest crisis of 1790, the mutiny at Nancy. Despite their gravity, none of the previous conflicts between officers and men equalled the scope of this disorder which verged on civil war and

---

[1] 'Idées présentées au Comité Militaire par M. Emmery, l'un de ses membres, le 26 Juin 1790', Maclure Collection, vol. 848.
[2] Bouillé, *Mémoires*, p. 140. The figure of 27 German hussar squadrons is confusing because there were only 24 hussar squadrons in the cavalry. Bouillé probably meant simply squadrons of German-speaking mounted troops, mostly hussars.
[3] Details of the law can be found in documents in A.G., X^b 14, 31, and 42, and in A.D. Bas-Rhin IL 1439.

climaxed the wave of insubordination of the prior thirteen months.[1]

On a superficial examination, the three regiments garrisoned at Nancy would appear to be the least likely to mutiny. The King's Own (Du Roi) Infantry was unique among the line infantry, twice the size of all the other regiments with a much higher ratio of officers to men. The other units, the Swiss regiment of Châteauvieux and the Mestre de Camp Général Cavalry, were the kinds of regiments— foreign and cavalry—that had generally maintained the best discipline since the beginning of the Revolution. The revolutionary experience of these units, however, belied any assumptions based on their general characteristics. Both the Swiss and the cavalry regiment had been among the forces that served in Paris during July 1789; and, although they had maintained good discipline since then, they had been directly exposed to revolutionary propaganda and military insubordination among their fellow-soldiers. The men of the King's Own Infantry, stationed in Nancy since 1783, had indicated their pro-revolutionary sentiments clearly and early. Within a month of the fall of the Bastille soldiers of this regiment had demonstrated in the streets of Nancy in support of the Third Estate.[2] In addition, four soldiers, either on leave or deserters, had participated in the attack on the Bastille;[3] and twenty-two others subsequently enlisted in three of the six divisions of the paid National Guard of Paris.

Since the summer of 1789 soldiers in the three regiments, especially those in the King's Own Infantry, established close ties with pro-revolutionary citizens of Nancy. On 19 April 1790 many soldiers attended the federation ceremony in that city, despite the opposition of their officers. Some joined the local Jacobin club and

---

[1] Almost every moderately detailed history of this period or of the army contains some information on the Nancy affair. The basic sources for the following discussion, unless otherwise indicated, are: Georges Bourdeau, 'L'Affaire de Nancy—31 août 1790', *Annales de l'Est*, XII (1898), 280–92; Bouillé, *Mémoires*, pp. 138, 145–61, and 389–90; 'Rapport de MM. Duveyrier et B.-C. Cahier, Commissaires nommés par le Roi, pour l'exécution des décrets de l'Assemblée Nationale, relatifs aux troubles de Nanci, Remis à M. la Tour-du-Pin, Ministre de la Guerre, le Jeudi 14 Octobre 1790' and 'Rapport des Comités réunis Militaire, de Rapports et des Recherches, sur l'Affaire de Nanci par M. de Sillery', Maclure Collection, vol. 831. My special thanks are due to William Baldwin who has most generously shared with me the results of his intensive research on Nancy at this period. His study, when completed, will undoubtedly constitute the most thorough investigation of the mutiny available and a much more detailed examination of military responses to the Revolution than this general study can accomplish.

[2] Choppin, *Les Hussards*, p. 246.

[3] Durieux, *Vainqueurs de la Bastille, passim.*

more socialized with radical elements of the Nancy National Guard. Led by the grenadiers, a number of soldiers in the King's Own Infantry had established a 'soldiers' committee' which maintained contacts with similar groups in other regiments. At the same time, relations between officers and soldiers and between officers and pro-revolutionary civilians deteriorated. The officers prohibited their soldiers from wearing the new national cockade, until the king authorized it. Suspect soldiers were dishonourably discharged. Enlisted men, especially those associated with the soldiers' committee, were insulted and mistreated by officers; and some were arrested. Some of the young noble officers in the King's Own Infantry even bribed soldiers to pick quarrels with members of the National Guard. On 19 July the officers outlawed the soldiers' committee. In early August the grenadiers of the King's Own Infantry were insulted by being taken off guard-duty.

On 9 August the decisions made by the National Assembly three days earlier became known at Nancy. The abolition of associations within military units vindicated the position of the officers; but, on the other hand, the decision to audit unit funds justified complaints made by the soldiers' committee shortly before its disestablishment. The same day the soldiers of the King's Own Infantry confined their officers to quarters and arrested the regimental quartermaster-treasurer. The Military Commandant of Nancy, General de Noue, wanted to declare martial law, but was dissuaded by the municipal officials who feared that this extreme measure would only further inflame the soldiers and the many civilians who sympathized with them. When the quartermaster gave the soldiers the 150,000 *livres* which they demanded, they released him with a receipt for this sum.

The success of the King's Own soldiers led to insubordination on the part of the rest of the garrison. On 10 August two representatives of the soldiers of the Châteauvieux regiment complained to their officers about the discipline and administration of this regiment. In response the Swiss officers had the two soldiers publicly whipped the next day. Such brutality rallied the two French regiments and many civilians behind the soldiers and led to their forced release from arrest. On 12 August pickets of soldiers confined the Swiss officers to their quarters and forced them to distribute 27,000 *livres* to the soldiers of Châteauvieux. General de Noue again attempted to make the municipality declare martial law, but again it refused because of popular support for the soldiers. Two days later the cavalrymen of

Mestre de Camp Général held their officers in confinement until a partial payment of the 48,000 *livres* that they demanded was handed over. Simultaneously, the men of the King's Own Infantry deputed eight soldiers to present their case and that of their comrades to the National Assembly.

The local officials and officers at Nancy had, in the meantime, sent their own version of the recent events to Paris and requested that firm action be taken to end the crisis. The Minister of War and the Military Committee of the Assembly decided to make an example of the regiments at Nancy in the hope that the quick repression of this insubordination would serve to limit or eliminate the general unrest in the army. Lafayette strongly supported such action; in a letter of 18 August he wrote to Bouillé: 'It seems to me, my dear cousin, that we ought to strike a blow which will impress the entire army, and stop by a severe example the general dissolution which is going on.'[1] On 16 August the Assembly decreed that if the soldiers at Nancy did not cease their insubordination in twenty-four hours, they would be guilty of high treason. Bouillé would be the Assembly's agent in enforcing this decision. On 17 August the eight representatives of the soldiers were arrested in Paris.

The decree of 16 August became known at Nancy three days later. On 20 August soldiers of the three regiments signed a declaration of submission to the National Assembly and the King and promised that they would observe perfect discipline. The soldiers asked that their deputies to the Assembly be released. The calm which had existed since 16 August continued until the twenty-fourth.

On that day General de Malseigne arrived in Nancy to check the regimental accounts and restore order. This cantankerous officer so insulted and abused the Swiss for their conduct that within twenty-four hours of his arrival he had to barricade himself in General de Noue's quarters while besieged by the irate soldiers of Châteauvieux. Having succeeded only in exacerbating the situation, Malseigne managed to bring it to the brink of civil war by dashing off to Lunéville on 28 August, in order to rally the regiment of Carabiniers stationed there against the Nancy garrison. This move convinced the two French regiments that rumours of 'an aristocratic plot', which had been circulating in Nancy, were in fact true. The soldiers arrested their officers, including the commandant, and sent a contingent to pursue Malseigne. They also raided the royal arsenal

[1] Lafayette, *Mémoires*, I. 383.

at Nancy and distributed weapons to their supporters in the National Guard.

At Lunéville, the civil officials and the Carabiniers decided to turn Malseigne over to his pursuers from Nancy. And by the afternoon of 30 August the General was in the custody of the troops and insurgent elements of the National Guard in Nancy. By this time, however, a more serious problem had presented itself, the approach of the hostile army under Bouillé.

In execution of his commission from the Assembly, Bouillé had gathered an army of almost 4,500 men, all but 700 of whom were regulars and many of whom were from foreign regiments. By the evening of 30 August this force was outside Nancy. To the delegates sent out by the municipal officials and the troops Bouillé offered unconditional terms, complete surrender within twenty-four hours. He demanded the immediate release of Generals Malseigne and Noue and the surrender of the four most mutinous soldiers in each of the three line regiments. The soldiers, impressed by Bouillé's authority from the Assembly, decided to capitulate on the thirty-first. As an advance guard of Bouillé's troops approached one of the city gates, however, firing began. The Swiss of Châteauvieux, who manned this sector, and unidentified snipers in this part of the city put up a violent resistance which lasted three hours. It was nearly nightfall before Bouillé was master of Nancy, after suffering over a hundred casualties.[1]

Swift and harsh repression followed. By the next morning all three regiments had been marched out of Nancy. The local Jacobin club was closed, although there was no evidence to implicate it directly in the mutiny. Even the city's National Guard was disbanded, temporarily. The most severe punishment was meted out to the Swiss soldiers. One soldier of the Châteauvieux Infantry (a member of the soldiers' committee) was broken on the wheel, twenty-two others were hanged, forty-one were condemned to the galleys for 30 years, and seventy-four soldiers were punished within the regiment. Other soldiers of the garrison and scores of civilians were imprisoned. The two French regiments involved in the mutiny were disbanded, only to be recreated in early 1791.

In the shocked aftermath of the Nancy affair there was a lull in insubordination until the following spring, although some incidents

[1] The estimates of casualties vary widely. One of the more judicious estimations can be found in Chilly, *La Tour du Pin*, pp. 241–4.

did occur during this period. In the summer of 1790, however, it appeared to many that the entire army was collapsing into anarchy. More than one-third of the Royal Army experienced some form of insubordination during 1790, mostly before autumn. Not only was this problem markedly more widespread than in 1789 (when it had affected about one-fifth of all regular army units), but in 1790 80 per cent of the cases of insubordination involved direct confrontations between officers and men, unmistakable evidence of the soldiers' increasing self-confidence and aggressiveness.[1]

Although somewhat less significant than during the previous year, civilian support continued to be an important factor in the incidents of insubordination during 1790; over 40 per cent of the line units that displayed insubordinate behaviour in that year received some form of encouragement from civilians, particularly local National Guard units (e.g. at Lille, Hesdin, Perpignan, Nancy).[2] In addition, the actions and attitude of the National Assembly encouraged soldiers to defy their superiors. The Assembly's concern for improving the conditions of soldiers and ending the abuses to which they were subjected convinced many soldiers that the legislature sincerely wished to redress their complaints. This led many of the mutinous troops to believe that they had at least the tacit sanction of the Assembly in their independent efforts to improve their lot.

The fundamental issue in most cases of insubordination during 1790 remained military conditions—the use of unit funds, the right of soldiers to fraternize with civilians, and the officer's abuse of their authority; and the basic problem was still the alienation between soldiers and officers. In 1790, however, the political implications of this division were made more explicit. In the conflict between the regiments in Lille, for example, opposing units were identified on the basis of their reactions to the Revolution. At Perpignan and Nancy the officers were associated with an 'aristocratic plot'. Increasingly, professional and social differences were defined in political terms. A new dimension was being added to the conflict between 'patriotic'

[1] See the section in Appendix I on the 'Incidence of Insubordination'. In the selected sample used for 1788–92, 25 of the 73 units studied (34·2%) suffered insubordination in 1790; of the 104 units for which I have data for that year, 38 (36·5%) experienced a breakdown in discipline. In both sets of data 80% or more of these incidents consisted of open defiance of officers by soldiers; the remainder of the examples of insubordination took the form of excessive desertions.

[2] In the sample for the period 1788–92, 11 of the 25 units guilty of insubordination in 1790 had close relations with civilians. Of 38 such examples in 1790 alone, 16 units had similar ties.

soldiers and 'aristocratic' officers that would ultimately lead to the complete renovation of the officer corps of the line army.

In 1789 only a few high-ranking officers of the court aristocracy had emigrated with the Comte d'Artois. Most officers remained at their posts, despite their reservations about the revolutionary policies of the National Assembly. While few noble officers were unhappy to see the end of the preference accorded to the court nobility or the abolition of venality, most were reluctant to accept the principle of equality which would put their social inferiors on the same level as them. The abolition of hereditary nobility in June 1790 increased noble uneasiness and tended to unify the court and pro-vincial aristocracy in the face of a common enemy.[1] On the other hand, a substantial minority of the established officers—who would later constitute an important element in the armies of the Revolution —continued to perform their duties with the same devotion as before 1789. They did so for a variety of reasons: because they sincerely embraced the new principles, out of a sense of professional com-mitment, and due to the new opportunities opened to them by the new regime.[2] Yet even dedicated professionals had difficulty in coping with political charges against them and the mounting in-subordination of their troops. As the Minister of War noted on 4 July 1790, the massive insubordination in the Royal Army was creating 'a military democracy' which would drive the officers to emigrate.[3]

VARENNES AND THE DEFECTION
OF THE OFFICERS

A number of factors contributed to the relative calm after the Nancy mutiny. The severity of this clash undoubtedly had a sobering effect on all but the hottest heads. The thoroughly repressive nature of the

[1] Hartmann, *Les Officiers de l'armée royale*, pp. 142–9 and Donald Greer. *The Inci-dence of the Emigration During the French Revolution* (Gloucester, Mass., 1966), p. 23.

[2] One example of how the frustrations engendered by the Old Regime aroused revolu-tionary activity, even among the nobility, is recounted in 'Rapport des Messieurs J. Godard et J. Robin, Commissaires civils, Envoyés par le Roi, dans le Département du Lot, en execution du Décret de l'Assemblée Nationale du 13 Décembre 1790', Maclure Collection, vol. 832. These deputies determined that one of the leaders of a peasant uprising in the Lot over the redemption of feudal obligations was M. Jean Linars, a noble whose pedigree dated back four centuries. Linars, however, had become bitterly opposed to the Old Regime because he had been victimized by 'injustices relative to his military advancement'.

[3] 'Discours de M. de la Tour du Pin, Ministre et Secrétaire d'État au Départment de la Guerre, à la Séance du 4 Juin 1790', Maclure Collection, vol. 848.

reaction to the mutiny dulled revolutionary enthusiasm among many troops and civilians. Some officers even began to take their duties more responsibly. Although dishonourable discharges and even bribes continued to be used to insure discipline,[1] more positive action was taken as well. The proportion of officers on leave between the autumn of 1790 and the spring of 1791 declined by 10 per cent or more compared to the previous year;[2] and this facilitated supervision of the activities of enlisted men. Nonetheless, the underlying animosity between soldiers and officers, although temporarily muted, remained the fundamental element in intra-military relations.

In the spring of 1791 the wave of insubordination which had swept the Royal Army during the previous spring and summer revived; and the distinctive characteristics which marked this movement in 1790—growing belligerence and political awareness on the part of the soldiers—became more pronounced. Many contemporaries and later historians have blamed this situation on the Assembly's decision of 1 May 1791 to allow military personnel to attend political clubs when off-duty, a right which had been denied them since the previous September. Although there was a chronological coincidence between this decree and the upsurge of insubordination, and although in a number of instances local political groups did indeed encourage insubordination among soldiers, neither sole nor even major responsibility for the insubordination during the spring of 1791 can be attributed to the clubs. Like other conspiracy theses, so comforting in their exoneration of all but a handful of evil-doers, this argument is too facile and ignores contradictory facts.

For one thing, many soldiers continued to attend political clubs during the comparatively quiet winter of 1790–1, despite the official prohibition. In February 1791 General Biron wrote to General Rochambeau that a large number of soldiers garrisoned at Amiens, Lille, and elsewhere were frequenting local Jacobin clubs.[3]

---

[1] E.g. the commander of the regiment of Grenoble Artillery discharged 26 soldiers in October 1790; see A.G., X^d 15. The previous month, the general who inspected the men of the Metz Artillery gave every soldier a 'gratification', despite the Assembly's prohibition against this practice; see A.G., X^d 7.

[2] Data on periods of leave in 1790–1 is scarcer than for the previous year, but in five infantry regiments only 38% of the officers took semester leaves. See A.G., X^b 168, 169, 172, and 173.

[3] Letter from Biron to Rochambeau, dated Amiens, 16 Feb. 1791 in A.G., B^{1*} 208.

Between late March and mid-April soldiers from the detachment of the 54th (Royal Rousillon) Infantry,[1] stationed in Blois, attended the Jacobin club in that city. When their officers protested, the club supported the soldiers and denounced the officers as hostile to the Revolution.[2] Despite close ties between the Jacobins and the soldiers, discipline was not destroyed. Soldiers' unauthorized attendance at political clubs during late 1790 and early 1791 did not necessarily disrupt the relative calm within the army during this period; and it is impossible to argue that the legalization of this practice suddenly opened the floodgates to insubordination in the spring.

Furthermore in two-thirds of the cases of insubordination in 1791 there was no evidence of civilian interference at all, whether from political clubs or unorganized citizens.[3] Most often the hostility between officers and soldiers simply did not require the intervention of civilians to burst into insubordination or mutiny. For example, in mid-April 1791 a quarrel between a captain and a corporal of the 6th (La Reine) Dragoons, garrisoned at Laon, resulted in the Corporal's arrest. His comrades reacted by insulting their officers publicly and refusing to obey their orders until the Captain was punished too. This insubordination ended only when the Captain was tried, found guilty of insulting the Corporal first, and sentenced to one month of 'forced arrest in his quarters [guarded] by a sentinel'.[4] In another incident, the men of the 36th (Anjou) Infantry who had shown their enthusiasm for the Revolution on a number of occasions (e.g. by celebrating a *fédération* with the National Guard of Tours in May 1790, by holding ceremonies in honour of Mirabeau in April 1791), strongly suspected that their officers held opposite sentiments. By mid-May 1791 the soldiers of the first battalion, at Saint-Servan, were convinced that many of their officers were planning to emigrate to the English island of Jersey. This led to increased hostility and

[1] The names of all regiments were changed to numbers on 1 Jan. 1791; see Appendix II.

[2] For fuller details, see Pierre Dufay, *Les Sociétés populaires et l'armée (1791–1794)* (Paris, 1913), pp. 61–71. Excerpts from the minutes of the Blois club are in Jean-Paul Bertaud, *Valmy: La Démocratie en armes* (Paris, 1970), pp. 171–72.

[3] Of the 73 line units studied for the period 1788–92, 23 experienced insubordination in 1791; of these, only 7 (30·4%) had developed close ties with civilians. Of 97 units for which I have data for 1791 only, 31 exhibited insubordination, and 12 of these had civilian support (38·7%).

[4] Letters from Biron to Rochambeau, dated 16 Apr. 1791, and to Duportail, dated 24 Apr., 1 May, and 2 May 1791, in A.G., B1* 208.

acts of insubordination; and in the next five months most of the officers did in fact desert the regiment.[1]

Civilian support for the soldiers was still a significant element in military insubordination, although its importance decreased as the Revolution progressed. The essential cause of insubordination, however, existed within, not outside, the Royal Army. Civilians often provided encouragement to the soldiers and the clubs sometimes offered a forum for them to voice their complaints. But, it was conditions in the army that created the complaints, and it was the Revolution, but its overthrow of traditional authority, that allowed them to be expressed as they were. One of the most serious mutinies of 1791 graphically illustrates this situation and shows that in order to redress their military grievances, some soldiers were prepared even to defy the National Assembly.

Since the early Revolution hostility had been building up between the soldiers and officers of the 38th (Dauphiné) Infantry. In November 1789 disorders had broken out in Toulon, where the regiment had been garrisoned for two years. Some of the officers aroused the animosity of the inhabitants by wearing the black cockade of Austria, which was associated with counter-revolution; and there was a brief insurrection in the grenadier company in connection with this incident.[2] As a result of large-scale desertion (111 between September 1789 and September 1790), twenty dishonourable discharges, and the almost total cessation of recruitment (only 34 recruits during the same period), order was restored in the unit at the price of a drastic reduction in strength.[3] In August 1790 the regiment was moved to Nîmes; and the following February a large detachment of the regiment helped to preserve order during conflicts between the Catholics and Protestants of Uzès.[4]

In May 1791 the soldiers of the 38th revolted against their officers.[5] On 20 May a deputation from the grenadier company presented a list of complaints to the commanding officer of the

[1] See Anon., 'Historique du 36ᵉ Régiment d' Infanterie. 1ʳᵉ Partie (1791–1815)', pp. 1–35; A.N. H¹⁴⁵³, letter from Berchény to Saint-Priest, dated 15 May 1790; A.N., F⁷ 3679¹, letter from the directory of the district of Saint-Malo to the directory of the Ille-et-Vilaine, dated 17 May 1791; and A.G., Xᵇ 174.

[2] D'Izarny-Gargas, *38ᵐᵉ Régiment d'Infanterie*, pp. 105–6 and Chilly, *La Tour du Pin*, pp. 54–5.

[3] See the inspection report for 22 Sept. 1790 in A.G., Xᵇ 51.

[4] D'Izarny-Gargas, *38ᵐᵉ Régiment d'Infanterie*, p. 109.

[5] The following account, unless otherwise noted, is based upon the documents in A.N., Dxv5, dossier 45.

regiment, Lieutenant-Colonel Roqueville; most of these concerned ways by which the soldiers had been cheated by the officers, e.g. inadequate replacement of uniforms, withholding of funds due to the soldiers, and the forced purchase of certain supplies from the regiment. The next day Roqueville held a meeting of the officers and advised them to arm themselves. The soldiers, in turn, took up weapons and arrested a number of officers. They then asked the municipal officials of Nîmes and the Military Commandant of the region, General D'Albignac, to intervene. D'Albignac suspended the officers provisionally and requested the government to send commissioners to investigate the situation. On 22 May the soldiers chased almost all the officers, fifty in all, from the regiment, and appointed a new commander, Captain Pecault.

The reaction of the government was to insist that the soldiers accept their officers back; no commissioners were sent out nor, as the soldiers repeatedly requested, were new officers appointed. To justify their position, the soldiers made public their charges against the officers. Besides the accusations of cheating, the soldiers also claimed that the officers had frequently inflicted illegal and excessive punishments, that they often treated the soldiers in degrading fashion, and that some of them had displayed a marked hostility towards the Revolution and its supporters. The government still would not take action until the soldiers received the officers back. The soldiers refused and again presented their case against the officers. On 28 August the National Assembly passed a decree ordering the soldiers to return to obedience under their old officers and threatened severe punishments if this were not done.

The soldiers protested their devotion to the Assembly but remained adamant. Civil authorities now took up the cause of the men, many of whom were natives of the region.[1] Officials of the department of the Guard and the municipality of Nîmes testified to the good conduct of the soldiers and the legitimacy of the complaints. The municipality, National Guard, and Jacobin club of Uzès all supported the soldiers' case and praised their patriotism. Similar petitions to the National Assembly came from officials and clubs of some nearby towns, Saint-Gilles, Vallabrèques, Aiguesmortes, and

[1] Of the 884 soldiers in the regiment at the inspection of 22 Sept. 1790, 140 (15·8%) were from Languedoc, 260 (29·4%) were from Provence, and 105 (11·9%) were from Dauphiné. In all, three-quarters of the regiment were from the Midi. See A.G., X^b 51.

Genolhac. On the other hand, the Minister of War, Duportail, argued that the officers had been dismissed from their functions without any legal proceedings and had the undeniable right to return to their posts; and that since the soldiers were not obeying either military or civil authority, they were in a state of insurrection and must be punished. General D'Albignac, who had left Nîmes, informed the Assembly that the military discipline of the entire army depended on the punishment of the 38th Infantry.

The National Assembly, once again frightened by the spectre of military mutiny, condemned it in the strongest possible language. By the time the Assembly had passed its decree of 28 August, however, the attempted flight of the King and the reaction of European powers to this event had greatly increased the likelihood of war. The National Assembly and the Legislative Assembly, which succeeded it on 1 October 1791, did not punish the men of the 38th as had been threatened. The possibility that severe punishment of this regiment might only spread insubordination further in the army, and the unquestionable patriotism of the soldiers of the 38th precluded such action. Only a few officers of the regiment were allowed to return to it, and most of the former officers were ultimately replaced.[1]

Although a somewhat extreme case, the mutiny of the 38th Infantry exemplified the increasing pressures to which the Royal Army officer corps was being subjected. Many officers regretted the reordering of politics and society initiated by the Revolution, and particularly resented changes affecting the army. A more immediate problem was the insults and mistreatment which a number of officers suffered at the hands of their men; this alienated not only those directly involved, but others who were not personally subjected to such treatment. The general collapse of authority and discipline was frustrating to practically all officers. In addition, those officers who had already emigrated encouraged others to join them; they appealed to honour and ambition; they offered bribes; and they threatened those who refused to join them with the revocation of their commission after the 'restoration'.[2] By early 1791 some 1,200 noble officers had joined in Condé's attempt to create an army of

---

[1] The regiment did not regain its full complement of officers until the autumn of 1792. See A.G., X^b 175.

[2] Greer, *Incidence of Emigration*, pp. 24-5 and Mme de La Tour du Pin, *Mémoires*, p. 155.

émigrés and others had enlisted in smaller forces composed of exiles, such as the 'Black Bands of Mirabeau'.[1]

Yet until mid-1791 a large majority of the pre-revolutionary officers were still at their posts.[2] The spirit of professionalism developed over the previous quarter-century, their economic dependence upon the state, and strong sense of loyalty to the King firmly bound the French nobility, especially the lower nobility, to military service. A new oath of loyalty to the nation, the law, and the King was decreed by the Assembly on 11 June 1791. This oath was to be in writing and signed by each individual officer, not taken orally and collectively as previously;[3] it combined the threat of possible legal action with an appeal to the officers' honour. It might have succeeded in ensuring the adhesion of most officers to the new regime had not the King completely altered the situation by attempting to flee his kingdom, only a week and a half after the Assembly's decree.

Since October 1790 the King and General Bouillé had been considering plans to provide adequate armed protection so that the King might leave Paris safely.[4] Various garrison towns, such as Metz, Besançon, Valenciennes, were proposed as royalist rallying-points; but all were rejected, because the townspeople or garrisons were hostile, because of their distance from Paris, or because the route to them was unsuitable. Finally Montmédy was selected as a place where the King could rally forces loyal to him and repress the Revolution.

To cover the projected flight Bouillé selected units that he felt he could depend upon. He chose four German and two Swiss infantry regiments, and detachments from ten cavalry units, including four hussar regiments.[5] Bouillé took the further precaution of sending potentially unreliable officers in these units on leave.

---

[1] Poisson, *L'Armée et la Garde Nationale*, I. 280-1. Also see Mirabeau's correspondence in A.N., 119 AP.

[2] It is impossible to be at all precise about the number of officers present for duty at any specific date. Records on officers were much less rigorously maintained than those on soldiers, and greater discretion was allowed them in matters concerning leave.

[3] Hartmann, *Les Officiers de l'armée royale*, pp. 222-9.

[4] The best account of the army's role in the flight to Varennes is Michel de Lombarès, 'Varennes ou la fin d'un régime (21 juin 1791)', *Revue historique de l'armée*, 1960, Nos. 3 and 4, pp. 33-6 and 45-62 and 1961, No. 1, pp. 23-36. Unless otherwise noted, the following details of this episode are based on this article.

[5] The German regiments were the 94th (Royal Hesse Darmstadt), 96th (Nasssau), 98th (Bouillon), and 99th (Royal Deux-Ponts) Infantry. The Swiss units were the 66th

The arrangements for the flight were badly mismanaged in Paris. Most importantly, the royal entourage was many hours behind schedule when it left the Tuileries early in the morning of 21 June. The military units, largely ignorant of their mission, arrived at pre-determined rendezvous, waited for hours, and then, suspecting that whoever they were to meet had passed, returned to their stations. The royal party would later arrive to find no escort. Meanwhile, the officers who were privy to the plot were having increasing difficulties in hiding or explaining such large troop movements. The delays also increased the danger of even the hand-picked troops turning against their officers.

On the morning of 21 June a detachment of thirty men from the 1st (Royal) Dragoons arrived, as directed, in Sainte-Menehould. The townspeople were suspicious of their mission; a detachment of the 6th (Lazun) Hussars had spent the previous night there and had been jeered when they departed earlier that morning. The National Guard was called out and three or four hundred muskets were distributed to citizens. Some townspeople mixed with the dragoons and brought them drinks. When the captain commanding the detachment tried to leave the town that night, the National Guard prevented the troops' departure. Shortly afterwards, news of the King's flight reached Sainte-Menehould. The troops were forced to disarm; the captain was arrested; and the dragoons were put under the orders of National Guard officers.

The same afternoon a forty-man detachment of the 6th Hussars arrived at Pont-de-Somme-Vesle. While awaiting the arrival of the King, some hussars mixed with the inhabitants. When the King failed to arrive the contingent was moved back to Varennes.

A detachment of the 13th (Monsieur) Dragoons had been at Clermont-en-Argonne since 20 June to assist the royal flight. By the afternoon of the next day the King's party had still not arrived and townspeople passed the time talking with the soldiers. Rumours of the attempted flight began to spread. By 11 p.m. the commander of the detachment, Colonel Charles de Damas, one of the leaders of the plot, ordered the departure of his unit. The National Guard was

(Castella) and 100th (Reinach) Infantry. The cavalry detachments were from the 1st (Berchény), 2nd (Chamborant), 3rd (Esterhazy), and 6th (Lazun) Hussars; the 1st (Royal), 7th (Dauphin), and 13th (Monsieur) Dragoons; the 3rd (Flandre) and 12th (Champagne) Chasseurs; and the 15th (Royal Allemand) Cavalry. See Bouillé, *Mémoires*, p. 410.

called out to stop the dragoons. Rather than risk violence, and dubious of the loyalty of his men, Damas left his troops and departed with a small escort for Varennes.

At Varennes two companies of the 6th Hussars had been detached to protect the King and his family. When the evening came on 21 June and the King had not yet arrived, the commander of this detachment, an 18-year-old second-lieutenant named Rohrig, allowed his men to go to their scattered quarters to sleep. Around 10 p.m. Rohrig was ordered to form his two companies; but the hussars, many of whom had been drinking during the day, could not easily be found and put into formation. More than an hour later, when the King's coach arrived in the town, the hussars had not yet assembled. About midnight the Duc de Choiseul, who commanded the 1st Dragoons, and Colonel de Damas arrived in Varennes and managed to assemble about forty hussars. Meanwhile, another detachment of the 6th Hussars arrived from Pont-de-Somme-Vesle. While the officers were organizing this group and their comrades, some eighty hussars in all, officers of the National Guard arrived and explained that the King had been arrested. Some fighting took place between line officers and the National Guard; but when a National Guard officer informed the hussars that they were under his orders, he was greeted by cries of 'Long live the Nation!'

When Bouillé himself arrived in Varennes, accompanied by the 15th (Royal Allemand) Cavalry, the King, guarded by a large contingent of National Guard and armed civilians, had already departed more than an hour before. Further pursuit was hopeless. Bouillé's troops were exhausted and, except for the men of the 15th Cavalry to whom he had earlier distributed four hundred *louis*, he could not count on the line troops in the area.[1] There was only one alternative now left; Bouillé emigrated.

The King's attempted flight and the reaction to it constituted one of the most important events of the early Revolution. The fiction of the King's allegiance to the Revolution was now fully exposed. Simultaneously the danger of war became a much more real possibility, even a probability. Whatever were the King's ultimate intentions—and these were never fully known, perhaps least of all to the King—the attempted flight entailed an appeal to force, whether simply on the part of the loyal units in the line army or, more likely, by the intervention of foreign forces as well. Had the

[1] Ibid., pp. 240–4.

King succeeded in gaining the frontier, it is impossible to see how civil war could have been avoided.

The flight to Varennes also marked a turning-point in the development of the Royal Army; it had an immediate and widespread impact on both officers and men. Until mid-1791 the major drain on military personnel had been the desertion of soldiers; afterwards, it became the emigration of officers. This change not only had important practical effects but also was of considerable symbolic importance. While officers had emigrated before the Varennes episode and soldiers deserted after it, generally, before then disagreements between officers and men led to the departure, voluntary or forced, of the soldiers; after Varennes it was the officers who felt obliged to leave. Varennes made the recalcitrant officer rather than the insubordinate soldier the 'outsider'.

The attempted flight and subsequent apprehension of Louis XVI proved conclusively to many officers that the King was a prisoner in his own country. Furthermore, by his own example he had shown that emigration was not dereliction of duty. Whatever remaining uncertainty many officers felt regarding emigration was resolved by the new oath of loyalty imposed on army officers by the Assembly shortly after the flight; it made no mention of the King! Hundreds, then thousands of officers considered their last obligation to service now severed, and resigned their commissions and emigrated. By August some 1,500 officers had refused to take the new oath in the presence of the commissioners of the Assembly.[1] Others simply resigned their commissions or left the army without a resignation. Some units lost nearly all of their officers; and by the end of 1791 perhaps as many as 6,000 officers had emigrated from France,[2] over 60 per cent of the authorized officer strength of the line army.

The political crisis created by the King's flight and the officers' reaction to it confirmed many of the soldiers' suspicions. Now there seemed to be conclusive proof (albeit after the fact) that previous charges about officers' enmity to the new regime were well founded. Every new resignation and emigration reinforced this attitude and

---

[1] Hartmann, *Les Officiers de l'armée royale*, pp. 225 and 271–88. For more specific reactions in some of the frontier departments where most line units were stationed, see 'Rapport des commissaires de l'Assemblée Nationale, Envoyés dans les départmens du Rhin et des Vosges' and 'Rapport des commissaires de l'Assemblée Nationale, Envoyés dans les départemens de la Meuse, de la Moselle et des Ardennes; fait par M. de Montesquiou, Député de Paris, le 13 Juillet 1791', in the Maclure Collection, vol. 832.

[2] Greer, *Incidence of Emigration*, p. 26.

further eroded confidence in those officers who remained at their duties. This distrust and the hostility which it engendered led, in turn, to a new wave of mutinies in the summer of 1791.

Shortly after the King's arrest the men of the 17th (Auvergne) Infantry stationed in Phalsbourg began to wear the national cockade on their uniforms and ordered the officers to do the same. The sergeants started a club at which they and their subordinates discussed taking over the regimental colours and funds and chasing off all the officers. On 29 June their plans were put into effect. At 5 p.m. the soldiers of the 17th were drawn up in formation, with loaded muskets, by their N.C.O.s. The sergeant-majors of the regiment then ordered all the officers to leave Phalsbourg within two hours. The officers had no choice but to comply. When a new colonel was appointed to the regiment in late July, he ordered all the officers to return; but only seven did so. Almost the entire officer complement of the regiment had to be replaced.[1]

When the news of the King's flight reached the first battalion of the 27th (Lyonnais) Infantry at Montpellier, the troops immediately assembled in formation and seized the regimental colours and unit funds. Relations between the officers and men of this unit had been badly strained since the previous December when some officers had been charged with attacking members of the Jacobin club in Aix. The action of the soldiers in June led more officers to leave the regiment, some by resigning and others by taking extended leave. By 1 January 1792 there were eighteen officer vacancies in the regiment; and the soldiers, who said that the officers had completely lost their confidence, wanted to select their own officers, who, they promised, would be 'patriot leaders'.[2]

When the officers of the 58th (Rouergue) Infantry, stationed in Blois, had taken the oath required by the Assembly after the King's flight, they had added a declaration that the absence of the King's name from the oath in no way changed the constitution '. . . which assures to France a monarchial government . . .'. The local Jacobin club and a number of soldiers of the 58th who attended the club denounced this action publicly. As a result, four soldiers were imprisoned for insubordination. When all efforts to free these men

[1] A.G., X^b 168 and Pages-Xatart, 'Auvergne—17ᵉᵐᵉ Régiment d'Infanterie', pp. 195–220.

[2] Lieutenant Carnot, 'Le Régiment de Lyonnais (27ᵉ de Ligne) pendant la Révolution française, 1789–1793', pp. 42–8 and the letter from the N.C.O.s and soldiers of the 27th to the Minister of War, dated 3 Feb. 1792, in A.G., X^b 40.

failed, the soldiers of the second battalion mutinied and were supported by the club. As the fighting spread and some inhabitants of Blois joined it, the local officials convinced the commander of the area to release the four soldiers, pending a trial. This satisfied the mutinous soldiers who then returned to their barracks. Shortly afterwards the regiment was transferred to Lorraine. The four soldiers were left behind in the custody of the civil officials and released in late Octber.[1]

Other incidents of insubordination occurred at Perpignan, Wissembourg, Landrecies, Saintes, and elsewhere in the latter half of 1791.[2] Although not all of these developed into full-scale mutinies and although the incidence of insubordination declined slightly from 1790, the situation of the line army was alarming. Nearly one-third of the Royal Army units experienced some form of insubordination during the year and in over 90 per cent of these cases soldiers openly challenged the authority of their officers.[3] Indeed, the slight decrease in the scope of this problem was more than balanced by the increased intensity of these confrontations. Rather than merely confronting their superiors with demands, soldiers in 1791 were prepared to take matters fully into their own hands; in the case of the 38th and of the 17th Infantry the troops assumed complete control of the regiment and its operation. Along with this growing independence on the part of the soldiers, the most prominent feature of military insubordination in 1791 was the increasingly political character of attacks upon the officers, especially after Varennes. Soldiers were not only more insistent about redress of their military grievances but also more ready to link these with complaints about the political unreliability of their superiors.

THE COMING OF WAR

Before the flight to Varennes many officers had found their situation in the Royal Army very difficult; after this, most found it impossible. The shock created by the King's flight and its implications greatly

[1] For full details, see Dufay, *Sociétés populaires et l'armée*, pp. 107–83.

[2] On these affairs, see respectively A.N., F⁹ 45; A.G., X^b 22; Maclure Collection, vol. 831, the letter from M. Bouillé, dated 3 Sept. 1791; and D. Hauterive, *L'Armée sous la Révolution*, p. 170.

[3] Of the 73 units sampled from 1788 to 1792, 23 (31·5%) suffered from insubordination in 1791; and of the latter, 21 (91·3%) involved direct hostile confrontations with officers, and only 2 consisted of excessive desertion. Of 97 units for which I have information for 1791 only, there were incidents of insubordination in 31 (32%), of which 29 cases consisted of open defiance of officers by soldiers (93·5%).

accelerated the process of change which had been going on since 1789. Most officers gave up all hope of reasserting authority over their men and abandoned the army. Officers who accepted the new changes, such as the most recent oath and the temporary suspension of the King, were judged insincere and were suspected of remaining at their posts only the better to serve the cause of counter-revolution. Simultaneously, émigrés and other royalists brought increased pressures to bear on officers to emigrate.[1] In this atmosphere even remaining personal ties disintegrated. For example, in the autumn of 1791 Captain Mautort of the 8th (Austrasie) Infantry visited some of the soldiers who had served with him for five years in India. Despite some lingering affection, Mautort concluded '. . . it was no longer the same'; and he decided to emigrate.[2] His was not an isolated case.

On 16 October 1791, the Minister of War, Duportail reported that there were 1,932 officer vacancies in the infantry and cavalry, for which only 764 replacements had been appointed.[3] Between 15 September and 1 December 2,160 officers emigrated.[4] Some units suffered more than others from emigration, but in every regiment of the line army there were officer vacancies due to resignation and emigration. In early 1792 most of the officers of the 40th Infantry resigned or simply left the regiment because of the insubordination of their soldiers. By the end of February there were only five officers left—one captain, two lieutenants, and two second-lieutenants; except for the captain, all were officers of fortune.[5] When the soldiers of the 45th refused to assemble for the reading of a new regulation on 25 February 1792, most of the officers resigned their commissions, claiming that they had borne such behaviour too long. By 6 March there were only thirteen officers present with the regiment; except for the colonel, none of these was above the rank of lieutenant. The Minister of War upbraided the soldiers for their conduct and urged the officers to return, but to no avail. Replacements had to be provided to fill the vacancies.[6]

---

[1] Hartmann, Les Officiers de l'armée royale, pp. 310–12.
[2] Mautort, Mémoires, p. 403.
[3] Revol, Histoire de l'armée française, p. 133 and Hartmann, Les Officiers de l'armée royale, p. 366.
[4] Arthur Chuquet, La Première invasion prussienne (11 août–2 septembre 1792) (Paris, 1886), p. 40. (Vol. I of Les Guerres de la Révolution.)
[5] A.G., X^b 176.
[6] A.G., X^b 178.

When the first battalion of the 48th Infantry received its new flags in late February, the soldiers refused to send their old colours to Paris, as the regulations required, but instead deposited them in one of the churches of Rennes, where the battalion was stationed. The soldiers claimed that this practice had been 'consecrated since time immemorial'. The lieutenant-colonel commanding the battalion and four other officers resigned in protest against this patent disobedience of the law. The city officials of Rennes, who firmly supported the soldiers, thereupon arrested all five. The Ministers of War and of Justice protested against this unwarranted interference in a purely military matter; but the officers were not returned to their unit.[1] In early May the soldiers of the 93rd Infantry sent away twenty-seven of their officers whom they accused of being counter-revolutionaries, a charge supported by the National Guard of Apt, where the regiment had been quartered briefly in late April. Although the officers were subsequently exonerated, only two ever returned to the regiment. By November, twenty-six N.C.O.s of the regiment had been promoted to officer, and eleven of these were already captains.[2]

During the period from 15 September 1791 to 1 December 1792, one-third of the units in the line army lost one-third or more of their authorized officer strength as a result of resignations, illegal absences, and emigrations.[3] This created an enormous strain on the cadres of these units, particularly since many of them were already under-strength in officers by the autumn of 1791. Political developments, while they constituted an important factor in the decision of many officers to leave the service, were not solely responsible for this state of affairs. As the above examples indicate, the insubordinate actions of their troops determined many officers to resign or emigrate.

[1] See the letters of these ministers to the Minister of the Interior, dated 8 and 10 Mar. 1792 respectively, in A.N., F[7] 3679[1].

[2] See the letter from the National Guard of Apt to the directory of the Bouches-du-Rhône, dated 23 Apr. 1792, in A.N., F[7] 3659[3]; A.D. Isère L 68; and Arthur Chuquet, *Lettres de 1792* (Paris, 1911), pp. 296-9.

[3] The source for the statistics on officer emigration is *État des Officiers de tous grades déserteurs ou émigrés classés par régiment* (Paris, 1793). Although incomplete and sometimes imprecise, this provides a generally reliable list and was used by Donald Greer in his *Incidence of Emigration*. It could not be used for all line units in 1792 because it contains desertions only to August for some units, especially a number of cavalry regiments. The basis for the statistical conclusion reached here was 150 units (94 infantry regiments, 12 light infantry battalions, 36 cavalry regiments, and 8 artillery regiments) of which 50 lost one-third or more of their officers between Sept. 1791 and Dec. 1792.

More than half (26 of 50) of the units which lost one-third or more of their officers had experienced large-scale insubordination during the early years of the Revolution.[1] The nearly total separation between officers and men that existed in the Royal Army was probably of even more fundamental importance. Although the statistical evidence is not conclusive because of the incompleteness of many records, it appears that there is a high correlation between the excessive losses of officers and certain factors which are indicative of this estrangement. Of the fifty units that lost one-third or more of their officer complement, I have found records on officers' periods of leave in 1789–90 for thirteen regiments. In nine of these thirteen regiments one-half or more of the officers were on leave during this crucial time.[2] Similarly, I have uncovered data on officers engaged in training during the period 1788–90 for fourteen of the fifty units that suffered excessively from the departure of officers. In only one of these fourteen regiments was there one officer in each company charged with training, as required by regulations; in most regiments there was not even an officer assigned to this duty for every two companies.[3] In such cases the departure of many officers was the final stage in a long process of alienation.

Most of the replacements to fill the officer vacancies came from the ranks of the N.C.O.s. Unlike the majority of noble officers, they knew their own men intimately; they shared essentially the same living conditions as the soldiers, and since the Revolution often exercised the only really effective authority over them. The N.C.O.s, especially the sergeants, had extensive military service and at least some general education, but until 1789 their ambitions in the army had been frustrated. The Revolution brought them greatly expanded opportunities for advancement, and most of them embraced it warmly. Since the beginning of the Revolution their role in the conflict between soldiers and officers had become progressively more militant. In 1789 very few N.C.O.s had actively or publicly defied their officers; they were too professional and had too much at stake to act precipitately. The expressed their sympathy for the new order passively, especially by winking at the desertions of soldiers in

[1] For the sources of information on insubordination, see Appendix I, the section entitled 'Incidence of Insubordination'.

[2] Data on officers' periods of leave can be found in A.G., X^b 14, 28, 31, 40, 42, 46, 49, 53, 73 and X^c 31, 50, 81, 83.

[3] Information on officers involved in training is in A.G., X^b 14, 25, 28, 31, 46, 49, 53, 73, 103 and X^c 31, 40, 50, 81, 83.

their units. By 1790 many sergeants were willing to represent the soldiers in what they considered legitimate complaints against their superiors. In 1791 and 1792 N.C.O.s organized and led mutinies, notably the revolts of the 38th Infantry at Nîmes and the 17th Infantry at Phalsbourg. Their experience and accepted leadership made them critical figures in the struggle between officers and men.

The hostility of many officers to the Revolution, intensified after the King's attempted flight, provided many N.C.O.s with an opportunity to serve both the new regime and their personal ambitions by purging the army of counter-revolutionary officers. Certainly there were a number of cynics who encouraged insubordination solely for their own advancement; and undoubtedly there were some idealists motivated only by revolutionary sentiments. For most of the N.C.O.s, however, self-interest and political principles were complementary motives which intermingled. This combination is exemplified in a letter to the Minister of War from a sergeant in the 29th Infantry, dated 24 August 1791. The Sergeant complained that the decrees of the National Assembly on the appointment of officers were not being faithfully executed in his regiment. In particular, he named one of his officers who had rejected the new oath of loyalty but who had been recommended for promotion to captain. 'Here is the injustice that I place before your eyes', he concluded. 'It would be distasteful to me, who am a good citizen, that a man who has so little honour would command the company in which I am a simple sergeant with more love [of country] than he.'[1]

The position and role of the pre-revolutionary officers of fortune was strikingly similar. These men had generally the same background and the same, though slightly more successful career patterns. Their frustration and resentment at never being fully accepted as officers made them at least as hostile to the Old Regime as were the sergeants. While somewhat more cautious and less prominent than the N.C.O.s, they too contributed to undermining the authority of their noble superiors. The prevalence of grenadier companies, whose officers were largely or entirely promoted from the ranks, in incidents of insubordination is too common to be coincidental. Among the regiments in Paris in July 1789, the grenadier companies consistently lost an excessive number of deserters. Insubordination in the Forez (14th) Infantry in September 1789

[1] See A.G., X^b 172.

started among the grenadiers. The next month at Versailles the grenadier company of the Flandre (19th) Infantry lost more deserters than any other company of the regiment. In May 1790 it was a demonstration by the grenadiers of the Touraine (33rd) Infantry that started the troubles which led to the emigration of Colonel Mirabeau. At Aix in December of the same year, an officer of fortune, Lieutenant Ferriol of the grenadier company, stopped the soldiers of Lyonnais (27th) Infantry from attacking citizens, despite the orders of his superior officers. The mutiny of the 38th Infantry at Nîmes, which led to the forced expulsion of most of the officers from this regiment, began on 20 May 1791 when a deputation of grenadiers presented the complaints of the soldiers to the commanding officer.

Although these and many other examples provide primarily circumstantial evidence about the role of officers of fortune, their frequency is too great to be ignored. Condemned to rise no higher than lieutenant prior to 1789, many officers of fortune could and did take advantage of the revolutionary situation to advance themselves. At first passively and then more actively they took the side of soldiers against their superiors. By 1792 many officers from the enlisted ranks had become captains and a number had reached field grades because of the departure of noble officers. As with N.C.O.s, selfish ambitions were undoubtedly an important element in bringing officers of fortune into opposition to Old Regime officers; just as surely, personal advantage was not the sole motivation, as many nobles claimed. Devotion to service and patriotism also played a role. Sometimes the recently promoted officers were reluctant to accept the responsibilities thrust upon them. For example, by September 1792 the second battalion of the 50th Infantry had lost all but eight of its officers and was commanded by Captain Moulières, a former seminarian who had enlisted in the army and become an officer of fortune. Moulières requested the Minister of War to appoint a new lieutenant-colonel to take over his command because, he said, 'I am a *parvenu* officer, I have very weak eyesight, numerous infirmities, little ability for the command of a battalion but for the rest [I am] a very good patriot and ready to sacrifice what is left of my life for liberty.'[1]

Whatever their motives and roles, the officers of fortune and N.C.O.s of the Old Regime came to form an essential element in the officer corps of the Revolution. They brought to their new positions

[1] A.G., X^b 180.

a practical skill, a knowledge of their troops, a commitment to their
career, and a devotion to the Revolution that only a minority of the
pre-revolutionary officer corps possessed. During 1791 approximately 800 men were commissioned from the ranks; and together
with the men who had been made officers of fortune before that year,
the ex-rankers constituted about one-sixth of the officer corps. In
1792 another 2,200 soldiers were promoted to officers.[1] The results
of this policy were sometimes spectacular. In the 72nd Infantry an
officer of fortune name Pouilly, who had enlisted in the army in
1755, was a lieutenant at the outbreak of the Revolution. By the
beginning of 1793 he held the rank of colonel.[2] On 16 March 1791
there were seven officers of fortune in the 78th Infantry; on 23 May
there were thirty-five of them, well over half the officer complement
of the regiment.[3]

The declaration of war on 'the King of Bohemia and Hungary' by
the Legislative Assembly on 20 April 1792 set off a new wave of
emigration. The time for temporizing was passed; one had to choose
to fight for the Revolution or against it. To some officers the war and
the invasion of the foreign and *émigré* armies represented the last
chance to restore the King to power. Between the declaration of war
and mid-July 1792 nearly 600 more officers emigrated.[4] For some
regiments this entailed the loss of all or almost all of their remaining
officers, as happened in the 23rd Infantry and 12th Cavalry, both
stationed at Strasbourg on the German frontier.[5]

It was not only officers who emigrated after the declaration of war;
sometimes soldiers, especially in 'foreign' cavalry units followed the
officers in their desertion. On 6 May 1792 most of the regiment of the
15th (Royal Allemand) Cavalry crossed the frontier from Lorraine
into Germany and joined enemy forces there. In July 1789 this
regiment had charged crowds in Paris, and thus earned the undying
enmity of all supporters of the Revolution. The great popular
hostility towards the regiment increased cohesion within the unit;
and the continued use of the unit in repressive or counter-

---

[1] Scott, 'Regeneration of the Line Army', pp. 320 and 326.
[2] A.G., X^b 187.
[3] A.G., X^b 189.
[4] Greer, *Incidence of Emigration*, p. 28; Georges Sagnier, *La Désertion dans le Pas-de-Calais de 1792 à 1802* (Blangermont, 1965), p. 25; and Spencer Wilkinson, *The French Army before Napoleon* (Oxford, 1915), p. 117.
[5] Commandant R. Séreau, 'La Révolution vue de Strasbourg', *Revue historique de l'armée*. 1947, No. 4, pp. 91-106 and 1948, No. 1, pp. 55-63.

revolutionary missions intensified civilian distrust. In August 1790 a detachment of this regiment had helped to repress the mutiny at Nancy. In June 1791 the entire regiment had ridden with Bouillé to save the King. When all but about forty men of the regiment emigrated the following May, the regiment was struck from the rolls of the line army, to the joy of most patriots.[1] On 9 May most of the officers and about eighty men of the 1st Hussars also emigrated. This regiment too had sent detachments to Paris in July 1789 and to assist the King's flight in June 1791. While the regiment was on a reconnaissance mission in May 1792, the officers had tried to convince the entire unit to follow them into Germany; and they provided wine and promises of pillage to the soldiers. But the men were bitterly divided and fighting began. Most of the regiment and five officers returned to their garrison at Thionville while the rest deserted to the enemy.[2]

Three days later, all but 150 men of the 4th Hussars, which was stationed near Strasbourg, also emigrated to the enemy. The single loyal squadron was integrated into existing units, and like the 15th Cavalry this regiment was dropped from the cavalry organization of the French army.[3]

The 6th (Lauzun) Hussars had been employed on numerous occasions during the Revolution to support the cause of the King. In July 1789 a detachment of this regiment had been stationed in Paris to assist the plans of the court. In August 1790 men of this regiment made up part of the army used by Bouillé to crush the Nancy revolt. Shortly after this, at Belfort, some hussars and officers of the regiment, who had been attacked for their role in the Nancy affair, staged a royalist demonstration in which a number of civilians were hurt. In June 1791 detachments of the regiment were posted to protect the attempted flight of the King; but many of the soldiers were won over by the citizens of Varennes. In August 1792 seventy men of the regiment joined some officers and deserted to the enemy.[4]

[1] Mathiez, *La Victoire en l'an II*, p. 72, and Choppin, *Les Hussards*, p. 205. All cavalry regiments from the 16th Cavalry on were then moved up one number, a source of some subsequent confusion.

[2] A.G., X^c 237, 'Extrait d'une Lettre de Thionville en date du 12 May relative à la défection des hussards de Berchény', and Commandant Ogier d'Ivry, *Historique du 1er Régiment de Hussards* (Valence, 1901), pp. 51–9.

[3] Mathiez, *La Victoire en l'an II*, p. 72 and Choppin, *Les Hussards*, p. 205. All hussar regiments, beginning with the 5th, were moved up one number.

[4] Capitaine C. Voisin, *Historique du 6me Hussards* (Libourne, 1888), pp. 1–25; A.G., X^c 245; and the uncoded troop register for this regiment in the Archives de la Guerre.

In each of these cases a number of similar factors played a role. All of these units were German-speaking, and so somewhat removed from most French civilians. More importantly, each of them had at one time or another been employed in a function generally considered to be anti-revolutionary. This had led to considerable civilian antipathy toward them, which increased cohesion within these regiments and helped officers to maintain their authority. The final test of this authority came when the officers decided to emigrate.

The outbreak of war had intensified the motives which officers had to emigrate. Furthermore, it added a new motivation—fear for their lives. Even in the most violent military conflicts, such as Nancy, very few officers had been murdered; and in the rare instances of this, it was usually civilians who were responsible, although some soldiers might have participated. The military setbacks suffered by the French early in the war often gave rise to panic; and in their panic the soldiers sometimes turned violently on their officers who, they felt, had betrayed them.

Shortly after the declaration of war the French began to mount an offensive against the Austrian Netherlands (Belgium). One column, under General Théobald Dillon, began its advance against Tournai on 28 April. The following day the French forces crossed into Austrian territory. When large enemy units appeared to halt this advance, Dillon, as had been pre-arranged, gave orders to withdraw. Some contingents of cavalry, including the 6th Chasseurs, who were to protect the retreat, began to panic. Dillon appeared among the troops and tried to prevent a rout, but was shot and wounded by a cavalryman. As the troops began to pour back into Lille, a rumour of treason by the officers spread. Dillon became the focus of this charge and was murdered by his own soldiers.[1]

Simultaneously, another force, under General Biron, had advanced against Mons. As this column approached Le Quiévrain on 29 April, two cavalry regiments, the 5th and the 6th Dragoons, at the first contact with enemy forces panicked. The men of these units quickly spread their fear by crying to the rest of the column: 'Every man for himself!', 'We are betrayed!' Biron was forced to order a retreat while he tried to restore order among his troops. Although he

---

[1] 'Relation du mouvement exécuté les 28 et 29 avril par un détachement de la garnison de Lille, commandé par M. Théobald Dillon, Maréchal de camp' and 'Relation de l'assassinat de M. Théobald Dillon, Maréchal-de-camp, Commis à Lille, le 29 Avril 1792', Maclure Collection, vol. 983.

escaped the fate of Dillon, Biron and other officers immediately became the object of the soldiers' fear and hatred and were accused of having betrayed the soldiers. Two officers and twenty-six soldiers were subsequently tried in July for their parts in the incident. Twenty-four of the soldiers were found guilty of the charges brought against them; but none received a punishment of more than 30 days in prison. The one officer found guilty, a second-lieutenant, had emigrated.[1]

For many officers these incidents proved that they commanded a horde of undisciplined savages, who, even when guilty of the most base cowardice, would be protected by the revolutionary authorities. To save their honour, as well as their lives, they decided to emigrate.[2] For many soldiers, on the other hand, these cases confirmed their worst suspicions about their officers.

Events in Paris yet further compounded the motives which many officers had to emigrate. On 20 June 1792 a crowd of Parisians invaded the Tuileries and for over two hours paraded before Louis XVI demanding certain concessions from him, such as the abolition of the royal veto. Many officers of moderate political views were appalled by the insult to the King.[3] General Lafayette, who commanded one of the three French field armies, returned from the front with petitions from the army condemning the events of 20 June, and demanded the closing of the Jacobin clubs. Less than eight weeks later the greatest political change of the Revolution took place when crowds of Parisians, supported by local and provincial National Guard elements, attacked the royal palace and forced the King to flee for his life to the Legislative Assembly. On 10 August 1792 the sovereign people overthrew the French monarchy.

This dramatic development would soon force the political reorganization of France along republican and democratic lines. A more immediate and pressing concern of the Assembly was the reaction of the army. On 11 August, the executive council, which had provisionally replaced the King, sent out commissioners to all armies. These agents were to require a new oath of loyalty with no mention at all of the King. They also had the power to suspend,

---

[1] For an account of the incident and trial, see A.G., B^{13} 69.

[2] Hartmann, *Les Officiers de l'armée royale*, pp. 446–9.

[3] For one example of this reaction, see Claude Simon, *Correspondance de Claude Simon, Lieutenant de Grenadiers du régiment du Walsh (no. 92) aux armées du Nord, des Ardennes et de Sambre-et-Meuse, 1792–1793* (Grenoble, 1899), p. 18.

dismiss, and arrest any officer whom they suspected of disloyalty.[1] Until the allegiance of the army was assured, the changes brought about by 10 August might still be altered or even reversed by the intervention of the military.

This anxiety on the part of the Assembly was not unfounded. Most of the generals supported the constitutional monarchy and were appalled by its overthrow. General Arthur Dillon and many of his subordinate generals at first wanted to march on Paris and restore the King. Many other generals would have supported such a plan.[2] There was, however, serious doubt whether the troops would follow their commanders in such an attempt. In the Army of the Rhine most of the soldiers greeted the overthrow of the monarchy with pleasure.[3] Although elements of the Army of the Centre stationed at Sedan renewed their oath to the King when informed of this event, their commander, Lafayette, was dubious whether the same sentiment existed throughout his command.[4] The units of the Army of the Midi encamped at Barraux maintained complete calm when the news of 10 August was announced to them, possibly out of indifference.[5] Many officers, without strong political opinions, had little difficulty in accepting the accomplished fact.[6] Finally, despite a flurry of correspondence among them, none of the generals would risk taking the initiative by marching on Paris.

The reaction of Lafayette to 10 August both represented and compounded the dilemma of the Royal Army officer corps. Thoroughly committed to the constitutional monarchy, he

---

[1] Poisson, *L'Armée et la Garde Nationale*, I. 473 and Jean Jaurès, *Histoire socialiste de la Révolution française*, vol. IV (Paris, 1922), p. 164. A text of the Assembly's decree can be found in A.D. Isère L 56.

[2] Jaurès, *Histoire socialiste*, IV. 86; Reinhard, 'L'Armée et la Révolution', fascicule 2, pp. 58–63; Lafayette, *Mémoires*, I. 469 and 472; and Charles-François-Duperier Dumouriez, *Mémoires du Général Dumouriez*, vol. I (Paris, 1848), p. 243.

[3] Chef de bataillon Legrand, *La Justice militaire et la discipline à l'Armée du Rhin et à l'Armée de Rhin-et-Moselle (1792–1796)* (Paris, 1909), p. 16. This observation is based on eye-witness accounts. A report read at the meeting of the General Council of the Isère on 22 Aug. 1792 corroborates this observation; see A.D. Isère L 56.

[4] See the report read at the same meeting of the General Council of the Isère in A.D. Isère L 56 and Lafayette, *Mémoires*, I. 503.

[5] See the session of 17 Aug. 1792 of the General Council of the Isère in A.D. Isère L 56.

[6] John Money, *The History of the Campaign of 1792, between the Armies of France under Generals Dumourier, Valence, etc. and the Allies under the Duke of Brunswick; with an Account of What Passed in the Thuilleries on the 10th of August* (London, 1794), p. 91. Money was an English professional soldier serving as a general in the French army in 1792.

attempted on 13 August to have his entire army, the Army of the Centre, renew its oath to the King and the law, but many refused. His hopeless position, that of a legalist in a revolutionary situation, left him with no alternative; and on 21 August he emigrated with most of his staff, about twenty officers in all.[1] Rather than mitigating this treason, Lafayette's previous role in the Revolution magnified the significance of his emigration.[2] If Lafayette would desert France and the Revolution, then what royal officer could be trusted? Soldiers denounced suspect officers to the civil authorities and a number of them were removed from their functions, pending an investigation. Scores of officers, including the colonels of the 24th Infantry and 2nd Carabiniers, the lieutenant-colonel and two captains of the 11th Cavalry, were suspended for *incivisme*.[3]

Undoubtedly, emigrations and denunciations in the late summer and early autumn of 1792 would have been much more numerous had it not been for the fact that most officers who were not committed to the Revolution had already left military service. With all but a small proportion of the remaining officers there was little question of their loyalty; and some were 'zealous partisans of the Jacobins'.[4] In addition, the considerable changes in the officer personnel of most regiments had contributed to improved relations between officers and men. Sometimes even, soldiers of a unit protested against the suspension of their officers and testified to the officers' devotion to the new regime. The soldiers and officers of the 3rd Dragoons and the 49th Infantry, for example, objected to the suspension of their colonels, arguing in both cases that their commanders were not only brave soldiers but good citizens.[5]

These last examples indicate that our description of the general situation in the line army during this period requires some qualification: there were exceptions to the common hostility between officers and men which so bitterly divided the army in the early Revolution.

---

[1] Lafayette, *Mémoires*, I, 471, 476, and 499 and Reinhard, 'L'Armée et la Révolution', fascicule 2, pp. 57–8.

[2] The change in attitude towards Lafayette is graphically indicated by two letters dated 29 July and 21 Aug. 1792, from a lieutenant in his army in Simon, *Correspondance*, pp. 24 and 26–8.

[3] Dumouriez, *Mémoires*, I, 252–3; D'Hauterive, *L'Armée sous la Révolution*, pp. 234–5; and A.N., Dxv 3, dossier 26, pièce 7.

[4] Thus did Lt. Simon describe some of the officers serving with him in August 1792; see Simon, *Correspondance*, p. 28.

[5] A.N., Dxv 2, dossier 11, pièce 32 and A.G., X^b 180, letter from the council of administration of the 49th Infantry, dated 31 Jan. 1793.

Just as there were some soldiers—particularly in foreign cavalry units—who opposed the Revolution and eventually emigrated, there were also officers—even from the nobility—who accepted the political changes and served well and loyally in the armies of the Revolution. The great majority of officers who had resigned or emigrated by the autumn of 1792 were indeed Old Regime nobles;[1] however, a large number of aristocratic officers remained in the army, roughly 3,000. Most of these were provincial nobles whose only career had been in military service. They found in the Revolution much greater opportunity for advancement than they could ever have expected before 1789. Prior to the Revolution only the most fortunate of these nobles could reach the grade of lieutenant-colonel; by 1792 many commanded regiments, and the rank of general was not beyond reach. Officers who were apolitical professionals or owed a higher allegiance to France than to the monarchy *and* who could retain the confidence of their troops continued to pursue their careers under the Republic.

An analysis of military insubordination during 1792 confirms the fact that relations between soldiers in the line army and their officers —both recently commissioned N.C.O.s and trusted officers from the Old Regime—had substantially improved. In 1792 the incidence of insubordination was half what it had been during the previous two years, affecting approximately one-sixth of the line units as compared to one-third in 1790 and 1791.[2] Such a striking departure from the trend since 1789 could not have occurred without a significant improvement in the relations between officers and men. On the other hand, certain tendencies exhibited by insubordinate troops earlier in the Revolution continued during 1792. Virtually all incidents of insubordination in that year took the form of open and hostile defiance of officers by soldiers under their command, a trend that had been progressively intensifying since the beginning of the

---

[1] Greer, *Incidence of Emigration*, pp. 33, 90, and 112. Greer estimates that over 75% of the officers who emigrated were nobles; however, he classifies all non-nobles as 'bourgeois or recently ennobled', a somewhat inexact category. Most of these officers emigrated before 1793.

[2] See the section in Appendix I on 'Incidence of Insubordination'. Of the 73 units sampled for the entire period 1788–92, only 9 regiments (12·3%) experienced insubordination in 1792. Among 92 units studied for 1792 only, there were 18 examples of insubordination (19·6%). Four cases of excessive desertions—in the 15th Cavalry and the 1st, 4th, and 6th Hussars—have not been included because they constitute emigrations rather than desertions and the soldiers who were involved followed, rather than defied, their officers.

Revolution. Similarly, the tendency towards more independent action by insubordinate soldiers and correspondingly less reliance upon civilian support also continued.[1] In 1789 approximately half of the line units that experienced insubordination had close relations with civilians; in 1790 this declined to about 40 per cent; for 1791 the figure was around one-third; and by 1792 only one-fifth of the insubordinate units received encouragement from civilian elements. The soldiers' distrust of and antagonism towards pre-revolutionary officers had ultimately found justification in the resignation or emigration of a majority of the Old Regime officer corps; and since the Nancy mutiny the government's efforts to control military insubordination had been largely ineffective. As a result, the soldiers had resolved many internal military problems by themselves, without outside intervention. This, in turn, had led to a more cohesive, but also more independent, military establishment.

In little more than three years, between the summer of 1789 and the autumn of 1792, the most dramatic changes had taken in the Royal Army. Many of these developments arose directly from dynamic conditions in the army itself. The most critical problem was the hostility between soldiers and officers. Divided by the chasm of birth in an estate society, the two enjoyed entirely different conditions of military service, including duties, rights, and prerogatives. The promise of the Revolution to redress past inequities led, in the army, to an outburst of complaints on the part of the soldiers. Naturally, the soldiers directed their objections primarily against the situation in the Royal Army: the monopolization of high ranks by nobles, harsh and sometimes inequitable discipline, the disdain with which they were treated by their superiors, and peculation on the part of their officers. The drastic political and social changes introduced by the revolutionary authorities, largely at the expense of the former privileged groups, and popular support from pro-revolutionary citizens encouraged the soldiers to translate their complaints against noble officers into political terms; and as divisions within both civil and miltary society deepened, this tendency increased.

For their part, the officers failed to grasp the importance of these changes and responded, as in the past, without any realization of or concern for the situation of the men under their orders. Legislative

[1] Among the 73 units sampled for the entire period of the early Revolution, 9 were insubordinate during 1792 and only 2 of these had close ties with civilians. Of the 92 studied for 1792 alone, 18 were insubordinate and 4 of them had civilian support.

reforms and mounting troop insubordination left the officers frustrated and increasingly alienated from the government and their subordinates. The attempted flight of the King in mid-1791 destroyed for a majority of officers what remained of their devotion to military service. Angered by their loss of social status, hostile to the new regime, and faced with a complete breakdown of their authority over their men, they left the army and often their homeland by the thousands. Resignations and emigrations by officers created a hopeless cycle: each officer who left his duties prompted further distrust of those who remained; this distrust often resulted in more insubordination; and this, in turn, led to additional resignations and emigrations.

As the officers lost control over the line army, the soldiers increased their role. A majority of the vacancies created by the departure of noble officers were filled by soldiers promoted from the ranks. These men, who were often the natural leaders of the enlisted men, had, like the soldiers in general, displayed an increasing militancy in their conflicts with officers; not only did they challenge their superiors' authority more and more directly, but they became less and less dependent upon support or encouragement from civilian sources. By 1792 the internal structure of the line army had been substantially renovated; and the soldiers, as a result of their struggles against noble officers, were largely responsible for this. Such a development had increased cohesion within the army and had given the soldiers a greater sense of their own dignity and strength; at the same time, it had given them experience in acting independently of, and sometimes in defiance of, established authorities.

Although many of the changes that had taken place in the army were the result of intra-military conflicts, developments outside the army also played an essential role. For example, while better officer–soldier relations certainly improved discipline in 1792, the coming of war also affected insubordination. It is not by chance that 60 per cent of all cases of disobedience or defiance of officers in 1792 occurred before the declaration of war, and more than three-quarters took place before the end of June. The war, especially the imminent danger of combat, reduced the immediacy of other problems and emphasized the necessity of discipline for mutual survival. Likewise, the substantial increase in desertions during 1792—spread rather evenly over almost all line units—was due, at least in part, to the war, in which serious personal danger, wretched physical conditions, and the chaos created by combat provided both motives and means for increased desertion. Despite some connections the war did not, of course, develop out of conditions within the line army. Rather, the declaration of war resulted from developments within the larger society of which the army was only a part; and it is to the question of civil-military relations that we must now proceed, in order to comprehend fully the relationship between the Revolution and the Royal Army.

CHAPTER IV

CIVIL-MILITARY RELATIONS, 1790–2

THROUGHOUT THE early Revolution there was continual interaction between civil and military developments. Civilian influences even played some role in the fundamentally military events discussed in the previous chapter. Although its importance declined steadily, civilian support or encouragement of insubordination was a factor in the conflicts between soldiers and officers during this period. In addition, political crises, such as the flight to Varennes and the uprising of 10 August 1792, had an immediate and profound impact upon conditions in the Royal Army. Finally, government policies— e.g. regarding the attendance of soldiers at political meetings, the inspection of military accounts, responses to insubordination, and the decision to go to war—exercised great influence over the situation within the army. Indeed, it could not have been otherwise. By the late eighteenth century there were frequent contacts between soldiers and civilians, in garrison towns, during troop movements, and while the soldiers were on leave. Also, in the last twenty-five years of the Old Regime the government had devoted much attention to the regular army. The Revolution intensified these civil-military contacts.

The most important effect of the Revolution was to fragment authority and create a situation in which contending institutions and groups vied for power: the King and the Assembly, local and national officials, opposing local factions, civil and military authorities, and—as we have seen at some length—officers and soldiers. Central to all of these issues was control over the armed forces, a crucial element in gaining and exercising political influence. Besides being the primary instrument in foreign relations, the Royal Army was also the sole agency capable of enforcing internal policies on a national scale. The mounted constables of the *maréchaussée* were simply too few in number to police the countryside even in normal times; and the recently created National Guard units were not only organized on a local basis but controlled by local officials as well. Consequently, opposing political groups were vitally concerned with the fate of the regular army, although their attitudes and

policies towards it varied widely. Generally, conservatives supported strict adherence to discipline and passive obedience by
soldiers towards officers. Politically radical elements, who were
often associated with lower social classes, fostered insubordination
within the army, which they viewed as the traditional vehicle of
repression by the upper classes. The moderates simultaneously
favoured sufficient discipline to ensure the maintenance of order and
enough political commitment to the new regime by both officers and
men to avoid the army becoming a tool of counter-revolution.

Thus, the line army was deeply involved in the process of revolution, being both a major instrument affecting its course and a
primary concern in the formation of its policies. In order to study
these phenomena more closely, we shall now proceed to deal with
the three most significant areas of civil-military relations: the police
role of the army, the factors which led to its politicization, and the
military policies of the government.

THE LINE ARMY AS POLICE

The events of July 1789 had clearly demonstrated the decisive role
that the Royal Army played in its capacity of a police agency.[1]
Regardless of the specific circumstances, the reaction of the army
could determine whether and how well law and order would be
enforced and, to this degree, could decide what authority would be
recognized. Within a month of the attack on the Bastille, the National Assembly asserted its right to control the police functions of
the regular army. On 10 August 1789 the Assembly decreed that
local officials could requisition line troops to assist the *maréchaussée*
and National Guard in keeping public order in the countryside and
towns of France. The decree also prohibited the employment of
regulars against civilians except on the orders of civil officers, and
required that such orders be read publicly to the troops before-
hand.[2] Control over the use of line units in civil disturbances was
not only an essential attribute of the sovereignty which the Assembly
was claiming for itself, but at the same time represented a very

---

[1] For a general description of the sources and methods used in this section, see
Appendix I, 'Police Functions of the Army'.

[2] For further details, see Colonel Henri-Joseph de Buttet, 'La Mission de Monsieur de
la Chapelle, Maréchal de camp commandant les troupes envoyées à Lyon pour le
rétablissement des barrières et ses rapports avec la municipalité (septembre 1790 à
janvier 1791)', *Actes du quatre-vingt-neuvième congrès national des sociétés savantes:
Lyon, 1964*, tome 2, vol. I (Paris, 1965), p. 223.

politic decision in light of the unsettled conditions that persisted. During the last six months of 1789 the Minister of War received more than 700 requests for line units from local authorities, many more than could possibly be filled.[1] Despite fluctuations from time to time, internal police duties would remain a major function of the regular army until the outbreak of war.

The types of disturbance in which the army was employed varied as widely as did French society in the eighteenth century; but they can be classified in seven general categories, according to the primary issues involved. Line troops were used as police in the general maintenance of order (usually in a preventive capacity where their mere presence served to discourage disorder), in the suppression of banditry, in halting anti-feudal violence, in religious conflicts, in restoring order among mutinous troops, in quelling or preventing food and grain disturbances, and in controlling civilian political struggles. Of course many disturbances involved a number of different issues; but usually one predominated or subsumed the others.

Frequently line units and detachments were sent, usually at the request of local officials, to regions where there were threatening indications of trouble although no violence had yet occurred. During the first three months of 1790, for example, detachments of the Artois and Rohan Infantry and of the Conti and Orléans Dragoons were used, along with local National Guard units, to patrol the countryside around Rennes.[2] Similarly, the Lyonnais Infantry was continually furnishing detachments to police the interior of Provence in the spring of 1790.[3] That same summer regular contingents were dispatched to keep order in a number of towns and cities of France, e.g. the Royal Guyenne Cavalry at Bourbon-Lancy, the Royal Roussillon Cavalry at the village of Puy-Notre-Dame near Saumur, the Royal Champage Cavalry at Vernon, the Royal Piémont Cavalry at Bourges. In each case, civil officials credited the presence of these forces with being responsible for the preservation of peace.[4]

[1] Chilly, *La Tour du Pin*, pp. 53-5.

[2] See the letters of the commanding officer of one detachment, dated 9 Feb. 1790, and of La Tour du Pin, dated 9 Mar. 1790, in A.D., Ille-et-Vilaine C 4701.

[3] Letter of the Marquis de Miran to the Minister of War, dated 15 Apr. 1790, in A.G., YA 447.

[4] Letters of Berchény to Saint-Priest, dated 29 May, 5 June, 2 July, and 16 Aug. 1790, in A.N., H^{1453}; and the letter of La Tour du Pin to Saint-Priest, dated 19 July 1790, in A.N., F^{9}41.

Royal Army elements continued to be used in the early Revolution, as they had been before 1789, to stop or repress brigandage. In late March 1790 a detachment of the Chartres Dragoons, together with local *maréchaussée* and National Guard elements, broke up a band of tobacco smugglers near Le Mans. Less than two months afterwards the Royal Piémont Cavalry helped to seize 'a wagon of [unidentified] contraband' at Nevers.[1] A much larger police action carried out by line troops was the attempt to control raids by 'brigands' from the papal possessions of Avignon and the Comtat Venaissin into neighbouring French territory. Throughout 1790 and until September 1791, when the papal areas were annexed by France, regular units in the region kept busy attempting to prevent the incursion of armed bands from the enclaves into nearby departments of France.[2]

Royal Army detachments were also employed in the summer of 1789 to protect property in Flandre, Alsace, and Franche-Comté against the peasant uprisings which had resulted in the abolition of feudalism.[3] The subsequent legal distinctions between different different types of feudal obligations and the requirement of compensation for some of them, however, resulted in new waves of anti-feudal violence which line units were again called upon to suppress. In January and February 1790, for example, a detachment of the Auvergne Chasseurs was employed separately and together with National Guard and *maréchaussée* contingents to halt the disorders over redeemable dues in southern Auvergne.[4] Sporadic peasant resistance continued, and later in the same year peasants in the newly formed department of the Lot attacked and destroyed the property of local lords; in reaction some nobles armed themselves to defend their property.[5] Detachments of line regiments, including the Royal Pologne Cavalry and the Languedoc Infantry,

[1] Letters of Berchény to Saint-Priest, dated 28 Mar. and 16 May 1790, in A.N., H1453.

[2] See the dossier on troubles around Avignon, 1790-2, in A.N., F73659¹.

[3] Lefebvre, *Grande Peur*, pp. 129–39.

[4] M. Leymarie, 'Féodalité et mouvements populaires à Maurs (Cantal) et aux environs en 1789 et 1790', *Annales historiques de la Révolution française*, XLIV (1972), 94–7.

[5] A full account of these troubles can be found in 'Rapport des Messieurs J. Godard et J. Robin, Commissaires civils, Envoyés par le Roi, dans le Département du Lot, en exécution du Décret de l'Assemblée Nationale du 13 Décembre 1790', Maclure Collection, vol. 832. The defensive measures taken by local nobles are particularly interesting because they gave substance to rumours about armed assemblies of nobles bent on counter-revolution. One wonders how many other claims of counter-revolutionary plots were based on similar evidence.

were summoned from their garrisons at Montauban and Figeac in early December. The peasants, however, were not intimidated and viewed the troops, who were simply enforcing the decrees of the National Assembly, as the accomplices of their former lords. On 3–4 December one band of armed peasants besieged a detachment of the Languedoc Infantry in a church in the small town of Gourdon. Only the intervention of the municipal officials deterred the crowd from lynching the soldiers who were released unharmed but had to leave the town. Throughout the incident, and others like it in the department, the regulars maintained complete discipline in the face of violent civilian hostility.[1]

In some regions of France, notably Languedoc, religious conflicts, which were frequently reinforced by social and economic differences and which took on a new and more intense political form in the early Revolution, also required the intervention of line troops. In May 1790 the Languedoc Infantry, despite some internal divisions between officers and men, helped to restore order in the Montauban following a bloody skirmish between pro-revolutionary Protestants and anti-revolutionary Catholics.[2] During even more bitter fighting between the same antagonists at Nîmes in May and June 1790, the regiment of Guyenne Infantry observed what the municipal officials called 'an incredible subordination'.[3] Such discipline was maintained despite the strong political overtones of the conflict and the sympathy of many of the soldiers for the 'patriot' Protestants. In the course of a similar conflict at Uzès in February 1791, the regiment of Lorraine Dragoons, which was called out of its garrison in that city to restore order, displayed exemplary moderation even after two of the dragoons had been seriously wounded.[4] In May 1791 when a crowd at Colmar in Alsace protested against

---

[1] Ibid. In late December 1790 and January 1791 the royal commissioners described some of the troops quartered at Cahors as being 'in open war with the inhabitants'.

[2] Daniel Ligou, *Montauban à la fin de l'ancien régime et aux débuts de la Révolution, 1787–1794* (Paris, 1958), pp. 228–44.

[3] For further details on this affair, which unfortunately cannot be treated in detail here, see the 'Rapport de l'affaire de Nîmes fait à l'Assemblée Nationale, au nom des comités des rapports et des recherches, par Charles-Jean-Marie Alquier, Député du Département de la Charente inférieure. Le 19 Février 1791', Maclure Collection, vol. 832. The most comprehensive treatment of the whole situation at Nîmes is in James N. Hood, 'The Riots in Nîmes in 1790 and the origins of a popular counterrevolutionary movement', (Princeton Univ. Ph.D., 1969); see esp. pp. 247–9 for the role of the Guyenne Infantry.

[4] 'Récit des événemens arrivés à Uzès les 13 et 14 février 1791, et jours suivans jusqu'au 22', Maclure Collection, vol. 832.

the closing of the Augustinian church there and threatened to chase from the town all priests who had taken the oath required by the government, the regiment of Alsace Chasseurs helped the National Guard to police Colmar and refused to be drawn into the quarrel.[1]

Even when called upon to police fellow-soldiers some units performed their duty without incident. The most spectacular example of this was the suppression of the Nancy mutiny in August 1790. On this occasion Bouillé's army consisted of six élite companies from three French regiments (the Auxerrois, Auvergne, and Hainaut Infantry), three battalions of Swiss infantry from the regiments of Castella and Vigier, one battalion of the Royal-Liégeois Infantry, three dragoon detachments (from the regiments of Royal, Monsieur, and Condé Dragoons), five squadrons of heavy cavalry (from the regiments of Royal Normandie and Royal Allemand), and a detachment each of Lauzun Hussars and Hainaut Chasseurs, as well as some 800 troops of the National Guard.[2] None of these shirked the presumably unpleasant duty of repressing their mutinous comrades; and some of the Swiss soldiers seem to have been brutally vindictive. A number of peculiar circumstances help to explain this display of discipline. The astute Boullé handpicked these troops and intentionally selected a large proportion of foreign units (over half of the regulars). Of even greater importance, when Bouillé's force was about to enter the city, elements of it came under fire and had to fight their way into Nancy, a situation sufficient to explain the absence of any sentiments of comradeship. Under less extreme circumstances other units were reluctant or even insubordinate when commanded to use force against soldiers. For example, during the conflict between the soldiers of the Salm-Salm Infantry and General Bouillé over unit funds in the summer of 1790, the Condé Dragoons and the rest of the soldiers garrisoned at Metz refused to march against the rebellious troops. The same attitude was displayed by men in the 25th (Poitou) and 31st (Aunis) Infantry on the opposite side of the Atlantic in early 1791, when detachments of these regiments would not obey orders to repress the mutiny of two colonial regiments in the West Indies.[3]

[1] 'Rapport fait à l'Assemblée Nationale à l'occasion des événemens qui ont eu lieu à Colmar les 21, 22, 23 Mai dernier, au nom des Comités réunis Diplomatique, Militaire, Ecclésiastique, des Recherches et des Rapports, par M. Salle, Député du Département de la Meurthe', Maclure Collection, vol. 832.

[2] Chilly, La Tour du Pin, pp. 240–1.

[3] This incident is treated in Belhomme, Histoire de l'infanterie, III. 460–1.

Probably the most common type of employment of line troops in a police role involved disturbances over food.[1] As we have already seen, the protection of food convoys, stores, and markets took up a great deal of the Royal Army's energies in 1789. Although there were seasonal and regional variations, this function continued to require the services of numerous line units and detachments in the following years. In early May 1790 men of the Royal Roussillon Cavalry had to assist the Saumur National Guard in halting the pillage of grain wagons. When the inhabitants of the village of Lucenay in Bourbonnais seized foodstuffs and sold them at 'popular' prices in mid-June of the same year, a detachment of sixteen men of the Royal Guyenne Cavalry was required to restore order. On 4 September 1790 a detachment of fifty troops of the Royal Picardie was called to Angers by the municipality because a crowd of women attacked a grain merchant. Upon their arrival, the troops too were attacked by the women when they tried to protect the merchant's property, and martial law had to be declared in the city. At Saint-Malo less than two weeks later both National Guard troops and soldiers of the Forez Infantry were used to repress a grain riot which began when a large crowd attacked some grain boats. The arrest of some twenty leaders of this riot helped to re-establish order.[2]

From December 1790 until the spring of 1791 one of the primary concerns of the military commandant of the former province of Picardie, General Biron, was the protection of grain shipments to Paris along the Saint-Quentin Canal.[3] During this period Biron was constantly shifting units and detachments, especially of cavalry, from one town or area in his jurisdiction to another, in order to stop the attempts of local people to interfere with the shipments to Paris. For example, in early January 1791 the general sent detach-

[1] In the sample used in this study political disturbances barely outnumbered those over food, 71 to 70. As already indicated, however, this probably reflects a bias in the sources consulted, rather than the actual situation. Scores or even hundreds of local archives would have to be examined for greater precision.

[2] See 'Relation de ce qui s'est passé à Angers le 6 7bre 1790', in A.N., H^1453 and the letter from De Bordy to Guignard, dated Oct. 1790, in A.N., F^7 3679^1. On the basis of this and numerous other archival data it is clear that the view of the period Nov. 1789–Aug. 1791 as being free of major food crises is at least partially erroneous and requires revision. See George Rudé, *The Crowd in History: A Study of Popular Disturbances in France and England, 1730–1848* (New York, 1964), pp. 109–10.

[3] Information on these problems comes from the correspondence of Biron in A.G., B^1* 208 and 209. My special thanks to John Lynn who brought this to my attention.

ments of the Berry Cavalry and La Reine Dragoons from Amiens to Chauny to 'assure the circulation and transport of grain on the Saint-Quentin Canal'. Three weeks later he sent a detachment of the Colonel Général Hussars to the same place for the same purpose, since the other two detachments had been transferred to other danger spots. In early March troops had to be dispatched along the canal between Dollon and Chauny because local peasants had filled the canal there with stones to stop the grain boats. In mid-March detachments of the Toul Artillery were called from La Fère to posts along the canal to protect shipments. Biron had to refuse additional troops requested by the municipality of Saint-Quentin because he did not have enough men. Other towns, such as Guise, were refused any troops at all simply because the demands on Biron's command were too great.

In November 1791 the 22nd Infantry was used to quiet agitation over the availability of grain at Saint-Omer. A detachment of the same regiment was sent to Hazebrouck the following February, when a crowd of armed civilians attacked and pillaged half a dozen grain wagons on the highway near the town. At the same time in Bergues a detachment of dragoons and some soldiers of the local National Guard were called upon to avoid a similar incident; and although they did maintain order, the soldiers performed their duty 'only with the greatest repugnance'.[1]

While most line troops performed these missions faithfully, if sometimes unenthusiastically, there were instances when soldiers expressed more than simple reluctance. At Douai in mid-March 1791 a crowd of people demanded that the grain of some merchants be confiscated and sold at reduced prices. When the merchants objected, the people attacked the home of one of the larger merchants, M. Nicolon. The National Guard and line troops from the garrison of Douai were called out to keep order; both forces however, sympathized with the rioters. The military commander of the garrison had to inform the department directory on 17 March that the soldiers '. . . had said that they were ready to march outside [the country] against the enemy if he made them, but that in the interior they would not move'. In these circumstances the

---

[1] See the letter from Rochambeau to D'Elbecq dated 30 Nov. 1791; letters of the district directory of Hazebrouck to the departmental directory of the Nord, dated 11 and 13 Feb. 1792; and the letter from the municipal officers of Bergues to the directory of the Nord, dated 13 Feb. 1792; all in A.N., F⁷3683⁵.

authorities were helpless when Nicolon was lynched shortly afterwards.[1]

An even more serious food disturbance took place in early 1792 at Dunkerque, a major transit centre for grain shipments. On 13 February a grain convoy of eleven wagons arrived at this port for shipment to the Midi. A crowd of nearly 500 persons seized four of the wagons upon their arrival. Pillaging continued the next day, and the garrison at Dunkerque, including elements of the 1st and 78th Infantry and the 10th Cavalry, was summoned to assist the National Guard in restoring order. The people had declared that they would allow no grain to leave the port; and houses of local grain merchants were attacked and destroyed. At 11 a.m. on 14 February martial law was declared; a detachment of the 3rd Dragoons and contingents of the National Guard of the surrounding area were called to Dunkerque to reinforce the troops already there. By the next day comparative calm had been re-established; but the commanders of both the National Guard and the line units informed the commandant of the garrison that their troops could not be depended upon to protect any grain shipments leaving the city. The National Guard had been very reluctant 'to prevent the pillage of the property of their fellow citizens' during the previous day; and some line troops had refused to fire on grain pillagers. Fortunately, no further incidents broke out and martial law ended on 24 February after six people had been killed and more than sixty injured.[2]

The final category of disturbances in which regular troops were employed comprises those conflicts whose origins were predominantly political. Of all types of disturbance, these had the most immediate bearing on the survival of the new regime and exercised the greatest influence on the response of the line army. Because of these pecularities and because of their intimate connection with the politicization of the army, political struggles will be dealt with separately, after a brief analysis of the police role of the Royal Army in the other kinds of civil unrest.

Despite the problems that attended the employment of the regular army in police functions, generally the units used for such duties displayed a strong sense of discipline. Of 233 incidents between

---

[1] Letter from the directory of the Nord to Duportail, dated 18 Mar. 1791, in A.N., F⁷3683⁵.

[2] See the correspondence of various local officials between 14 and 23 Feb. 1792 in A.N., F⁷3683⁵.

1788 and 1792 in which regulars performed police missions, only 1 in 8—30 in all—resulted in insubordination. Although it is impossible to claim any high degree of scientific accuracy for this sample, a number of interesting indications can be drawn from it. After 1789 the incidence of insubordination among troops serving in a police capacity declined dramatically, from over one-fifth to well under one-tenth. Furthermore, the rate of insubordination in these units was markedly below the general rate of insubordination within the army after 1789. This indicates that the authorities learned an important lesson from the reactions of the soldiers during the crisis of that year and the subsequent collapse of discipline. Whenever possible thereafter, they took much more care in the selection of line units to be used as police. Civilian officials and military commanders, like General Bouillé, realized the importance of calculating the discipline and loyalty of regular units to be used in these functions, although their estimations were not always accurate.

The stakes were great when line troops were called in to deal with civil disturbances. If the soldiers performed their duty without question, order was preserved and the power of established authorities was consolidated. On the other hand, if the troops refused to obey orders, law enforcement broke down, the authority of the officials was dangerously undermined, and the crisis was usually intensified, since the impotence of the officials became obvious and since insubordinate soldiers often supported or joined the very people whom they were supposed to control.[1] Every effort, therefore, had to be made to ensure that only well-disciplined, 'sure' forces were employed as police.

The great problem of civil and military officers was to determine what factors best guaranteed discipline. One clear concern of the authorities was to use troops without ties with the populace they were to police. The prevalence of foreign units in police functions reflected this concern. A number of officers advocated the withdrawal of all army units from garrison towns to isolated camps, far from civilian contacts and influences.[2] When conditions allowed, regulars were drawn from distant garrisons to keep order. In late

[1] For a more extensive treatment of this problem, see my article, 'Problems of Law and Order During 1790, the "Peaceful" Year of the French Revolution', *American Historical Review*, LXXX (1975), 859–88.

[2] See, for example, Sébastien-Joseph Comeau de Charry, *Souvenirs des guerres d'Allemagne pendant la Révolution et l'Empire* (Paris, 1900), pp. 41–2.

October 1790, for example, the regiment of Royal Roussillon Infantry was called from its garrison at Poitiers to restore peace at Issoudun in the neighbouring department of the Indre, although other units were stationed closer to the trouble. Firm action by this regiment led to the restoration of municipal officers who had been forcibly deposed, and justified the precautions taken.[1] Of course, in emergencies such planning was not always possible.

Factors other than careful selection contributed to the discipline exhibited by regulars during police actions. Hostility, and especially violence, between civilians and soldiers almost guaranteed firm discipline on the part of the troops. We have already seen examples of this in 1789 in the cases of the Royal Allemand Cavalry at Paris and the Bourbon Infantry at Caen. Other examples of similar situations after 1789 will be discussed later in this chapter, e.g. the Swiss regiment of Ernest Infantry at Marseille between 1790 and 1792 and the 12th (Dauphin) Cavalry in Franche-Comté during late 1791 and early 1792. The very presence of soldiers summoned to maintain order often created antagonism on the part of civilians. When citizens expressed this hostility toward soldiers, cohesion and discipline among the troops increased, as did antipathy towards civilians. Violence almost inevitably created an unbridgeable gap between the two. In approximately a quarter (63 out of 233) of the incidents in which regulars acted as police, violence resulted. In only *one* of these cases did the soldiers subsequently break discipline.[2] More than any other factor, violent confrontations ensured discipline on the part of the army in its police role. When treated as oppressors, soldiers usually acted as oppressors.

Just as the coming of war helped to restore discipline within the army, it also had a major impact upon its police functions and on civil-military relations in general. First of all, the war and the need it created for trained forces at the front led to the drastic curtailment of the police role of regulars. Despite inadequacies in our sample, it is striking that of those examples of police action by line

[1] Elements of the Royal Comtois Infantry and Royal Cravattes Cavalry were stationed at Blois and Vendôme, both closer to Issoudun than Poitiers. See Dufay *Sociétés populaires et l'armée*, pp. 51-2 and 54-5 and Anon. 'Historique du 10e Régiment de Cuirassiers', a manuscript history received at the Archives de la Guerre on 23 Jan. 1892, pp. 7-8.

[2] This was the incident that occurred at Douai in mid-March 1791, described above, when troops of the garrison at first assisted the National Guard in repressing a grain riot, but subsequently informed their superiors that they would not march against French citizens again.

units in 1792, approximately 70 per cent took place before the declaration of war and almost 90 per cent occurred before mid-year.

Simultaneously, civilian regard for the military improved markedly as the soldiers became the defenders of the nation and the Revolution against their foreign enemies. By removing an onerous burden from the responsibility of the army and by improving the prestige of military service, the war fostered better discipline and morale among line troops.

The factors which contributed to insubordination among troops performing police duties are, essentially, the opposite of the elements just discussed. Close and friendly relations between soldiers and civilians tended to undermine the reliability of the troops when they were called upon to police civil disturbances. Similar social and regional origins provided a basis for identification between soldiers and civilians, as did a sense of suffering comparable inequities at the hands of their social superiors.

Personal contact between soldiers and civilians strengthened the ties established by common social background. The propagandizing of the troops called to Paris in the summer of 1789 entailed not only an exposition of military injustices but also close contacts with civilian agitators. The numerous stories of soldiers drinking with civilian troublemakers (most frequently presented by contemporary and subsequent opponents of the Revolution) miss the point when they claim that resulting insubordination was due to alcohol. Cafés and wineshops in France have always been more important as centres of social intercourse than as places in which to become drunk. Soldiers garrisoned for years in the same locality who spent their off-duty hours working and socializing with local inhabitants inevitably formed individual and even organizational ties with these civilians. Quite simply, discipline was strained beyond the breaking-point when soldiers were ordered to use force against people with whom they had established personal relationships.

Even when such ties did not exist, certain conditions frequently had the effect of dissolving the bonds of discipline. The most striking example of this is the high proportion of insubordination among line units involved in political disturbances. Although only one-eighth of the line units suffered from insubordination while engaged in all kinds of police activity, one-third of those called upon to police political struggles became insubordinate and 80 per cent of all insubordination connected with police functions arose during conflicts between opposing political groups. When used for the general maintenance of order, in apprehending criminals, in upholding the law against anti-feudal riots, in calming religious disputes, in military police activities, and in protecting food supplies, soldiers could normally be depended upon to carry out their orders. However distasteful such duties might have been, they were generally viewed as customary and legitimate functions of the regular army. In the atmosphere of revolutionary change that had developed since 1789, political questions, especially conflicting claims to legitimacy, were much less easily resolved.

In the military conflicts described in the previous chapter the soldiers were on familiar ground. Long-standing complaints and civilian support allowed them to challenge their superiors; and the successes that they achieved in these struggles progressively increased their confidence. Indeed, line troops were usually more obedient to civil authorities than to their military commanders. When opposing civilian groups claimed to represent legitimate authority, however, the duty of the soldiers became confused. In such situations even well-disciplined and 'select' units could determine their allegiance on their own. Frequently, this meant that the troops supported those groups with which they most closely identified, even when this meant defying the established authorities in the name of the Revolution. The most notable and consequential incident like this had occurred in Paris during the summer of 1789. The problem, however, did not disappear after 14 July; rather, the continuing involvement of regular units in civilian political struggles constituted an important element in the politicization of the line army.

THE POLICIZATION OF THE ARMY

Only a minority—albeit a substantial one—of the line troops who were involved in political conflicts became insubordinate; most kept good discipline. For example, after local elections in the late spring and early summer of 1790, line units had to be employed in Touraine, Bourbonnais, Nivernais, and Alsace to restore peace among disgruntled political opponents. In all cases the troops carried out their mission with order and dispatch.[1] Similarly, detachments of regu-

[1] See the letters from Berchény to Saint-Priest, dated 29 May, 1 June, and 19 June 1790, in A.N., H¹⁴⁵³ and the report of the lieutenant of the maréchaussée of Strasbourg, dated 24 July 1790, in A.N., F⁷3686¹.

lars obediently suppressed tax revolts in Berry, Touraine, and Picardie during the first half of the same year, although in the last case some soldiers privately encouraged retail merchants in La Fère to refuse to pay duties.[1] When discipline among the troops did collapse, however, the impact on both soldiers and civilians was enormous.

One of the most vivid examples of the role of the military in political conflicts among civilians is an incident involving the Lyonnais Infantry at Aix-en-Provence in December 1790. The colonel of this regiment, the Comte de Fezensac, had kept good order in his unit since the Revolution by combining tolerance and firmness. He made no objections to his men attending the Jacobin club of Aix and even went to a meeting himself. At the same time, during the first half of 1790 he dishonourably discharged about fifty soldiers whom he considered troublemakers; and in September he dissolved a club formed by some corporals of the regiment to correspond with other units.[2] Relations between the troops and local authorities were good; in July 1790 the municipality petitioned the Minister of War to retain the regiment in Aix where it had been stationed since late 1787.[3] A local political quarrel, however, destroyed this comparatively happy situation.

In December two pro-revolutionary clubs in the area, the *Amis de la Constitution* and the *Société des frères anti-politiques*, alarmed by the formation of a third reputedly counter-revolutionary organization, decided to combine and held a unification ceremony in Aix on Sunday, 12 December.[4] During the festivities fighting broke out between the members of the two clubs and hostile observers, among whom were some officers of the Lyonnais Infantry. The local authorities called out the National Guard, arrested a number of suspects (including eleven Lyonnais officers), ordered the regiment to leave the city, and summoned military assistance from Marseille.

Before these orders could be executed, other officers of the regiment, who had remained in the barracks area just outside the city

[1] See the letters of Bercheny to Saint-Priest, dated 29 and 30 May 1790, in A.N., H[1453] and R. B. Rose, 'Tax Revolt and Popular Organization in Picardy, 1789–1791', *Past and Present*, No. 43 (May 1969), pp. 99–100.

[2] Carnot, 'Régiment de Lyonnais pendant la Révolution', pp. 13–14 and 21–2.

[3] Letter from the Mayor and municipal officers of Aix to La Tour du Pin, dated 2 July 1790, in A.N., F[9]40.

[4] Unless otherwise noted, this description of the events at Aix is based upon the report of the royal commissioners on the troubles at Aix, dated 23 Feb. 1791, in A.N., F[7]3659[1] and documents in A.D., Bouches-du-Rhône L 423bis and L 3245.

gates, called out the troops, distributed ammunition, and ordered the unit into the city to rescue their fellow-officers. Second-Lieutenant Ferriol of the grenadier company, however, halted his men and pointed out that without civilian authorization such intervention was illegal. Ferriol, an officer of fortune who had served in the regiment for 33 years, all but two of them as an enlisted man, enjoyed an authority among the men far beyond his rank.[1] The soldiers in the other companies refused to march despite threats and entreaties by their officers. The men returned to their barracks, and, in compliance with the orders of the civil officials, left Aix for Tarascon early the next morning.

The violence broke the fragile calm that until then had existed in the city and in the regiment. Civil strife grew in Aix and wealthier residents began to flee the city. Although the officers of the Lyonnais Infantry were released in June 1791 after a trial failed to implicate them in a counter-revolutionary plot, the soldiers refused to accept them back into the regiment. Because of the hostility of the troops ten other officers refused to return to the unit after their semester leave. The crisis at Aix had destroyed the bonds between officers and men and insubordination continued to plague the regiment throughout 1791.[2]

This incident is a prime example of the interaction of civil and military factors in a political conflict; at the same time, it provides specific evidence of a number of circumstances previously discussed in more general terms. The establishment of the soldiers' club and attendance at the Jacobin society indicated some dissatisfaction with the conditions of military service and support for the Revolution among the soldiers. The dishonourable discharges and hostility toward pro-revolutionary organizations on the part of some officers indicated the officers' concern for the maintenance of discipline and their opposition to major revolutionary change. These attitudes paralleled divisions among the citizens of Aix, which were formally expressed by the establishment of rival political organizations. The violence that erupted on 12 December exacerbated these differences. The soldiers, under the leadership of an ex-ranker, rejected the authority of their officers and thereby recognized the

---

[1] Details on Ferriol's service are in Carnot, 'Régiment de Lyonnais pendant la Révolution', p. 25.

[2] Ibid., pp. 34–50 contains information on conditions within the regiment after Dec. 1790.

supremacy of civilian officials. This reaction guaranteed the victory of the pro-revolutionary faction in Aix and created a decisive rupture between the officers and men of the Lyonnais Infantry. The effects of military and civilian actions were mutual; and one major result of this crisis was to increase the level of political consciousness among the soldiers.

Other political crises led to more complex interactions between soldiers and civilians. Long before the outbreak of the Revolution many of the inhabitants of Marseille had opposed the stationing of regular troops in their city because they viewed this as an infringement on and a threat to municipal autonomy.[1] The decentralizing tendencies of the early Revolution increased such sentiments. In late 1789 and early 1790 the military commandant of Marseille, the Marquis de Miran, was asked again and again to remove all line units garrisoned there. This opposition to a garrison was not, however, shared by all the inhabitants. Miran was convinced that 'all respectable citizens' (by which he meant the wealthier elements of the city) would evacuate Marseille if the troops were withdrawn because this would leave the city at the mercy of 'the mob'. The troops stayed, but any incident could create a major crisis.

Such an incident was touched off by the haughty and irascible behaviour of the colonel of the Royal Marine Infantry, garrisoned in Marseille. On the evening of 20 March 1790 while entering one of the city gates, Colonel D'Ambert berated and insulted the National Guardsmen on duty there. A crowd of Marseillais, infuriated by this conduct and demanding the Colonel's head, forced him to seek sanctuary in the city hall the next day and refused to be appeased by attempts at conciliation by municipal officials. Soldiers in his regiment meanwhile used the occasion to denounce D'Ambert in an address to the King that claimed he had defrauded them of some 200,000 *livres* over the previous eight years. Even a majority of his subordinate officers wrote to the Minister of War to request his removal. The Colonel responded by condemning his detractors and promising severe retribution.

On 8 April a hearing was held regarding D'Ambert's case and the court ordered his release. It was only with great difficulty and

---

[1] The primary sources for the description of the situation in Marseille can be found in A.N., F⁷3659¹, which was most useful for civil–military relations, and A.G., YA 447, which provided more detailed information on conditions within the regiment of Royal Marine Infantry.

thanks to a strong escort of the National Guard that he managed to leave Marseille unharmed the next morning. The judge who presided over his hearing, M. Chomel, did not escape so easily; his home was looted; he was denounced to the National Assembly as 'a dishonest judge'; and ultimately he was forced to flee the city. D'Ambert never rejoined his regiment; he was suspended from his functions in October 1790 and resigned his commission in July 1791. In early 1792, however, the intrepid Colonel demanded both his rank and his command restored!

The military and civil repercussions of this incident appeared quickly. Regardless of its own opposition to the Colonel, D'Ambert's regiment could not be kept in Marseille without risking further provocation; and on 22 April it withdrew from the city. This trouble, however, had destroyed disciplinary restraints and a month later the grenadier company initiated a mutiny which drove away most of the regiment's officers. Order was not restored in the unit until November. Within Marseille the D'Ambert incident provided justification for and impetus to the cause of those who opposed a garrison, especially the local Jacobin club. Public opinion now demanded the evacuation of all regular troops and the assumption of their duties by the National Guard.

On 30 April the citizens of Marseille took matters into their own hands; while the National Guard occupied Fort Notre Dame de la Garde, one of the three fortresses that guarded and dominated the city, municipal officials summoned the commanders of the other two forts, Saint-Jean and Saint-Nicolas, to hand them over to the National Guard as well. The soldiers of the Vexin Infantry, which garrisoned the forts, endorsed the seizures; but the officers were divided over what to do. Fort Saint-Nicolas was given up without trouble; but Major de Beausset, who commanded Fort Saint-Jean, prepared to resist. Division within his own command, however, dissuaded Beausset and on 1 May he too surrendered. The attitude of the soldiers of the Vexin Infantry, many of whom had been won over by the opponents of a garrison before 30 April, had facilitated this transfer. At the same time, their reaction had completely alienated the soldiers from most of their officers. The extent of this alienation was strikingly revealed on 2 May when Major de Beausset, on his way to justify his conduct to the municipality, was lynched in the street by a crowd that included men from his own regiment. When the soldiers of the Vexin Infantry departed from

Marseille five months later many citizens expressed their best wishes and gratitude to the troops.

The municipal officials of Marseille, supported by a large portion of the populace, the Jacobin club, the National Guard, and the soldiers of the regular garrison, had successfully defied the central authorities who had consistently rejected all demands that the National Guard replace the line troops in the city. By October Forts Saint-Jean and Saint-Nicolas had been demolished and all regular units, except the Swiss regiment of Ernest Infantry, had been withdrawn from Marseille. Without changing his official position the King had been forced to surrender his authority tacitly. The 'respectable citizens' of the city were convinced that the *canaille* now controlled Marseille.

The lone Swiss regiment remaining in the city, frequently insulted and continually harassed, was isolated from any but hostile contact with civilians who resented its continued presence. Violent confrontations between the personnel of this regiment and the Marseillais occurred in December 1790, and in May, June, and October 1791. Officers and men drew closer together in their mutual alienation from the populace. In late February 1792 the situation reached its inevitable climax; upon returning from a brief mission to Aix, the Ernest Infantry found itself surrounded by a large force of armed Marseillais who demanded that the Swiss lay down their weapons. The commanding officer, Major Watteville, decided that no cause would be served by resistance and ordered his reluctant troops to comply. When the regiment attempted to reorganize in Toulon and Lorgues, hostile townspeople refused to receive it, and ultimately the unit retired to Switzerland, leaving the service of France in May 1792.[1]

Like Marseille, Lyon also was the scene of internal strife in the early Revolution and here too the role of the military was of paramount importance.[2] In June and July 1789 crowds attacked the government toll-gates, which levied duties on foodstuffs entering

---

[1] On the lot of this unfortunate regiment, see the following: letter of Bessières, dated 1 Jan. 1791, in A.G., YA 447; letters of Lt-.Col. D'Olivier, dated 28 May 1791, and Debourge, dated 19 June 1791, in A.N., F⁷3659¹; letter of La Roque Dourdon, dated 18 Oct. 1791, in A.N., F⁷3659²; the inspection reports for 1790 and 1791 and the dossier marked 'Affaire du Régiment Suisse d'Ernest 1792' in A.G., Xᴳ 87; Bernard Eude, 'L'Émigration militaire à Nice au début de la Révolution (1789–1792)', *Revue historique de l'armée*, 1971, No. 4, p. 16; and Poisson, *L'Armée et la Garde Nationale*, I. 377–9.

[2] The account of the troubles at Lyon is based upon Buttet, 'Mission de M. de la Chapelle' and the section 'Lyon 1790' in A.G., YA 447, unless otherwise noted.

the city, and pillaged the royal arsenal. Economic unrest found political expression the following February when rioters again attacked the arsenal and forced the recently elected mayor, Imbert, who was described as the candidate 'of the formerly privileged and richest and most respectable people', to flee from Lyon. Continuing food shortages gave rise to further disturbances in June and July 1790 during which the toll-gates were again destroyed. The municipal authorities were unable to cope with the disorders, since the popular clubs and a substantial part of the National Guard sympathized with the crowds. Line troops, including the Swiss regiment of Sonnenberg Infantry and the German regiment of La Marck Infantry, were called into the city to keep order. The presence of these units, however, increased tensions in the bitterly divided city. When a Swiss soldier was lynched by a crowd in late July 1790, the municipality declared martial law and the government appointed General de la Chapelle military commandant of Lyon.

La Chapelle's command included not only the line units within the city but other regular forces within marching distance of Lyon, some 4,700 men in all. With this army at his disposal La Chapelle was able to restore order; but many Lyonnais viewed this as the repression of the poorer citizens for the benefit of the rich. The re-establishment of the toll-gates and resumption of duties confirmed this view. Resentment against the General also developed because of his persistent refusal to arm the local National Guard with weapons from the royal arsenal. As he noted in a letter to the Minister of War, it was only his superiority in armed force that allowed La Chapelle to dominate the situation.

Suspicion of and hostility towards La Chapelle mounted during the autumn of 1790 as rumours of counter-revolutionary plots, centering on Lyon and involving officers and troops of the Royal Army, circulated through the city. The fact that *émigrés* were making such plans and that royalist agents did visit some officers of the Lyon garrison intensified this distrust.[1] The local Jacobin club, elements of the National Guard, and what La Chapelle called 'the lowest class of people' demanded that the arsenal be turned over to citizens and that all royal troops, but especially the foreign units, be withdrawn from the city. The Jacobins further insisted that La Chapelle be removed, charging that he intended 'to subjugate the city'. The municipal officials publicly defended the General and the

[1] See an example of royalist methods in Mautort, *Mémoires*, pp. 393-4.

regulars, claiming that La Chapelle had always been moderate and wise in the exercise of force and that the troops' conduct was irreproachable; they added, however, that the line units could never be employed except on their orders. Like moderate, bourgeois officials elsewhere in France, these 'honest citizens' faced a dilemma. On one hand they feared disorders by the masses and saw the line army the most effective defence against this; on the other hand, aware of the threat of counter-revolution, they did not want to leave the army a passive instrument in the hands of aristocratic officers.

Refusing to rely on official assurances, the opponents of a garrison began to spread propaganda among the soldiers and to undermine discipline. They were most successful among the soldiers and N.C.O.s of the Guyenne Infantry, who earlier that year while stationed in Nîmes had shown sympathy for pro-revolutionary Protestants in their struggle against anti-revolutionary Catholics. On 9 November La Chapelle reported that most of the second battalion of this regiment 'identified absolutely with inhabitants of the lowest class', and that in the first battalion 'all the N.C.O.s without exception are corrupted to the same degree'. Such sympathies spread to other French units, and by 13 November La Chapelle wrote to the Minister of War that if it were not for the two foreign regiments in Lyon, he could not answer for the city for twenty-four hours. The General was hardly exaggerating. The following month when a detachment of the Metz Artillery was ordered to train its guns upon rioting silkworkers in the Croix-Rousse suburb of Lyon, the cannoneers threatened to kill their commander, Lieutenant Comeau de Charry, if he fired on 'the nation'.[1]

General La Chapelle's position had become untenable by the end of the year: he was under constant criticism from the Jacobins, most of the National Guard, and a large segment of the inhabitants; he was losing control of the soldiers in his command; and his major support in Lyon, the civil officials, themselves exercised only a very dubious authority. On 2 January 1791 he was relieved of his command; and by 1792 he had emigrated and was serving as a Major-general in the army of the *émigrés*, thus confirming—after the fact—many of the charges levelled against him.

---

[1] Comeau de Charry, *Souvenirs*, pp. 34–7.

The removal of La Chapelle did not restore peace to Lyon; the controversy over the presence of regular troops and the political and social implications of this continued.[1] In October 1791, 3,300 active citizens petitioned the Assembly to withdraw the garrison, arguing that it was ruining the economy of the city and that only 'the rich and the merchants' benefited from it. Shortly afterwards, 105 residents in an address to the King claimed that they, the large property-owners and taxpayers, were the true citizens of the city and they wanted a regular garrison. Their opponents they labelled a 'factious society' desiring only anarchy. Lyon with its numerous workers, they maintained, 'ought to have an armed force capable of opposing their insurrections against proprietors and commercial leaders'. In response, the lower classes of the city sent yet another petition, with 10,190 signatures, to the Assembly urging the replacement of regulars by the National Guard. Despite their numbers, the opponents of a garrison lost their case to the fewer but wealthier citizens and the garrison remained.

The incidents at Marseille and Lyon, despite their peculiarities, displayed important similarities that help to elucidate the complexities of civil-military relations in a revolutionary atmosphere, and the effects of these relations. Both cities had a heterogeneous population, divided by social and economic differences to which the Revolution gave political expression. In both cities the wealthier and politically more conservative classes desired the presence of royal troops to police the poorer and more radical elements of the populace. As a result of revolutionary changes, the latter had greatly expanded their expectations and had developed the means of implementing them, notably by direct popular action, through influence within the National Guard, and by means of the Jacobin clubs. These were used to put pressure on municipal officials to demand the withdrawal of regular units. In Marseille the civil authorities sided with these elements and forced the removal of most of the troops. In Lyon the officials, more sympathetic to the desires of wealthy merchants and more frightened by the threat of counter-revolution, favoured the retention of a garrison, whose employment they hoped to control. In both cases those opposed to a a garrison were not content to press for a troop withdrawal but also attempted to instigate insubordination among the soldiers.

[1] Details on these later developments are contained in the dossier 'Affaire de Lyon, novembre 1791' in A.G., YA 447.

The soldiers, already alienated from their officers by the situation within their regiments, were readily drawn into the local political conflict and gave at least passive support to the radical groups, thus tacitly recognizing their authority. This, in turn, further debilitated discipline and led to such insubordinate behaviour as that exhibited by the men of Vexin, Royal Marine, and Guyenne Regiments. When civilians did not try to seduce the troops but rather antagonized them as was done to the foreign units in both cities, the soldiers maintained discipline and thereby served the interests of the established authorities. Whatever their reactions, officers and soldiers became critical factors in the civil conflicts and at the same time developed an increased political commitment of their own.

While these three examples—the troubles at Aix, Marseille, and Lyon—offer striking evidence of the politicization of the army and its importance, they are not intended to infer that military personnel always divided along the same lines or that civilian disputes were the only means of injecting political ideas into the army. Soldiers, especially in foreign units, sometimes allowed their discipline and devotion to their officers to determine their politics. For example, at Belfort on 21 October 1790 the officers of the Royal Liégeois Infantry and of the Lauzun Hussars paraded around the city at the head of their men crying: 'Long live the king!' and 'To the devil with the nation!' Both these regiments, composed mostly of foreigners and foreign-speaking Frenchmen, had contributed detachments to the suppression of the revolt at Nancy; and they had subsequently been insulted for their role in this by the citizens of Belfort. During the demonstration of 21 October the officers and men achieved their revenge. Many of them, carrying white handkerchiefs at the end of their unsheathed swords, insulted, mistreated, and wounded local inhabitants. The Minister of War, usually anxious to expose the rioting of soldiers, withheld disclosure of this event from the Assembly for three days. After it was revealed, some deputies demanded that, as with the units involved in the Nancy affair, these regiments be disbanded. Instead, an attempt was made to assign individual responsibility. The colonel and major of the Royal Liégeois, which was considered the more culpable of the two regiments, were imprisoned; and an investigation of other officers implicated in the affair was undertaken. The two units were withdrawn from Belfort. The colonel and major, who faced the possibility of being charged with high treason, soon escaped from prison and emigrated from France.[1]

By mid-1791 the city of Arles was bitterly divided (particularly over control of the National Guard and the treatment of priests who rejected the oath to the Civil Constitution of the Clergy) into two political factions, the royalist Chiffonistes and the radical Monnediers. During the last three months of the year the dispute took on a more violent form, and line troops had to be called into the city. The soldiers in one of these units, a 200-man detachment of the 28th Infantry, soon showed that their sympathies were with the Monnediers and they began to insult and threaten 'the aristocrats' of Arles in public. The conservative city officials decried this action and confined the troops to their barracks. On the other hand, in February 1792 the same officials succeeded in having a large detachment of the 77th Infantry, a German regiment reputed to be counter-revolutionary, stationed in their city. The municipal officers gave free rein to these troops and by March 'patriots' were being shot in their homes while the streets of Arles echoed with shouts of 'Long live the King!' and 'Long Live the émigrés!' Only the military occupation of Arles by the departmental National Guard and the withdrawal of the 77th Infantry ended this opposition to the Revolution.[2]

In early December 1791 fighting occurred between troops of the 12th Cavalry and National Guardsmen near Besançon in Franche Comté. The cause of the conflict is unclear but very quickly rumours spread that the cavalrymen were counter-revolutionaries determined to burn, to pillage, and to slaughter good citizens. Popular hostility to the regiment reached fever-pitch, although the rumours had no foundation; and inhabitants and officials of the region insulted and humiliated it wherever it passed during the next four months. On 11 April 1792 fourteen officers and thirty-seven enlisted

---

[1] See 'Extrait des procédures criminelles du Tribunal du District de Belfort', A.N., F⁹45; 'Rapport fait à l'Assemblée Nationale dans la séance du samedi 30 octobre, au nom des Comités militaires et des rapports, sur les événemens arrivés le 21 Octobre à Béfort, par Muguet dit Nanthou, Député de la Haute-Saône', Maclure Collection, vol. 832; and 'Discours des officiers du Régiment des Lauzun Hussards à l'Assemblée Nationale', Maclure Collection, vol. 874.

[2] See the pertinent documents in A.D., Bouches-du-Rhône L289; letters of the royal commissioners at Arles to the Minister of the Interior, dated 28 Oct. and 27 Nov. 1791, and the letter of the municipality of Arles, dated 28 Feb. 1792 in A.N., F⁷3659²; and the report to the departmental council of the Bouches-du-Rhône, dated 15 Mar. 1792, in A.N., F⁷3659³.

men left the regimental encampment near Altkirch in Alsace and emigrated to Germany. Later testimony by officers who remained with the unit claimed that most of the men who emigrated did so because of the continual hostility to which they were subjected. Public antagonism toward the unit continued, nevertheless, and in May 1792 only five officers remained in this regiment whose commanding officer was, by then, a second-lieutenant.[1]

These examples show that, just as not all noble officers opposed the Revolution, so too not all the soldiers warmly welcomed it. One basis for anti-revolutionary sentiment among soldiers was the relationship between them and their officers; personal ties and firm discipline led the men of some units to endorse the same politics as their superiors. At least equally important was civilian pressure. Civilians could not only win soldiers to their cause by fraternal treatment and seductive propaganda; they could also drive troops into the opposite camp by violence and hostility. Of special broader political significance was antagonism towards the foreign regiments of the line army.

Suspicion of foreign units had increased steadily in the early Revolution, especially among the more ardent revolutionaries; and the Swiss were the most deeply distrusted of all. The Swiss regiments were the most thoroughly foreign in composition and generally the best-disciplined elements in the Royal Army. Furthermore, because of their special contracts with the King, the Swiss cantons retained considerable control over these units even when they were in French service.[2] The cantons directly controlled the appointment of officers and regulated the conduct of troops. For example, the Swiss were forbidden to attend political clubs even after this right had been granted to all other units of the Royal Army. Because of their normally tighter discipline, the Swiss had performed more than their share of police duties since 1789 and this had aroused antagonism on the part of many Frenchmen. By 1792, civilian suspicion of and hostility towards these foreigners resulted in a number of violent confrontations. Besides the conflict between the regiment of Ernest Infantry and the Marseillais, other incidents occurred that increased civilian distrust of the Swiss. At Douai in January 1792 soldiers of the 86th (Courten) Swiss fought

[1] A.N., Dxv 5, dossier 45, pièce 33 and A.G., X^c 115.
[2] For an example of the problems created by the special status of Swiss regiments, see the letter from Montmorin to De Lassart, dated 30 Aug. 1791, in A.N., F^{9}45.

with troops of the 74th Infantry following allegations that the foreigners were counter-revolutionaries. Soldiers in French regiments, members of the National Guard and civilians at Schilligheim in May and at Strasbourg in June accused the Swiss of the 69th (Vigier) Infantry of being mercenaries and instigated violent quarrels with them.[1] The stout defence of the Tuileries by the Swiss Guards on 10 August 1792 led to further denunciations of all foreign and especially Swiss units for their anti-revolutionary sentiments.[2] On 20 August the Assembly ordered the discharge of all Swiss regiments. The next month the 101st Infantry, formerly the Royal Liégeois Regiment, was also dismissed. After its counter-revolutionary demonstration at Belfort in autumn 1790 this foreign regiment had been the object of countless complaints for its political sympathies. In mid-August 1792 a large number of soldiers deserted and sought refuge with the municipal authorities of Grenoble and Lyon. The soldiers declared '. . . that they would rather rot in dungeons than return to a regiment whose officers were so openly the enemies of the French Revolution'.[3] On 21 September the regiment was officially disbanded.

Although other factors, such as their foreign composition and the limitations on French control over them, played a role in the decision to discharge these units, the primary consideration was political. The central government, in the midst of a major and as yet unsuccessful war, dismissed these regiments, containing some 12,000 trained soldiers in all, because their loyalty towards France and the Revolution was suspect. While this judgement is impossible to evaluate precisely and while it was certainly erroneous in some individual cases, the general conduct of these mercenaries, particularly their subordination to their officers even in the face of civil crises, did indeed constitute a threat to the revolutionary regime.

Willingly or unwillingly, the Royal Army had become a critical political instrument and its personnel were compelled to make political decisions. As the previous examples illustrate, this de-

---

[1] On these incidents, see the correspondence between 7 and 23 Jan. 1792 in A.N., F⁷ 3683⁵; A.D., Bas-Rhin 1L 1439; and letter from the directory of the Bas-Rhin to M. Roland, dated 14 June 1792, in A.N., F⁷ 3686¹.

[2] See the denunciation by Carrier at the Jacobin club of Lyon on 16 Aug. in A.N., Dxv 3, dossier 39, pièce 3 and the reaction of Marat in Michel Vovelle, ed., *Marat : Textes Choisis* (Paris, 1963), p. 189.

[3] A.D., Isère L 56 and L 68 and Chuquet, *Lettres de 1792*, pp. 1 and 94–5.

velopment often arose from the direct involvement of the military in civilian struggles. But the politicization of the army was not simply the result of fortuitous circumstances; organized efforts were made to propagandize and to provide political education for officers and men. We have already discussed a number of instances in which National Guard units and political organizations, both pro- and counter-revolutionary, influenced the attitude of military personnel. In addition the press, especially the radical press, tried to win the loyalty of the troops. For example, Marat wrote in the issue of *L'Ami du peuple* of 2 June 1790 that the preservation of the Revolution required the support of the soldiers whom he urged to question orders from superiors, lest they lend themselves to oppression.[1] Other newspapers, such as the *Courrier de Paris*, attacked existing military discipline as inimical to the principles of the Revolution.[2]

The most extensive attempt to politicize the army was the federation movement of the early Revolution. Arising spontaneously in different areas of France, this series of celebrations aimed at the commemoration of national and revolutionary sentiments in an atmosphere of fraternity. A common element in these festivities was the exchange of promises of friendship between Royal Army and National Guard units in order to bind together soldier-citizens and citizen-soldiers. During the spring of 1790 a number of these ceremonies took place. The regiment of Languedoc Infantry made such a pact with the National Guard of Montauban, to which the National Guard of Toulouse subsequently adhered. Guardsmen in Franche-Comté did the same with the Royal Étranger Cavalry, as did the Conti Infantry with the National Guard of Amiens.[3] These activities strengthened bonds between soldiers and some civilians, usually the most actively pro-revolutionary elements of the civil populace, but at the same time they tended to undermine the authority of officers over their men. The National Guard of Orléans held such a celebration on 8 May 1790 and invited the regiment of Royal Comtois Infantry to send representatives. Despite the desire of some soldiers to attend, the officers of the regiment refused, and this increased hostility towards the officers. A

[1] Vovelle, *Marat*, p. 164.
[2] The commanding officer of the Conti Infantry complained about the *Courrier de Paris* to the Minister of War; see Poisson, *L'Armeé et la Garde Nationale*, I. 220.
[3] Leverrier, *Naissance de l'armée nationale*, p. 52.

similar federation was scheduled for Tours on 16 May. Five companies of the Anjou Infantry garrisoned there, led by the grenadier
company, revolted against their officers the day before and took an
oath of federation with the National Guard of the nearby region.[1]
Some line units made federations among themselves; for example,
the regiments of the Beauce and Normandie Infantry took an oath
of fraternity, defence of the fatherland, and hatred of aristocracy;
and these soldiers invited other units of the army to adhere to their
pledge.[2]

Most deputies of the National Assembly approved of the movement, and the King had little choice but to authorize federations
himself on 4 June 1790. In response to popular initiative the government organized a national federation to be celebrated in Paris on 14
July 1790. Each regiment of line infantry was to send one officer,
one N.C.O., and four soldiers; each cavalry regiment, one officer,
one N.C.O., and two enlisted men; and special arrangements were
made for deputies from other branches. All the military representatives, officers and men alike, were selected on the basis of length of
service; consequently, a substantial proportion of the officers were
ex-rankers with long army experience.[3] After detailed and extensive
preparations, involving the determination of seniority and the funds
to pay for the deputies' expenses, hundreds of line soldiers mixed
with National Guardsmen and simple citizens of all ages and social
ranks in this fraternal high-point of the Revolution. It is impossible
to determine accurately the effects of this event upon the army; but
it seems safe to assume that the military representatives brought
back to their units an increased sense of political participation and,
probably, a greater devotion to the Revolution.

The *fête de la fédération* of 14 July 1790 was the most spectacular
attempt by the French government, particularly the National
Assembly, to politicize the Royal Army, but was by no means the
only, or even the most important, official action by the central
authorities to influence military response to the Revolution. For,

---

[1] A.N., H^{1453}

[2] Poisson, *L'Armée et la Garde Nationale*, I. 223.

[3] Chilly, *La Tour du Pin*, p. 140. Administrative details on the military representation are in A.G., YA 305. Information on some of the soldier-deputies can be found in
A.G., X^c 31, 34, 35, 42, 50, 60, 66, 72, 79, 81, 83 and in the appropriate regimental
registers. Older men with long service records were typical of the military representatives; but none could match Lieutenant-General de Rostaing who made his first campaign in 1713 and had to refuse the honour because of physical incapacity!

besides the unofficial and immediate contacts which soldiers had with civilian politics, described in this section, the line army was directly affected by the military legislation of the early Revolution.

THE ASSEMBLY AND THE ARMY

From its inception the new legislature in France was in an ambivalent position. The deputies of the Constituent Assembly and its successor, the Legislative Assembly, attempted to effect a moderate revolution, an objective continually threatened by both counter-revolution and radicalization. The regular army, an essential instrument in exercising political authority, itself represented these opposing threats. Consequently, legislative ambivalence was evidenced nowhere more strikingly than in the government's military policies, particularly in matters involving discipline. The legislators wanted a well-disciplined force to maintain order, especially among the urban and rural masses; yet at the same time, unquestioning obedience by the soldiers would put dangerous power in the hands of noble officers, many of whom were hostile to the Revolution. The Assembly was never able to resolve this dilemma successfully and its handling of the internal problems of the army was an inconsistent series of responses to specific situations, rather than a coherent long-range plan. Unpredictable crises, such as the flight to Varennes and military reverses, only compounded the government's problems.

In dealing with other matters concerning the army—jurisdiction, organization, military justice, promotion, recruitment—the legislature was normally decisive and consistent. The Assembly very quickly asserted its authority over the Royal Army. Less than a month after the fall of the Bastille it required an oath of loyalty to 'the nation, the King, and the law' from all officers, at the head of their troops and in the presence of civil officials. Simultaneously the conditions under which regulars could be employed against civilians were defined. Proceeding to expand its control over the line army, in February 1790 the Assembly decreed that it would determine the annual military budget, the pay for all grades, the total strength, the conditions of enlistment and discharge, the service of foreign corps, and the laws governing military crimes.[1] While remaining its titular chief, the King retained little real authority over the Royal Army.

[1] Picq, *Législation militaire*, p. 8; Chilly, *La Tour du Pin*, pp. 283–4; and Jung, *Dubois-Crancé*, I. 133–4.

Despite their considerable political significance, these changes had little effect on conditions within the army. In order to implement revolutionary principles, answer the practical complaints of military personnel, and gain favour among the troops, the Assembly enacted other reforms in early 1790 to improve the lot of military men. Venality was abolished and all ranks were open to all citizens. A measure to go into effect on 1 May 1790 raised army pay, by *c*. 1 *sou* per day for the average infantryman with corresponding increases for other ranks and branches. The legislature also improved the status of soldiers by decreeing that sixteen years of honourable service entitled veterans to the full rights of active citizenship.[1] Since these reforms were implemented rather slowly, their immediate effect was negligible.[2] They did, nonetheless, convince many soldiers that the government was determined to redress their grievances and this led them to identify their interests with the Revolution, sentiments also fostered by the federation movement that was flourishing at the same time. These measures, however, did nothing to improve relations between officers and men; on the contrary, they sometimes encouraged insubordination by soldiers who were convinced their actions had official approval.

The general collapse of discipline during the first eight months of 1790 confused and appalled the moderate legislators; and their response was typically ambivalent. On the one hand, the Assembly outlawed the soldiers' committees as a source of insubordination; on the other hand, it lent credence to the soldiers' complaints of misuse of unit funds by ordering a general inspection of regimental accounts. The great mutiny at Nancy, set off by this very issue, brought an abrupt and decisive response from the government: the rebellion was ruthlessly suppressed. Indeed, the repression at Nancy was probably more severe than the Assembly intended; very quickly it returned to a more conciliatory and, again, ambivalent policy.

---

[1] Picq, *Législation militaire*, pp. 305-6 and Chilly, *La Tour du Pin*, pp. 283-4. For the complete pay-scale of the French army, see A.G., YA 437 which includes the variations according to branch and rank.

[2] An unsigned document dated 9 June 1790 in A.G., *Travail du Roi*, carton 446 indicates that venality remained in practice after its abolition. This document, a request for the appointment of Major de Montmorin to the colonelcy of the Flandre Infantry, notes that: 'The price of this regiment is 15,000 livres.' Another document, unsigned and undated, in the same carton says that the King has approved the appointment but desires 'that this nomination be kept secret and that its expedition be suspended until new orders'. Pay increases were notoriously slow and this contributed to the discontent in the Nancy garrison in August 1790.

Although the legislature forbade soldiers to attend political clubs and prohibited correspondence between units in the aftermath of Nancy, it simultaneously made further changes to benefit the soldier. In September 1790 the system of military justice was thoroughly revised. Virtually all forms of corporal punishment were abolished and the use of dishonourable discharges was provisionally proscribed.[1] In each unit a 'council of discipline', composed of seven officers, was established to supervise all regimental punishments and hear complaints. Its sessions were to be held publicly. For more serious offences military tribunals, composed of four officers, three enlisted men, and two judges of the same rank as the accused, passed verdicts; but a separate body composed of three civilian commissioners, *commissaires de guerres*, determined and pronounced sentences.[2] Like previous reforms, these changes were not immediately put into operation.[3]

During the same month the Assembly established new rules for advancement within the army.[4] For promotion to all non-commissioned ranks except adjutant, the men of the regiment holding the same rank as that in which the vacancy existed nominated candidates; the captain of the company with the 'open slot' selected three of the nominees; and the colonel chose one man from this list. Adjutants were selected by a vote of the unit's superior officers. Three-quarters of vacant second-lieutenancies in the infantry and cavalry were to be filled by competitive examinations, open to active citizens between 16 and 24 years of age who could meet the physical requirements and possessed a certificate of *civisme* from their municipality. The other quarter of the vacancies went to sergeants, alternately by seniority and by vote of all the officers of the unit. In the technical branches (artillery and engineers), examinations were the sole method of obtaining a second-lieutenant's commission.

Promotion to the grades of lieutenant and captain depended solely on seniority in the regiment. Two-thirds of the lieutenant-

[1] Godechot, *Institutions de la France*, p. 135. One corporal punishment maintained was the forced drinking of several tankards of water for soldiers found drunk.

[2] Picq, *Législation militaire*, p. 239 and L. Cahen and R. Guyot, *L'Oeuvre législative de la Révolution* (Paris, 1913), p. 286.

[3] Examples of deserters being punished by ten turns of the gauntlet by 100 men exist in A.G., B[13] 69. In late April 1791 the commissioner at Verdun complained that courts-martial there had not yet been organized on the new basis; see the letter of the Minister of Justice to Duportail, dated 4 June 1791, in A.N., F[9] 55.

[4] See Picq, *Législation militaire*, pp. 290-8.

colonels and colonels were promoted according to their length of service within their branch in peacetime and within their regiment during war. The appointment of the other one-third was at the choice of the King, although he could not promote anyone to these ranks who did not have at least two years service as captain. The grade of major was abolished and all majors automatically became lieutenant-colonels.

The number of generals was drastically reduced, from the hundreds who held general officer rank before the Revolution to ninety-four. Of these six could be marshals and thirty-four lieutenant-generals. Major- and lieutenant-generals were selected alternately on the basis of length of service and by choice of the King, provided his appointees had at least two years of service as colonel. The King alone selected marshals of France.

These reforms implemented many of the principles of the Revolution by establishing more humane, more equitable, and more rational conditions in the army. They attacked privilege and set up bureaucratic standards, based on experience and education. They also eliminated a number of abuses deeply resented in the army. While these changes did little or nothing to resolve the most fundamental military problem—the widening split between officers and men—they did prove that the new government could achieve substantial reform in certain areas. During the latter part of 1790 and early 1791 when internal military divisions were muted, the Assembly was able to continue its reform programme in an area fully within its competence, namely the reorganization of the line army.

In January 1791 most useless and redundant officer positions were eliminated and the total number of officers was reduced to 9,406. The strength and organization of every type of unit was established on new bases, except for the Swiss who retained their own organization. The former names of units, reminiscent of monarchical glories, were replaced by numerical designations.[1] Six months later all the foreign regiments in the French army—again with the exception of the Swiss—were fully assimilated, losing all distinctions of uniform, pay, and administration. This change was precipitated by the de-

---

[1] For further details on these changes, see Chassin, *Armée et Révolution*, pp. 78–9; Édouard Desbrière and Maurice Sautai, *La Cavalerie pendant la Révolution, du 14 juillet 1789 au 26 juin 1794: La Crise* (Paris, 1907), pp. 6–8 and 53–5; and Matti Lauerma, *L'Artillerie de campagne française pendant les guerres de la Révolution* (Helsinki, 1956), pp. 95–6. Also Appendix II.

mand of the soldiers of the German regiment of the 96th (formerly Nassau) Infantry who, after continual civilian harassment, tore all distinctive insignia from their uniforms and 'declared that they are French, and that they wished to serve as French'.[1] Under the pressure of this reaction, the Assembly formally abolished all differences between the German, Irish, and Liégeois regiments and the rest of the French infantry on 21 July 1791.

Despite the improved efficiency achieved by this reorganization, the line army faced an even more vital problem as the probability of war increased in 1791, a serious shortage of men. In August 1790 the official strength of the line army had been set at slightly more than 150,000 men: approximately 110,000 in the infantry, 30,000 in the cavalry, and 10,000 in the artillery.[2] By January 1791 the army was more than 20,000 men short of its authorized strength because of excessive desertions, disciplinary discharges, restrictions on recruitment efforts, and the disbanding of two regiments that had mutinied at Nancy.[3] This situation was a matter of grave concern to the government. Not only were there constant requests for line units to police the interior of the country; but also, by early 1791, foreign powers, often prodded by émigrés, were becoming increasingly hostile to the new regime in France. The National Assembly had to increase its armed forces in order to face both internal and foreign dangers.

In the past the militia had been called up to supplement the regular army during national crises. No institution of the Old Regime, however, had been more universally condemned in the cahiers of 1789 than this one; and the government could not dare to continue it, even had it so wished. On 28 January 1791 the Assembly tried to create a substitute by ordering the establishment of a force of 100,000 'auxiliary soldiers'. These troops were to be raised by voluntary enlistments and, in the event of war, would take over interior duties from the regular army in order to release it for service at the front. The new institution too closely resembled the hated militia to arouse popular response; and it failed miserably. It is

[1] A full description of developments in this regiment can be found in Lt. J.-B. Bouvier, 'Historique du 96ᵉ Régiment d'Infanterie de Ligne', I. 54–61. This handwritten and lavishly illustrated work was received at the Archives de la Guerre on 25 Oct. 1890.
[2] Chassin, Armée et Révolution, p. 97 and Chilly, La Tour du Pin, p. 299, as well as 'Rapport fait au nom du Comité Militaire au Séance du 28 Juillet 1790, par M. Alexandre Lameth', Maclure Collection, vol. 848.
[3] Scott, 'Regeneration of the Line Army', pp. 315–18.

unlikely that this force ever recruited more than 5–10 per cent of its manpower goal.[1]

For the Constituent Assembly the line army always remained the primary defence of France and its major military concern. As early as December 1789 a substantial majority of deputies had rejected Dubois-Crancé's proposal for a national citizen army based on the compulsory service of all able-bodied citizens; they opted instead for maintaining the regular army.[2] In 1791 this force still received top priority in the government's military policy. In March of that year the conditions of enlistment were improved and abuses associated in the past with recruitment were eliminated. Men between 16 and 40 years of age could enlist voluntarily, but those younger than 18 needed parental consent. Local civil officials were to supervise recruitment and could invalidate engagements if any fraud or violence had been employed. Only foreign regiments (which lost their identity four months later) could enrol foreigners; and no units were to enlist criminals, vagabonds, or beggars. Conditions for veteran soldiers were improved by increasing re-enlistment bonuses, limiting the term of re-enlistment to two or four years (in place of eight), allowing sergeants to resign with three months' notice, and assuring any soldier who had served twenty-four years or who had been injured in the line of duty that he would be cared for by the army as long as he wished.[3] As we shall see shortly, the new recruitment policies contributed to a very substantial increase in strength during the year preceding the outbreak of war.

The threat of hostilities also turned the attention of French military theoreticians to the improvement of tactics. The ordinance of 1 August 1791 prescribed new flexible rules for manœuvres, minutely described training, and set down methods of deployment. This ordinance, based essentially on the principles of Guibert, remained in effect throughout the wars of the Revolution and Napoleon.[4]

[1] Picq, *Législation militaire*, p. 76 and the section entitled 'La levée des Auxiliaires (28 Janvier 1791)' in A.G., X^w 73.

[2] See Jung, *Dubois-Crancé*, I. 23–4; Chassin, *Armée et Révolution*, pp. 62–4; and various documents on this debate in Maclure Collection, vol. 848.

[3] Picq, *Législation militaire*, pp. 77–9; Henri Choppin, *Notes sur l'organisation de l'armée pendant la Révolution, 4 août 1789–8 brumaire an IV* (Paris, 1873), pp. 17–18; and 'Décret sur le Recrutement, les Engagemens, les Rengagemens et les Congés, des 7 et 9 Mars 1791', Maclure Collection, vol. 848.

[4] Robert S. Quimby, *The Background of Napoleonic Warfare: The Theory of Military Tactics in Eighteenth-Century France* (New York, 1957), pp. 304–7.

Despite problems of implementation, the National Assembly had legislated an impressive array of military reforms in the first two years of the Revolution. It had established full constitutional control over the army. It had dramatically improved conditions by increasing pay, reforming military justice, and changing the bases for promotion. It had carried out a major transformation of the organizational framework and tactics of the line army. Yet, for all this, the Assembly remained largely ineffective in dealing with the internal problems of the army and continued to have many of its most important military decisions forced upon it by circumstances beyond its control.

The attempted flight of Louis XVI with its clear implications of an appeal to force was one such incident. On 21 June 1791 the Assembly called upon the frontier departments of northern and eastern France to furnish volunteers from the National Guard for active duty, in so far as their population and general situation warranted. On 3 July the number of these volunteers was set at 26,000. On 22 July the Assembly asked for 97,000 'national volunteers' from all of France; and on 17 August the total was set at 101,000.[1] These citizen soldiers were to be recruited, organized, and equipped by local civilian authorities. They enlisted for a term of one campaign only; they elected most of their officers and N.C.O.s; and they received a rate of pay about double that in the line army.

The creation of a new and distinct army, about two-thirds its size, could not but have important implications for the line army. Some of the personnel of the volunteers were drawn from the line army. By law, one of the two lieutenant-colonels in each of the volunteer battalions was required to have served as a captain in a line unit. Likewise, the adjutant and sergeant-major had to be selected from among former lieutenants and N.C.O.s of the line army.[2] In addition, many other veterans and even some men still on active duty in the regular army were elected officers by the volunteers. Nearly one-third of the subaltern officers of the volunteers of 1791 and a majority of the superior officers had pre-

---

[1] For general studies on the volunteers, see Camille Rousset, *Les Volontaires, 1791–1794* (Paris, 1892); G. Dumont, *Études sur l'armée pendant la Révolution. Première série: 1791. Bataillons de volontaires nationaux,* 2 vols. (Paris and Limoges, 1914); and Eugène Déprez, *Les Volontaires nationaux (1791–1793)* (Paris, 1908).

[2] Six, *Généraux de la Révolution,* p. 127.

viously served in the army.[1] The presence of such experienced cadres undoubtedly facilitated the organization and training of the volunteers.

The attractive conditions of service in the volunteer battalions—shorter enlistment, higher pay, better opportunity for promotion by election, less rigorous discipline, and service with men from the same area—lured many veterans and deserters from the line army. The proportion of men with prior service as regular troops varied from unit to unit, but there were some soldiers from the Royal Army in virtually every volunteer battalion.[2] In social background the volunteers were very similar to the soldiers of the line infantry; and, although younger and less experienced in general, under the leadership of line veterans they soon developed into a useful complement to the regular forces.[3]

The government at this time had no intention of supplanting the standing army with these new formations; quite to the contrary, it exerted every effort to bolster the strength of the line units while the volunteer battalions were being organized. On 3 July all infantry regiments, not yet so ordered, were required to increase the complement of both of their battalions to 750 men each; artillery regiments were instructed to do the same; and all cavalry squadrons were to be brought up to a strength of 170 men each.[4] In September the paid units of the Paris National Guard, composed largely of former French Guards and other line veterans, were disbanded and their personnel enrolled in newly created regular units: the 102nd, 103rd, and 104th Infantry Regiments and the 13th and 14th Light Infantry Battalions.

[1] Bertaud, *Valmy*, p. 205. This work is the only one, as far as I know, which provides data on the social origins of the volunteers of 1791 and 1792 on a national basis. Some information on the officers of specific battalions can be found in Jules Tintou, *Soldats limousins de la Révolution et de l'Empire* (Tulle, 1967), pp. 63–5, 72, 85, 102, and 114; Maxime Mangerel, *Le Capitaine Gerbaud, 1773–1799* (Paris, 1910), pp. 26 and 54–5; and Mathiez, *La Victoire en l'an II*, pp. 66–7.

[2] Bertaud, *Valmy*, p. 202.

[3] Approximately 37% of the line soldiers in 1789 were from urban areas; 34% of the volunteers of 1791 were urban in background. About 60% of the line troops had been artisans and shopkeepers in civilian life; 66% of the volunteers were from these groups. Slightly more than 20% of the line soldiers were peasants; about 15% of the volunteers were. Of all the groups in the middle classes of French society, members of the liberal professions were most prominent in the ranks of both the line troops and volunteers. These figures on the volunteers are from Bertaud, *Valmy*, pp. 199–200; for their age and military service, see p. 97.

[4] 'Décret de l'Assemblée Nationale [3 July 1791]', Maclure Collection, vol. 842.

During 1791 the line army enlisted more than 50,000 recruits; by the end of the year it had recovered from the losses of 1790 and had a total strength greater than at any time since the beginning of the Revolution. The reform of recruitment practices, the improvements in the treatment and status of line soldiers, and the immediate payment upon enlistment of a large bonus—approximately 100 *livres*—made the line army more attractive to many young Frenchmen than service in the volunteers. Indeed, although it appears that more soldiers left line units to join the volunteers, it is clear that many officers and soldiers also left the volunteer battalions to join the line army. Simple chance also affected recruitment. The choice of enlisting in a volunteer battalion or in a line regiment was often determined by the presence of a recruiter from one army or the other in the potential recruit's town or village. Certainly, the desire to defend France and the Revolution against hostile foreign powers, a trait usually attributed to the volunteers of 1791, cannot be denied the young men who enlisted in the regular army during that year.[1]

The crisis engendered by the King's flight led the Assembly to expand its military forces considerably; it also intensified the suspicions and antagonisms that troubled the line army. Even before this, the Assembly, in spite of its reorganization of military structure and operation, could not be sure that the army would serve it effectively and loyally. In the spring of 1791 it had taken new steps to insure the political loyalty of military personnel. In a measure directed against officers who might be hostile to the Revolution, a decree of 4 March prohibited captains who had not rejoined their regiments since 10 October 1789 from being appointed aides-de-camp. Reversing its previous position, in early May the Assembly restored to military personnel the right to attend political meetings while off duty, a right of which they had been deprived after the Nancy mutiny.[2] These decisions neither guaranteed allegiance nor healed the breach between officers and men.

The Varennes episode exploded tensions within the army. Following the King's arrest hundreds of officers refused the new civic oath which made no reference to the King; in subsequent months thousands resigned and emigrated; and by the end of 1791 a substantial majority of the pre-revolutionary officer corps had left the

---

[1] Scott, 'Regeneration of the Line Army', p. 322.
[2] Picq, *Législation militaire*, p. 285 and the decree of the National Assembly of 1 May 1791 in A.D., Bas-Rhin 1L 1439.

army. Both a cause and a result of this was a new wave of soldiers' mutinies that surpassed in intensity those of the previous two years. Meanwhile, rumours of foreign invasion swept the frontier regions of France, and civil disorders within the country multiplied. In Paris a demonstration of some 50,000 people supporting a radical revision of the new constitution led to the 'massacre of the Champ de Mars' on 17 July. More than ever before the Assembly needed a reliable army; and it made frantic efforts to restore military discipline and morale.

The government's problem was a massive and wellnigh insoluble one: to restore discipline among an insubordinate but largely loyal soldiery and simultaneously to assure the political allegiance of a disillusioned and hostile officer corps.[1] Almost of necessity the Assembly's policies were equivocal. On 24 June army commanders were authorized to suspend officers whose loyalty was suspect. A month later the legislature attempted to stem the tide of resignations and emigrations. All officers who had left their posts since 1 May without resigning and who had 'passed to the enemy' were to be treated as deserters; those who had resigned before emigrating were given six weeks to return to France before being put in the same category; those who had left their posts but remained in France were barred forever from military service.

On the other hand, on 30 June the Assembly formally admonished French soldiers that the strength of the new constitution depended upon their submission to the law and obedience to their officers. The next month unit councils, composed of officers, were empowered to dismiss enlisted men for insubordination, but only on the complaint of men in the unit of the same or lower rank. At the same time, the Assembly ordered the reinstatement of all officers who had been forced to leave their regiment, provided they took the new oath of allegiance. Furthermore, in units where officers had been chased off promotions were suspended until a thorough investigation had been conducted and any culpable participants punished. A decree of 6 August provided additional penalties, loss of citizenship and dishonourable discharge, for soldiers involved in 'seditions', while simultaneously guaranteeing the right of every

---

[1] Government legislation to resolve these problems, which is described in the following paragraphs, can be found in Cahen and Goyot, *L'Oeuvre législative de la Révolution*, p. 287; A.D., Bas Rhin 1L 1446 and 1L 1439; 'Décret de l'Assemblée Nationale du 30 Juin 1791, Concernant le changement des Drapeux dans l'Armée Françoise', Maclure Collection, vol. 842; and A.N., Dxv 5, dossier 45, pièce 12.

soldier to appeal to his superiors and even directly to the National Assembly. Continuing mutinies, especially that of the 38th Infantry at Nîmes and of the 17th Infantry at Phalsbourg, led to harsher legislation in late August. Specific procedures were established for the repression of military insurrections, and severe punishments, including the execution of N.C.O.s and twenty years in chains for privates, were set for recalcitrant mutineers.

Decrees and regulations were incapable of commanding the allegiance of officers or restoring trust and discipline among the soldiers. The bitter divisions within the army continued, to be resolved ultimately by the participants themselves. The impotence of the legislature was aggravated by its continued vacillation in dealing with military insubordination. On 14 September 1791 the Assembly largely reversed the harsh but decisive legislation of the previous month; it decreed a general amnesty for all army personnel accused, indicted, or convicted of any military offence since 1 June 1789 and ordered the release of those still in custody.[1]

At the beginning of October the Legislative Assembly replaced the National Assembly. One difficulty requiring immediate attention was the serious shortage of officers due to the exodus since June. This made it impossible to continue to demand examinations of most officer candidates; too many vacancies had developed in too short a time. On 29 November the Assembly ordered that half of the vacant second-lieutenancies in infantry and cavalry units should be filled by N.C.O.s in those units on the basis of length of service, although restrictions on the promotion of N.C.O.s in regiments where there had been mutinies were maintained. The other half of the appointments were to be allotted to members of the National Guard and volunteers. Line units soon began to approach their full complement of officers once again. Exams were still required of artillery and engineer officer candidates, but in February 1792 questions on the constitution were added to the tests.[2]

Despite the persistence of major problems, the line army exhibited clear signs of recovery by the beginning of 1792.[3] This revival was

---

[1] A copy of this law is in A.N., F⁷3683⁵.

[2] Picq, *Législation militaire*, p. 291 and Reinhard, 'Armée et Révolution', fascicule 1, p. 5.

[3] Most historians, ignoring or ignorant of the important changes in the line army during this period, describe the army by 1792 in the most pessimistic terms. See, for example, Hampson, *Social History*, p. 138; Soboul, *Armée nationale*, p. 70; and J. M. Thompson, *The French Revolution* (New York, 1966), p. 291.

the result of official policies, independent developments within the army, and the growing likelihood of war. Although regular units remained understrength, this was primarily due to the recent authorization of wartime complements, an increase of more than 350 men per infantry regiment; and recruitment was progressing satisfactorily. The reconstitution of the officer corps, still incomplete, was well under way; and the new officers were perhaps more skilled and certainly more devoted than the old. In addition, the voluntary and involuntary purge of noble officers and their replacement by men from the ranks was improving morale and discipline. Finally, as more and more regular forces were transferred to the frontiers, their involvement in civil conflicts declined and their prestige, as the backbone of national defence, increased.

With war a virtual certainty in the near future the Legislative Assembly devoted even more attention to the line army during the first months of 1792. In order to bring the strength of regular units to a war footing, it passed the decree of 25 January 1792, calling for new recruitment efforts by local authorities and improving the terms of enlistment. The age-limit for recruits was extended to 50 and the height requirements reduced to 5 feet 4 inches in the infantry and 5 feet 7 inches in the cavalry and artillery. The term of enlistment was restricted to three years, or less under certain conditions. Enlistment bonuses were retained, 80 *livres* in the infantry and 120 *livres* in other branches, with additional amounts for recruits with previous military service.[1]

Civil authorities on departmental and district levels co-operated in encouraging enlistments, and despite some problems of application—e.g. the recruitment of men who were physically unfit, objections to payment in paper *assignats*, uncertainty about the eligibility of married men—the results were impressive.[2] For example, when Colonel Boulard took command of the 60th Infantry in January 1792 he had only 768 men in his regiment; three months later there were over 1,200.[3] By early April at least four regiments stationed in the department of the Nord (the 1st, 24th, 36th, and 56th Infantry) had reached full strength and asked that no more

---

[1] This decree is reproduced in B.-C. Gournay, ed., *Journal militaire*, V (Paris, 1792), 67-71.
[2] A.G., X^d 7 and 16; A.D., Nord L 8546; and A.G., X^w 73 provide examples of these problems.
[3] See the letters of Boulard, dated 26 Mar. and 20 Apr. 1792, in A.G., X^b 184.

recruits be sent to them.[1] Meanwhile, regimental personnel and professional recruiters continued to enlist men by more traditional methods. By June 1792 over 24,000 men had enlisted in the line army.[2]

During the spring the Assembly took other steps to increase the army's strength and maintain it at the desired level. On 10 March it decreed that former members of the French Guards could re-enlist and draw pay at the same rate as if there had been no interruption of service.[3] The number of discharges in 1792 was drastically reduced, to about 40 per cent of the figure for the previous year.[4] Penalties for returned deserters were made more lenient, usually only a few months in prison, after which they returned to their unit.[5]

The men recruited into the line army by these policies, along with the soldiers who entered it before 1792, often displayed the patriotism and revolutionary fervour usually attributed exclusively to the volunteers. The men of the 5th Artillery, for example, wrote to the Assembly in March 1792. They had heard, they said, that a proposal had been made to increase the pay of line troops. In light of the great suffering in France and the pressing needs of the state, these soldiers asked that the proposal be withdrawn since they fought not for money, but for liberty. There were 229 signatures on this petition.[6] Earlier, in July 1791, the men of the 53rd and 81st Infantry Regiments had received a commendation from the National Assembly for their contributions to the refurbishing of the fortifications of Givet.[7] In December of the same year troops from the 23rd Infantry and 7th Chasseurs wrote to General Luckner that they would show 'the despots on the other bank of the Rhine' that they were invincible, and promised to defend the nation 'to the death'.[8] When the 34th Infantry marched into Châlons-sur-Marne on its way to the front on 1 April 1792, its entire complement was singing the *Ça ira*.[9]

---

[1] A.D., Nord L 8546.

[2] Desbrière and Sautai, *La Cavalerie, 1789–1794*, p. 66.

[3] A.G., X^w 73, dossier 1.

[4] Scott, 'Regeneration of the Line Army', p. 326. For a specific example of this policy, see a *mémoire*, dated 8 Mar. 1792, in A.G., X^d 7.

[5] There are a number of cases of this in A.G., B^{13} 69.

[6] 'Adresse des sous-officiers et soldats du cinquième régiment d'artillerie à l'Assemblée Nationale, lue à la Séance du 3 Avril 1792', Maclure Collection, vol. 1018.

[7] A.D., Bas-Rhin 38J 178.

[8] A.D., Bas-Rhin 38J 179.

[9] Mangerel, *Capitaine Gerbaud*, p. 58.

More than numbers and enthusiasm, however, was necessary. The new recruits had to be organized into units, equipped, and trained before they could usefully be employed in combat; and this could not be achieved overnight. Recognizing these problems, the government issued new regulations on 15 March 1792. Each line regiment was ordered to furnish one battalion at full strength plus the company of grenadiers from the second battalion for immediate front-line duty under the command of the colonel of the regiment. The second battalion, under the lieutenant-colonel, would remain behind to garrison fortifications and to equip and train recruits. In the cavalry, one squadron out of three or four in each regiment would be left behind the combat zone for the same purpose.[1]

To provide adequately for such forces was an enormous task. On 16 April 1792 the Assembly removed the supply of food and forage from the competence of the individual units and restored this function to private companies under contract to the state.[2] The burden of lodging and supplying troops in transit remained, as always, on the inhabitants of the areas through which the soldiers passed. With the enormous troop movements in early 1792, especially in the frontier departments of the north and east, public funds were required to enable many communities to meet these obligations.[3]

Before these preparations could be completed, France went to war in April 1792. The first months of the war proved that the recent changes in the army had not yet been fully assimilated and that the disorganization within the army during the first three years of the Revolution was not yet completely eliminated. In the earliest engagements many line troops broke and ran, complaining that they had been betrayed by their commanding officers. Desertion rates increased dramatically, doubling in the cavalry.[4] During the summer the military situation continued to deteriorate and foreign armies advanced into France.

The government responded with yet more massive mobilization.

---

[1] Picq, *Législation militaire*, p. 142.

[2] Ibid., p. 213.

[3] For examples of this, see A.D., Isère L 68, *passim* and the letters from the departmental directory of the Meuse to the Minister of the Interior, dated 15 May 1792, and from the Minister of the Interior to the departmental administrators of the Ardennes, dated 5 Nov. 1792, in A.N., F^{9}129.

[4] Scott, 'Regeneration of the Line Army', pp. 311 and 323-6.

In May 74,000 additional volunteers were called up to bring existing battalions to full strength and to man thirty-one new battalions. On 11 July the Assembly declared 'the fatherland in danger' and called for 33,600 more national volunteers.[1] For this levy, height requirements were abolished, the minimum age for enlistment was reduced from 18 to 16, and the previous distinction between active and passive citizens (only the former could officially serve in the National Guard) was ignored.[2] Like their predecessors, the volunteers of 1792 enlisted for one year, elected their officers, received the same pay, and enjoyed a relatively mild discipline. Local officials implemented the levy however they could in order to fulfil departmental quotas.[3] In general, these recruits came from lower social classes and more rural areas than in 1791. Approximately half their officers were former N.C.O.s in the line army.[4]

The concern of the Legislative Assembly to strengthen the volunteer battalions in no way implied neglect of the line army, which most legislators and almost all military men felt would bear the burden of the war. On 22 July the Assembly called upon the departments to furnish 50,000 recruits for the regular army. The conditions of enlistment and service were the same as those set in January. The truly innovative aspect of this decree was that, contrary to all previous legislation on recruitment of the line army, a quota, ranging from 100 to 2,400 men, was placed on each department. Furthermore, the departmental directories were to receive a sum of 10 *livres* for each recruit, to encourage the full implementation of the law and to defray the costs of supervising recruitment.[5] This decree and its predecessor in January were enormously successful. During 1792 more than 70,000 men enlisted in the line army, an impressive achievement under any circumstances and particularly impressive in view of the great competition for recruits from the volunteer battalions.[6]

[1] For details on this levy, see Gournay, *Journal militaire*, V. 422–9.

[2] Mathiez, *La Victoire en l'an II*, p. 74 and Albert Soboul, *Les Soldats de l'an II* (Paris, 1959), p. 192.

[3] Pierre Caron, *La Défense nationale de 1792 à 1795* (Paris, 1912), pp. 2–5.

[4] Mathiez, *La Victoire en l'an II*, pp. 78–9; Soboul, *Soldats de l'an II*, p. 87; Bertaud, *Valmy*, pp. 239 and 244; and Serge-William Serman and Jean-Paul Bertaud, *Vie et psychologie des combattants et gens de guerres: Questions de méthodes et de documentation, y compris l'iconographie. Armée francaise de terre: Officiers, sous-officiers et soldats, 1635–1945* (Paris, 1970), pp. 39 and 59.

[5] Gournay, *Journal militaire*, V. 415–34.

[6] Specific examples of the success of this policy can be found in Bernard Mouillard,

Because more advanced technical training was necessary for artillerymen, this branch could not afford the time to train raw recruits in the basic tasks of the soldier. Consequently, the artillery accepted only enlistees with previous military service.[1] This required the transfer of large numbers of infantrymen to artillery regiments during the summer of 1792. For example, 447 soldiers from ten infantry regiments joined the 5th Artillery in July and August; over 300 transferred into the 7th Artillery in August; and between August and September 195 men from six infantry regiments joined the 2nd Artillery.[2]

The influx of recruits into line units, especially infantry units, minimized the difference between the line regiments and the volunteer battalions. Dumouriez's observation in July 1792 that both regulars and volunteers were '. . . all equally new and inexperienced' was only a slight exaggeration.[3] This similarity would later facilitate the amalgamation of both forces into a single, homogeneous army; but at the time it complicated the already immense military task facing France.

Although the overthrow of the monarchy on 10 August 1792 committed the Assembly more thoroughly to a prosecution of the war against France's monarchial enemies, the foreign invaders continued to advance. By September, after the capitulation of Longwy and Verdun, Paris itself was in jeopardy. French authorities did all in their power to bolster the sagging front. Although they had been dismissed from French service only a short time before because of popular hostility, the discharged Swiss soldiers, well disciplined, fully trained, and ready for combat, were too attractive a source of manpower to be ignored; and every effort was made to enlist them. Between their official discharge on 20 August and the actual disbanding of these regiments in the autumn of 1792,

---

Le Recruitement de l'armée révolutionnare dans le Puy-de-Dôme (Clermont-Ferrand, 1926), pp. 13-14; Lieutenant de Cardenal, *Recrutement de l'armée en Périgord pendant la période révolutionnaire* (Perigueux, 1911), pp. 104-5 and 109; Choppin, *Notes sur l'organisation de l'armée*, p. 36; Sagnier, *Désertion dans le Pas-de-Calais*, p. 41; and A.G., X^w 73. See also Scott, 'Regeneration of the Line Army', p. 325.

[1] See the letter from the municipal officers of Douai, dated 6 Sept. 1792, A.G., I, X^w 73.

[2] See the uncoded troop registers for these units during the period specified for each of them.

[3] Dumouriez, *Mémoires*, I. 242. General Biron confirmed this observation in his letter to Servan, dated 7 Sept. 1792, in which he said: 'The majority of the line troops of the army is composed of recruits.' This quotation can be found in Bertaud, *Valmy*, p. 168.

between 3,000 and 4,000 Swiss soldiers enlisted in the French Army.[1]

Thus, the French government in its struggle to survive was making every effort to strengthen and improve the line army. Its policies, which ranged from well-conceived technical reforms to *ad hoc* emergency measures, helped to transform the regular army from a typical eighteenth-century institution into a prototype of the armies of the nineteenth and twentieth centuries.

The extensive and rapid changes undergone by the Royal Army in the first three years of the Revolution were a product of its own peculiar situation and of larger developments in civil society. While it continued to perform police functions as in the past, the revolutionary crisis drastically increased the demand for such service and involved numerous line units in political conflicts that often strained and sometimes broke traditional discipline. Inevitably the army became politicized. Its police role necessarily exposed its personnel to the disputes that divided the civilian population; and since the army's response could determine success or failure for opposing interests, civilian factions made great efforts to win officers and soldiers to their cause. Even had they so desired, military personnel could not have remained untouched by the political upheaval. Beyond this, officers and soldiers alike had a professional and personal interest in the policies of the Revolution; and they came to view and express this interest increasingly in political terms.

The highest revolutionary authorities, the deputies to the first two National Assemblies, were vitally concerned with the loyalty and efficiency of the line army and attempted to ensure these qualities by legislative reforms. Efforts were made to provide some political education for the armed forces, notably by the federation movement and the establishment of new revolutionary standards and principles. At the same time, the government substantially revised military organization and set new regulations governing the functioning of the army. Despite the impressive results of these reforms, however, the deputies were powerless to resolve the most critical internal problem of the army: the relentless conflict between soldiers and officers. Ultimately, this difficulty was solved by the independent action of the participants which resulted in a substantial

---

[1] Examples of the recruitment of the Swiss are in Bertaud, *Valmy*, p. 223; Jules Vassias, *Historique du 69e Régiment d'Infanterie (1672–1912)* (Paris, 1913), p. 35; A.D., Nord L 6760; and A.G., X^w 73.

reconstitution of the officer corps. By 1792 the line army was officered mostly by professional soldiers with extensive experience who were, for various reasons, committed to the Revolution. Under these professionals served a rank-and-file far more politicized than other contemporary armies.

Developments over which neither the government nor the army exercised complete control also had a profound influence upon civil-military relations. The most important of these was the war, which in a somewhat perverse way facilitated military recovery and led to the re-establishment of civilian authority over the army. The war and its early results encouraged further purges of officers considered politically unreliable and necessitated their rapid replacement by men more acceptable to both soldiers and civil officials. The war also led the legislature to implement revised and vastly expanded recruitment policies, including limited conscription, which revivified the ranks of the line army. In addition, the war helped to alleviate problems which arose from the politicization of the army. Many line troops had been displaying a growing tendency to intervene in political issues, often in support of the more radical civilian elements and independently of the established authorities. The incidents at Marseille, Lyon, and Arles treated above are examples of this. The war allowed the government to harness pro-revolutionary enthusiasm and direct it against foreign enemies. The early crises created by the war also pointed out the need to strengthen the authority of the central government over the army. The departure of most regular units for the front withdrew them from civilian disputes and virtually eliminated their police functions in the interior, duties which were often objectionable to the soldiers and almost always unpopular with citizens. Finally, the requirements of war demanded the induction of tens of thousands of civilians, increased the prestige of military service, and united soldiers and citizens in a common cause.

All the changes in the army since the beginning of the Revolution, from the earliest reforms in 1789 to the desperate measures of the government in the summer of 1792, whether brought about by intra-military quarrels, government policies, or the conditions imposed by the war, were now to be put to a critical test. In the early autumn of 1792 the line army had to prove whether or not it was capable of performing its primary mission of defending the country. Its success would determine the fate of France and the Revolution.

CHAPTER V

THE END OF THE LINE ARMY

IN THE critical campaign of 1792 the regular troops, along with the national volunteers, proved that they were indeed able to defend France against enemy attack. Although the French army was seriously weakened during that winter and suffered a series of military setbacks in 1793, the victories of the previous autumn assured the survival of the new regime.

In February 1793 the government made two major decisions affecting the army; it ordered the largest levy of troops up to that time and simultaneously decreed the amalgamation of the line army with the units of national volunteers. A number of considerations were responsible for this unprecedented decision. A national, citizen army—rather than the professional army associated with the development of the monarchy in France—alone appeared to be compatible with the prevailing political ideology. The practical difficulties arising from the maintenance of two separate armies seriously hampered national defence. And the extensive changes in the composition of the former Royal Army greatly facilitated such a merger. Although it had recovered from its most serious problems and constituted about three-quarters of the effective strength of all military forces, the line army was officially disestablished as a distinct organization in February 1793.

Besides providing a nucleus of organized and trained soldiers in the ranks of the new integrated army, regulars also contributed much of its leadership. Veterans of the old Royal Army alone could furnish the experience required to train and command the hundreds of thousands of recent recruits from the volunteers of 1791 and 1792, from the new levy of 300,000 men, and from the line army itself. (For, as a result of massive changes in personnel since 1789, even the regular army in 1793 was composed, in large measure, of civilians from all regions of the country who had only recently been inducted into military service.) A necessary corollary of this huge, national, citizen army was a professional officer corps that could effectively direct such a force. In 1793 the officers of the line army alone could accomplish this task. These men, who would lead the new armies of the Revolution and later those of the Empire, had the necessary experience and education. Despite variations in their civilian background, these officers, from second-lieutenant to lieutenant-general, possessed the professional qualifications required for the operation of a modern army.

THE WAR AND THE 'AMALGAM'

In the late summer of 1792 the foreign invasion of France continued to make progress. On 16 August an army under the Duke of Brunswick crossed the French frontier and soon laid siege to the fortress-town of Longwy. The garrison, composed of a regiment of hussars, a regiment of line infantry, and three battalions of volunteers, was commanded by Lieutenant-Colonel Lavergne-Champlorier, who had resigned from the line army as a captain before 1789, was selected as the commander of the National Guard of his canton, and then rejoined the line army with the coming of the war. Although prepared for a strong defence, Lavergne was forced by the civilian administration to capitulate on 23 August, because these officials feared further destruction of their town.[1]

The fall of Longwy greatly increased the threat to France but did not seem to dampen the ardour of the line soldiers. The men of the 67th Infantry sent an address to the Legislative Assembly promising that they would defend Neuf-Brisach more honourably than Longwy had been defended.[2] Louis-François Jeannet, a nephew of Danton and a second-lieutenant in the 5th Dragoons, had a more dramatic reaction to the fall of Longwy: 'We shall show them [enemies and traitors] that we are soldiers of the fatherland, that we know how to cleanse in their blood the opprobrium with which the cowardly garrison of Longwy has covered us.'[3]

Such sentiments were not sufficient, however, to turn back the Prussian and Austrian armies. Verdun, another key fortress, was put under siege. The officer in command of the garrison was Lieutenant-Colonel Beaurepaire, a former officer of fortune in the line army who had been elected commander of the 1st Battalion of the volunteers of the Maine-et-Loire. Like his counterpart at Longwy, Beaurepaire was pressured by the civilians of Verdun to surrender the place

---

[1] Chuquet, *Première invasion prussienne*, pp. 178–83.
[2] Chuquet, *Lettres de 1792*, p. 164.
[3] Ibid., p. 168.

rather than endure further bombardment. But before the official capitulation was signed on 3 September, Beaurepaire committed suicide rather than face such dishonour.[1] Now, Paris itself was directly threatened.

Dumouriez, who had taken command of Lafayette's army after his emigration, attempted to join his forces with the army of General Kellermann in Champagne, in order to stop the advance of Brunswick. On 16 September, near Montcheutin, elements of Dumouriez's army made contact with a small enemy force. Their reaction was to flee and as they fled they spread panic by crying that they had been betrayed and that all their generals had gone over to the enemy. Dumouriez and his subordinates finally succeeded in rallying their men after considerable effort. However, the flight of an army of 10,000 at the sight of 1,500 Prussian cavalrymen was not an incident to instil confidence.[2] Besides, the generals had little faith in the battalions of volunteers who now comprised a substantial portion of both Dumouriez's and Kellermann's armies. These soldiers had selected their own officers, often for reasons that had nothing to do with military ability. Furthermore, their rather lax discipline was a scandal to most line officers.[3]

When the armies of Dumouriez and Kellermann effected their juncture near Valmy on 19 September, there was little reason for confidence in a French victory. The very positioning of the opposing forces was cause for alarm; although the French had selected a strong position, it was located between the Prussians and the frontier. If the French were repulsed at Valmy, there was nothing to prevent a victory parade by Brunswick's army into Paris.

The battle at Valmy took place between 7 a.m. and 8 p.m. on 20 September.[4] Both opponents had suffered from fatiguing marches, poor weather, and a shortage of supplies. The French with 52,000 soldiers had an advantage in manpower over the Prussians whose forces amounted to 34,000. The Prussian cannon outnumbered the French artillery by 58 pieces to 40. In some ways the engagement was an example of the careful tactics of the eighteenth century: much manœuvring, little hand-to-hand fighting, few

---

[1] Chuquet, *Première invasion prussienne*, pp. 221-59.
[2] Dumouriez, *Mémoires*, I. 283-5 and Arthur Chuquet, *Valmy* (Paris, 1887), pp. 137-8.
[3] Dumouriez, *Mémoires*, I. 288 and Soboul, *Soldats de l'an II*, p. 169.
[4] No detailed description of the battle will be given here. For specific military details see Chuquet, *Valmy*; for a more general description of the situation in France and especially for information on the French combatants, see Bertaud, *Valmy*.

casualties, and victory by the army which retained its position on the battlefield. On the other hand, there were elements of the combat that presaged a 'new era': the use of massed artillery that decided the day, the songs and slogans of the French which made this a political as well as a military conflict, and the employment of large numbers of non-professional soldiers.

Almost all of the artillery and cavalry units used by the French at Valmy were from the line army. Nearly half of the infantry, however, was composed of volunteer battalions, which constituted 31 of the 75 infantry battalions at Valmy.[1] Moreover, more than half of the soldiers in the line units at Valmy had enlisted since the beginning of the Revolution, and more than a quarter of them had served in the army for less than one year.[2] There can be little doubt that line troops were largely, if not primarily responsible for the French victory of Valmy. It must be emphasized, however, that these line soldiers were quite different from what they had been before the Revolution. By their age and length of service they bore a closer resemblance to their comrades in the volunteer battalions than they did to the long-term, professional soldiers of the Old Regime.

The battle of Valmy turned back the foreign invasion and saved the new regime in France. The very day that the battle took place the National Convention, which shortly afterwards declared the Republic, began its sessions. For the line army too this victory represented a turning-point. Valmy was the first clear indication, if not conclusive evidence, that the army had survived the crises of the past three years. Most of the French troops, whether regulars or volunteers, were not committed to action and the combat itself was above all an artillery duel. Nonetheless, the French guns were served almost exclusively by men from the Royal Army, both artillerymen and former line infantrymen recently inducted into the artillery. Furthermore, although few infantry or cavalry troops were engaged except for reconnaissance, the French forces stood their ground and displayed considerable spirit under enemy bombardment. The success provided the French forces with the self-confidence that they had been lacking since the beginning of the war.

The French did not, however, press their advantage after the

---

[1] Godechot, *Institutions de la France*, p. 138.

[2] These proportions are based upon a 3% sample of six infantry and six cavalry regiments that served at Valmy. The proportion of men with brief service was somewhat higher in the infantry than in the cavalry.

victory. Despite their enthusiasm, they too, like the Prussians, were exhausted from their recent exertions. Furthermore, the generals were not entirely convinced that the tide had turned. Only days before the battle, the French soldiers had panicked; and there was no guarantee that they would not do so in their next confrontation with the enemy. Besides, Dumouriez saw in the recent victory an opportunity to conclude a separate peace with Prussia and even possibly an anti-Austrian alliance with that power. This would give Dumouriez the advantage that he needed to achieve successfully his pet project, the conquest of Belgium.[1]

Within a few days of Valmy, other French armies began to take the offensive. During the night of 21–22 September, General Montesquiou invaded Savoy and by the end of the month he had successfully occupied this region and Nice. On 29 September, General Custine began his invasion of the Rhineland from Alsace. Within a month his army had taken Spire, Worms, Mainz, and Frankfurt. On 23 October, General Kellermann ordered the firing of three salvoes to announce that no enemy remained on the soil of the Republic.[2] At the end of October, Dumouriez launched an army of 40,000 men into Belgium.

As Dumouriez advanced into Belgium he met an enemy army near Jemappes on 6 November. Dumouriez's army was composed largely of men, both line troops and volunteers, who had already seen service in combat. His infantry consisted of thirty-two battalions from the line army and thirty-eight battalions of volunteers. Dumouriez deployed his infantry in brigades, most of which were composed of both line and volunteer units. Besides ten regiments of regular cavalry, he had in his command four mounted free corps. His artillery was manned by men from line regiments.[3] Most of the officers were experienced veterans who together commanded forces approximately three times the strength of the enemy.

The different components of Dumouriez's army all fought well in this battle. An attack by his first line, including regular and volunteer battalions, was broken twice by Austrian fire; but the French continued to re-form and ultimately broke into the town of

[1] Arthur Chuquet, *La Retraite de Brunswick* (Paris, 1887), pp. 173–4 and Ramsay W. Phipps, *The Armies of the First French Republic and the Rise of the Marshals of Napoleon*, vol. I (London, 1926), p. 134.

[2] Chuquet, *Retraite de Brunswick*, p. 208 and Phipps, *Armies of the First Republic*, II. 31

[3] Arthur Chuquet, *Jemappes et la conquête de la Belgique* (Paris, 1890), pp. 72–3 and 106.

Jemappes. When a gap was made in the French line and some troops began to flee, the Duc de Chartres, who was later to become King Louis-Philippe, rallied the soldiers; and by throwing two cavalry regiments and two line infantry regiments into the breach, he was able to force the Austrian troops back. Later in the day, a more serious penetration of Dumouriez's right wing was halted and turned back when a number of the line and volunteer units in this sector rallied and, singing the *Marseillaise*, turned on their attackers and drove them off. By the end of the battle the Austrians had been thoroughly defeated and Belgium lay open to the French.[1]

Although Valmy was more important as a political and symbolic victory, Jemappes was a more significant proof of the military quality of the French army. At Valmy the French artillery had carried the day, but there had been little hand-to-hand combat. Although artillery was also of crucial importance at Jemappes, the French infantry and cavalry had shown themselves to be the equal of the Austrian troops. The French, of course, had a substantial numerical superiority; but, if they had not also had the ability and resoluteness to stand up to the enemy, no advantage in strength could have compensated for such fatal deficiencies. Both line and volunteer units proved that in addition to numbers and enthusiasm, they had courage and military competence in a pitched battle. Five line regiments and five volunteer battalions from the levy of 1791 were especially cited for their contributions to the victory.[2] According to Dumouriez: 'There was not a unit in the French army that was not [at one time] beaten, and that did not close with the enemy with cold steel.'[3]

The significance of these military successes in the autumn of 1792 —and the contribution of the men of the Royal Army to them—can hardly be exaggerated. Defeat would undoubtedly have changed the course of the Revolution in a drastic fashion and might well have substantially altered the fate of Europe during this period. The victories, however, represented a stage in the development of the Revolution and of the French army rather than a terminal point. Shortly afterwards the military situation deteriorated seriously and the army was completely reorganized.

During the winter of 1792–3 a series of problems, most of them

---

[1] Ibid., pp. 92–102. The casualties were about even, between 4,000 and 5,000 on each side.

[2] Ibid., p. 103.

[3] Dumouriez, *Mémoires*, I. 373.

beyond military control, led to the debilitation of the French armies. Tens of thousands of national volunteers who had enlisted for one campaign, i.e. until 1 December 1792, began to return to their families, homes, and jobs; by the beginning of 1793 some 60,000 had left the ranks. Having fulfilled their obligation and secured France against foreign attack, they refused to pursue the enemy beyond the frontiers.[1] In addition, totally inadequate logistical preparations created shortages of necessities: food, clothing, equipment, firewood, weapons, ammunition, forage, draft animals— virtually everything. Furthermore, the inefficiency and corruption of agencies responsible for supplying the army seriously hampered the delivery of those goods that were available.[2] Local resources could not compensate for these deficiencies because the inhabitants of occupied areas, especially Belgium, refused to accept payment for products and services in the paper *assignats* which had become the currency of the Revolution. This led to pillage by the soldiers which, in turn, aroused local hostility and sometimes violence against French troops.[3] This last situation compounded the feeling of isolation and loneliness that made homesickness, *mal du pays*, a serious problem among the French soldiers, many of whom were for the first time cut off from the secure and familiar confines of their village or town.[4]

Along with these difficulties and in part because of them, suspicion of the remaining noble officers—particularly at the highest echelons—flourished. The emigration of Lafayette lent credence to such attitudes and politicians, journalists, and Jacobin clubs encouraged them. Robespierre and Saint-Just feared that a successful

---

[1] Chuquet, *Jemappes*, pp. 130–3; Leverrier, *Naissance de l'armée nationale*, p. 298; and Baron Louis-Joseph Lahure, *Souvenirs de la vie militaire du lieutenant-général Baron L.-J. Lahure, 1787–1815* (Paris, 1895), pp. 32–3.

[2] Dumouriez, *Mémoires*, I. 387–403; Money, *Campaign of 1792*, pp. 202–4; Simon, *Correspondance*, p. 51; 'Observations générales sur l'administration des hôpitaux ambulans et sédentaires des armées de la République française', dated 1 Mar. 1793, Maclure Collection, vol. 967; Chuquet, *Jemappes*, pp. 166 and 173; and Charles Poisson, *Les Fournisseurs aux armées sous la Révolution française: Le Directoire des achats (1792–1793): J. Bidermann, Cousin, Marx-Berr* (Paris, 1932), esp. pp. 209, 223–4, 246–8, 231, and 295.

[3] The best-documented example of these conditions is Belgium. See Dumouriez, *Mémoires*, II. 12 and Poisson, *L'Armée et la Garde Nationale*, II. 124–8.

[4] On this fascinating problem, see the brilliant article of Marcel Reinhard, 'Nostalgie et service militaire pendant la Révolution', *Annales historiques de la Révolution française*, XXX (1958), 1–15 and Jean Robiquet, *La Vie quotidienne au temps de la Révolution* (Paris, 1938), pp. 186–7.

general might establish a military dictatorship. Marat, in October 1792, warned that '. . . almost all our generals and almost all our superior officers are creatures of the court.' Popular societies denounced noble officers as traitors.[1] A number of generals were purged from the army. Arthur Dillon was relieved of his command in October, despite his contributions to the military success. General Montesquiou, the conqueror of Nice and Savoy, emigrated in November rather than answer the charges against him. General Kellermann was exonerated from accusations made by General Custine in mid-November; but Custine's days were numbered.[2] The Ministry of War changed hands with alarming frequency. In October Servan resigned from his second term in that office and was replaced by Pache. The latter, a committed Jacobin, began extensive changes to democratize the army but was replaced by Beurnonville on 4 February 1793. Beurnonville's attempts to undo many of his predecessor's reforms increased the chaos.[3] Most of the generals remained suspect. Dumouriez, perhaps the most able and certainly the most mistrusted, was in fact making plans to turn his forces on Paris and become arbiter of the Revolution.[4]

Fortunately for the defence of France, these political developments had little direct effect upon the soldiers. During the winter of 1792–3 most line troops were stationed in battle zones, far removed from such controversies. Their attention was concentrated on the immediate problems facing them and they had little time or interest for anything else. The soldiers, volunteers and regulars alike, were largely unconcerned even with such a monumental event as the trial and execution of Louis XVI.[5] Major developments at home might briefly arouse the soldiers' concern '. . . but a shot or two fired on an outpost makes them look forward and forget the victims that fall behind them to consider those that are to fall before them'.[6] As the immediacy of political conflicts faded, the marked decline in instances of insubordination, that had begun with the war, continued during the first months of 1793. Desertion, usually related to the conditions of warfare, remained an important problem, but hostile confrontations between officers and men on the regimental level

[1] Bertaud, *Valmy*, pp. 125–7.
[2] Poisson, *L'Armée et la Garde Nationale*, II. 47–55.
[3] Mathiez, *French Revolution*, pp. 296–7 and Chuquet, *Jemappes*, pp. 144–6.
[4] Dumouriez, *Mémoires*, I. 397–8 and II. 86–7.
[5] Ibid., I. 409 and II. 14.
[6] Money, *Campaign of 1792*, pp. 297–8.

were rare.[1] These had been mitigated or ended in most units by the replacement of most Old Regime officers and by the increased dependence between soldiers and officers bred by combat. This is not to say that there were no conflicts within line regiments; denunciations and dismissals of noble officers did occur, but much less frequently.[2] By early 1793 nobles constituted only 15-20 per cent of the officer corps and many of them, especially in the lower grades, had the confidence and respect of their men. A more common but less violent competition emerged between N.C.O.s of the regular army and citizens from the National Guard or volunteer battalions for commissions in line units. The old soldiers often resented the appointment of outsiders, especially when they had little prior military experience.[3] This problem was part of a broader rivalry between the regulars and the volunteers. Although employed together for tactical purposes, the soldiers from both forces served in completely distinct organizations; and this sometimes led to controversies between 'the cornflowers' (named after the blue uniforms of the volunteers) and 'the white bottoms' of the former Royal Army.[4] These quarrels arose from the normal rivalry between different units and from the peculiar characteristics of the two armies. The line troops disdained the military qualities of the citizen-soldiers, and the volunteers distrusted the army which had so long served the Kings of France. Yet this rivalry can be, and sometimes is, emphasized to the exclusion of the bonds which existed between the soldiers of both armies. In April 1792 at the camp of Tiercelet, for example, the volunteers, who comprised about half of the 6,000 soldiers in the camp, did not have enough cartridges. The regular troops there shared theirs with the volunteers, and both groups took an oath of fraternity between them.[5] After the battle of Jemappes, the line soldiers congratulated the volunteers for their

---

[1] In Jan. and Feb. 1793 only 5 of the 73 units studied throughout the period 1788-93 suffered from problems of discipline. In every one of these cases the insubordination consisted of large-scale desertion (i.e. the desertion of 10% or more of the units' strength, projected over twelve months on the basis of desertions during the first two months of the year). In none of these instances does it appear that civilian encouragement played a role. See the section on 'Incidence of Insubordination' in Appendix I.

[2] For an example of continuing purges in line regiments, see Caron, *Défense nationale*, pp. 44-6.

[3] Examples of this rivalry can be found in A.G., X^b 172, letter of Col. Lagardeolle, dated 16 June 1792; A.G., X^b 163, letter of the N.C.O.s of the second battalion of the 4th Infantry, dated 29 Aug. 1792; and Mangerel, *Capitaine Gerbaud*, p. 89.

[4] Soboul, *Armée nationale*, p. 90.

[5] Bertaud, *Valmy*, p. 214.

important contribution to the victory, and all joined in fraternal celebrations.[1] Furthermore, some of the antagonisms which existed between the soldiers were totally unrelated to service in line or volunteer units. The soldiers on the front lines, both regulars and volunteers, resented those left behind in the depots; and many quarrels within the army, e.g. over the selection of new officers or the use of unit funds, arose from this rivalry which had nothing to do with 'blues' and 'whites'.[2]

A more serious problem for the government was the drastic decline in the strength of the French armies. In February 1793 there were *c*. 228,000 soldiers in the armies of the Republic (all but *c*. 50,000 of them in line units), while two months earlier there had been nearly 400,000. Furthermore, the enemies of France were beginning to rally from their unexpected defeats of the autumn. The situation required vigorous action and on 24 February 1793 the Convention ordered a new levy of 300,000 men to fill the depleted ranks of the army. All French males between 18 and 40 years of age who were bachelors or widowers without children were eligible for this requisition. Each department was to furnish a number of men in proportion to its population. The departments, in turn, settled on the requirements from each district and the districts passed these on to the communities. The required number of recruits was to be raised by voluntary enlistments or, failing that, by whatever means was decided upon by the local authorities. When enlistments failed to produce a sufficient number of men, the officials usually had recourse to selection by lot or by vote of all the citizens. Anyone selected by these means was allowed the alternative of providing a replacement.[3]

The response to the new levy varied considerably from one department to another; but, in all, only about half of the 300,000 men were in fact recruited. There were numerous abuses in the selection process which was sometimes used to punish a political minority. Many of the recruits were too young, too old, or otherwise physically unfit. Furthermore, the recruitment took much longer than the government desired.[4]

---

[1] Poisson, *L'Armée et la Garde Nationale*, II. 74.

[2] For an example of this problem, see Samuel Scott and Jean-Paul Bertaud, 'Le 104e Régiment de ligne: Gardes françaises et gardes nationaux parisiens aux armées de la Révolution (1792-1793)', *Études de la région parisienne*, no. 12 (Oct. 1966), p. 9.

[3] Caron, *Défense nationale*, p. 8 and Jaurès, *Histoire socialiste*, VI. 414-15.

[4] Mathiez, *La Victoire en l'an II*, pp. 109-14 and Soboul, *Soldats de l'an II*, pp. 108-12.

On 21 February, three days before ordering the levy of 300,000 men, the Convention had decreed the amalgamation of line and volunteer units into a single force with the same organization, uniform, pay, and regulations. Various mounted units, legions and free corps, which had been raised during the war were later organized as separate regiments of regular cavalry; the Amalgam ordered in February, however, was concerned primarily with the infantry. The new basic tactical unit of the French infantry was to be the 'demi-brigade', composed of two battalions of volunteers and one of line troops.

Since the outbreak of the war volunteer and line units had in fact been employed together in similar or identical formations; and the decree of the Convention simply formalized what was already a frequent practice. Such combinations, however, had been temporary and strictly tactical procedures. For the most part, the regulars and volunteers had served under completely distinct regimes. This situation had seriously hampered the efficient employment of French troops. The multiplicity of different types of units required an excessively complex administration. The varying number of effectives in the different units made it difficult for commanders to estimate accurately the forces under their orders. The higher pay of the volunteers was resented by the regulars and contributed to the hostility between the two forces. The instruction of thousands of new recruits could best be handled by a single agency. And finally, the large number of units multiplied the number of small, ineffective staffs and constituted a serious drain on the available number of experienced officers. Such considerations played an important role in Dubois-Crancé's decision to propose the Amalgam to the National Convention.[1]

The integration of the regular and volunteer forces has usually been presented as an effort to combine the revolutionary enthusiasm of the battalions of national volunteers with the professional skill of the regiments of the line army.[2] This was, undoubtedly, one of the purposes of this policy. However, the practical considerations noted above contributed very significantly to this decision in the crisis of early 1793. Also, it is a gratuitous assumption to assign a monopoly

[1] Charles-Louis Chassin, *L'Armée et la Révolution*, p. 164 and Jung, *Dubois-Crancé*, I. 363 and 368.
[2] See, for example, Levy-Schneider, 'L'Armée et la Convention', pp. 396–7; Soboul, *Soldats de l'an II*, p. 171; and Mathiez, *La Victoire en l'an II*, p. 147.

of patriotism to the volunteers. Since the outbreak of the Revolution the devotion of line troops to the new regime had been evidenced on numerous occasions. This enthusiasm had, if anything, increased since the declaration of war. In late August 1792 General Biron, who then commanded the Army of the Rhine, had written that the line troops '. . . are full of ardour and patriotism . . .'. In October of the same year Lazare Carnot, who was to gain fame as 'the Organizer of Victory' in 1793-4, wrote of one line regiment: '. . . the regiment cedes in nothing to the National Guards; all are equally consumed with patriotism.'[1] Finally, a large proportion of the regular troops had been recruited since 1789, a fact of which the authorities were not unaware, and these men could no more be considered professional soldiers than could the volunteers of 1791 and 1792.

To provide the cadres for the new demi-brigades and for the hundreds of thousands of new recruits who would soon be joining them, the Convention also established new regulations governing promotions.[2] Henceforth all corporals were to be elected by the soldiers in their units. Promotions to all higher grades from sergeant to *chef de bataillon* (as lieutenant-colonels were now designated) were to be based on election and seniority. Two-thirds of the appointments to these ranks were to be by elections in which all members of the battalion, who held the rank in which the vacancy existed, were to vote. The remaining one-third of the vacancies was to be filled according to seniority, measured by total length of service in the army. *Chefs de brigade*, the new designation for colonels, were to be selected solely on the basis of seniority. One-third of the general officers also were to be selected on the basis of seniority; and two-thirds were to be chosen by the executive power of the state. However, the appointment of generals was a matter in which the government always allowed itself much greater discretion than was provided for in the regulations. The only major exception to the above rules was in the case of artillery officers, since there could be no substitute for the skills required of these soldiers. One half of all artillery second-lieutenants were required to have successfully completed their education at an artillery school; and the other half were to be selected from among sergeants in this branch.

[1] Jean Jaurès, *L'Armée nouvelle* (Paris, 1915), pp. 163 and 168. Albert Soboul also testifies to the revolutionary devotion of the line soldiers in *Soldats de l'an II*, p. 170.

[2] For the regulations on promotions and their effects, see Jaurès, *Histoire socialiste*, VI, 398-400; Soboul, *Soldats de l'an II*, pp. 174-6; Poisson, *L'Armée et la Garde Nationale*, II. 174 and 188-9.

In general, the line troops, especially the N.C.O.s, benefited from the new laws on promotion. The appointments based on seniority were dominated by soldiers who had entered the army before the Revolution. Even elections to fill vacant grades tended to favour the experienced soldiers of the line army. In the combat zones where most of the French troops found themselves in early 1793, military experience far outweighed other criteria in the choice of a superior. Local prestige or social standing, which had been the basis for the election of many officers of the volunteers of 1791 and 1792 while the battalions were still organizing in their home areas, were of minimal value to soldiers engaged in combat on the frontiers. In these circumstances the skill and experience of old soldiers could mean the difference between life and death for those under their orders; and this situation often contributed to the election of line soldiers to command positions.

The Amalgam was essentially the merger of the regular army into the volunteers. For most matters it was the standards and regulations of the national volunteers that were imposed on the new, unified army. The election of officers, the rate of pay, the uniform were based on practices in effect in volunteer battalions. Many of these changes, notably the election of superiors and the higher pay, were warmly welcomed by the men of the regular army. Other changes were resented. Some soldiers were reluctant to give up the white uniform of the Royal Army which represented for them an honourable heritage not easily discarded. They even removed the buttons from their old clothing to sew on the newly issued blue uniforms of the national army. Many regulars objected to being placed on a par with the less-trained, less-disciplined volunteers.

The decree on the amalgamation of the line and volunteer units was but the first step towards a unified French army. The actual implementation of this decree was a very time-consuming process. It was not for many months—in some cases years—after this legislation that full integration was achieved.[1] It is impossible to assess accurately the importance of all the factors which contributed to the critical French military successes of 1793-4. National mobilization, the Terror, the employment of new tactics, division among the Allies, the fervour of citizen armies, all contributed to

[1] The current research of Jean-Paul Bertaud will clarify the great complexities involved in this process. Here I can only thank him for the information that he has provided to me on his preliminary findings.

almost unparalleled victory. Among these factors, whose relative importance cannot be evaluated, was the Amalgam. The merger of regular and volunteer forces greatly reduced the administrative difficulties and increased the military efficiency of the French armed forces. The line army, as it had emerged from the crisis of the Revolution, was an important element in the victories which consolidated the international position of France and assured the survival of the Revolution.

THE LINE ARMY IN 1793

By 1793 the organization and composition of the former Royal Army had changed substantially. Three line infantry regiments and two light infantry battalions had been created in late August 1791. During the next year twelve foreign regiments (eleven Swiss and the Liégeois) had been dismissed from French service. On the other hand, during 1792 five colonial regiments were incorporated into the line army as the 106th to the 110th Infantry. At the time of the Amalgam the regular infantry consisted of 98 line regiments and 14 battalions of light infantry, composed of approximately 125,000 and 8,500 soldiers respectively. Between 1792 and 1793 the cavalry lost two regiments, the Royal Allemand or 15th Cavalry and the Saxe or 4th Hussars, through emigration, while four new mounted units—free corps, legions, volunteers—were incorporated into the regular cavalry. Thus, in early 1793 this branch mustered about 35,000 enlisted men in 64 regiments of heavy and light cavalry. The Artillery of the Colonies was reorganized as the 8th Artillery Regiment by a decree of 27 August 1792 and by the following February twenty companies of mounted artillery had been formed. At this time the artillery included over 10,000 troops.

The total strength of the line army at the time of the decree ordering its amalgamation with the volunteers was between 175,000 and 180,000 men, excluding the officers. The army had considerably expanded its strength since 1789 and had made a remarkable recovery from the disintegration which threatened it during the first two years of the Revolution. Even more important, however, than the numerous changes in units and the significant increase in strength were the changes in the personnel who composed the line army.[1]

[1] The basis for determining the total strength of line units is explained in the section on 'Changes in Strength' in Appendix I. For a general discussion of the methods and

One of the striking aspects of the line soldiers of 1793 was their youth. Nearly 60 per cent of the private soldiers in all branches were between the ages of 18 and 25, about 10 per cent more than in 1789. This is almost exactly the same proportion as that of men in the same age group among the volunteers of 1792.[1] Another 5 per cent of the regulars were under 18 years of age. Only one-sixth of them were older than 30, and less than 4 per cent were older than 40. The non-commissioned officers, usually 5–15 years older than their men, were also rather young. Five-sixths of the corporals and more than three-quarters of the sergeants were 40 years old or younger. Only 3 per cent of all the N.C.O.s of the line army were older than 50. The youth and vigour so frequently described as characteristic of the volunteers were also hallmarks of the 'professional soldiers' of the line army.

The professional character of the line army at the time of the decree of the Amalgam is one of the most enduring preconceptions and misconceptions about this period of French history. Even such a competent historian as Jean Colin in discussing the Army of the Moselle in the spring of 1793 claims that one-third of Schauen- bourg's division was composed of 'professional soldiers'.[2] In fact 7 of the 20 infantry battalions in this command were line units; but by 1793 such a fact in no way necessarily implied a high degree of military professionalism. At the outbreak of the Revolution, when more than three-fifths of the regular troops had been in the army for four years or longer, such an assumption could be justified. In 1793 after the vicissitudes of the previous four years such an identification between line units and professional soldiers is not merely gratuitous, it is also erroneous.

In February 1793 over 38 per cent of the ordinary soldiers in all branches of the line army had less than one year of military service; in other words, their army experience was comparable to that of the volunteers of 1792. Almost 65 per cent of them had served for less

sources used to determine the composition of the regular troops, see the section 'Back- ground of the Soldiers' in the same appendix. The data contained in the *contrôles* for Feb. 1793 could not be checked against inspection reports since the last reports with information on the soldiers' backgrounds date from late 1791 or the first months of 1792. Because of the vast influx of recruits during the latter year, these reports were valueless in determining the composition of the army in early 1793.

[1] Bertaud, *Valmy*, p. 300.
[2] See Colin's introduction to *La Tactique et la discipline dans les armées de la Révolution : Correspondance du Général Schauenborg du 4 avril au 2 août 1793* (Paris, 1902), p. cxxix.

than four years in the army and so their length of service was comparable to that of men who had joined the National Guard since its creation—although regular army service was clearly more rigorous and demanding. A small proportion, less than 1 per cent, of the regulars had some prior service in the National Guard or in battalions of national volunteers. One soldier in nine had ten years or more of service, about half as many as in 1789. Desertions, dismissals, promotions, along with the normal attrition due to discharges and deaths, had in less than four years reversed the proportions of professionals and non-professionals, as measured by length of service. It was not only the youth of the majority of line soldiers that made them similar to their comrades in the volunteer battalions, but also their limited military experience. Although on the whole the regular troops still enjoyed an advantage in experience over the volunteers, the difference was one of degree—and not an overwhelming one, at that—rather than of kind.

The non-commissioned officers of the line army in 1793 were still drawn from soldiers with long service. Less than 5 per cent of the N.C.O.s in all the branches had served in the army for fewer than four years. More than two-thirds of the N.C.O.s had over ten years of service. In the line army, as in the volunteer units, these 'old' soldiers provided the essential knowledge and experience to train and lead the large numbers of fresh recruits who poured into the army in 1791 and 1792.

The frontier regions of northern and north-eastern France continued to furnish a disproportionately large number of recruits to the line army throughout the early Revolution. More than one-third of the infantry and almost half of the cavalry in 1793 were from these areas; and, although the proportion of artillery soldiers native to these regions had declined by over 10 per cent since 1789, still 6 artillerymen in 10 came from these areas. This is only to be expected. The long tradition of military service so well established in these sections of the country was exploited by the revolutionary government which imposed heavy requirements on the frontier departments in its troop levies. Furthermore, the military units ordered to the frontiers before and after the declaration of war recruited extensively in these regions. Finally, the fact that the frontier areas were most directly threatened by the war encouraged enlistment by the inhabitants who, quite literally, enrolled in the army to defend their homes and families.

The number of foreigners serving in the line army declined markedly between 1789 and 1793. The dismissal of the twelve Swiss and Liégeois regiments in 1792, of course, largely accounts for this development, despite the individual enlistments of many of these soldiers in line units. The abolition of all distinctions between French and foreign regiments and the subsequent recruitment of the former German and Irish regiments among French citizens also contributed to this result. From 1792 various 'legions' were created to absorb most of the foreign volunteers and deserters who enlisted in the French army. By February 1793, only about 4 per cent of the line army was composed of foreigners.

Another important change in the regional composition of the line army that had occurred by 1793 was an increase in the number of soldiers from western and southern France, e.g. Bretagne, Guyenne, Languedoc. With some variations according to branch, these regions contributed more recruits, not only in absolute numbers but also in proportion to their population, in 1793 than in 1789.[1] The primary factor responsible for this appears to have been the military legislation of 1792, especially the law of 22 July, which established quotas of recruits for each of the departments. Although the number of soldiers from the west and south remained disproportionately low in comparison with other regions of France, it did increase significantly; and in its regional composition the line army was more representative of the French nation in 1793 than it had been before the Revolution.

Official reductions in the height requirements for recruits and the unauthorized practice of enlisting those who did not meet even these criteria contributed to more representative recruitment, especially of southerners. Between 1789 and 1793 the proportion of infantrymen shorter than 5 feet 6 inches nearly doubled. By 1793 almost half the men in the light infantry, the least demanding of all branches in regard to height, were from the Midi. The average

---

[1] E.g. the area south of a line drawn from the mouth of the Gironde River to Savoy and including all of the Marche, Limousin, Auvergne, and Lyonnais contained about 36% of the population of France in 1789. In that year, about 20% of the enlisted men in the line army were from this area. Less than four years later, about 23% of the regular troops were from the same regions. While an increase of 3% is hardly remarkable, the brief period of time in which it occurred and the absolute number of men it affected do make it significant. In Feb. 1793 there were *c.* 9,000 more soldiers from the Midi serving in the line army than there had been only three years and eight months earlier. Similarly, the number of regular troops from the two western provinces of Bretagne and Poitou increased by *c.* 2,000 during the same period.

height of soldiers in the cavalry and artillery also declined. In the latter branch, however, three-quarters of the men were still 5 feet 8 inches or taller because the strenuous duties of the artilleryman necessitated big, presumably sturdy, soldiers. These changes reflected the increased manpower-needs created by war. Regardless of their stature, virtually no able-bodied men were barred from service in the regular army.

The broader bases of recruitment and the more national character of the line army in 1793 are also evidenced by changes in the rural–urban background of the regular troops. The proportion of soldiers in line infantry regiments who came from urban centres declined by almost 4 per cent; in early 1793 slightly less than one-third of these soldiers were from towns of 2,000 or more inhabitants.[1] Furthermore a somewhat higher proportion of infantrymen were from towns of less than 10,000 inhabitants in 1793 than in 1789. The decline in the number of soldiers from an urban background was most marked in the light infantry, where the proportion of such soldiers dropped by 15 per cent. By 1793 less than 30 per cent of the men in the light infantry were from urban areas. Thus, in the infantry as a whole the proportion of soldiers from rural communities approached more closely the proportion of such people in the general population, although urban centres continued to be over-represented among the recruits.

In the cavalry, on the contrary, the proportion of men from towns and cities increased by approximately $3\frac{1}{2}$ per cent; in February 1793 nearly 30 per cent of the enlisted men were from communities of more than 2,000 inhabitants. In this respect, the soldiers in this branch became more similar to their comrades in the infantry, while such a change made them somewhat less representative of the civilian population. This disproportionate number of recruits of urban origins in both the cavalry and infantry was probably an inevitable result of the method of mass recruitment employed in the early part of the war. The volunteers of 1791 and 1792 displayed almost exactly the same background as their counterparts in the line army. One-third of the volunteers of 1791 and nearly 30 per cent of the volunteers of 1792 were from towns of 2,000 or more inhabitants.[2]

---

[1] As with regional origins, the comparatively small changes in percentages, while not to be exaggerated, tend to minimize fairly substantial differences over a brief span of time.

[2] Bertaud, *Valmy*, pp. 291 and 302.

The greater facility of recruiting in population centres, the greater revolutionary enthusiasm of urban areas, and perhaps the greater economic hardship that existed in cities all contributed to a higher rate of enlistment in urban centres than in the countryside, where opposition to military service was often a deeply ingrained tradition.

Only the artillery was an exception to this pattern. With no significant variation between 1789 and 1793, the proportion of artillerymen from an urban background remained at $18\frac{1}{2}$ per cent, approximately the same proportion of urbans as in the population at large. This stability was due to the greater care with which recruits to this branch were selected. Every effort was made to ensure that men who enlisted in the artillery were big, strong country boys who would receive whatever education or training was necessary to perform their military duties after their enlistment. Such selectivity was felt to be essential to the efficient functioning of the artillery, the most specialized of the major branches. The other combat arms, which were trying to raise and train recruits for use in close combat as rapidly as possible, could not afford such discrimination.

The proportion of N.C.O.s, especially sergeants, from urban centres declined in the first years of the Revolution. Between 1789 and 1793 thousands of sergeants had been promoted to fill the vacancies created by the resignation, emigration, and forced retirement of officers. Their places were usually taken by the corporals of the former Royal Army who, as a group, were more rural in their origins than the sergeants whom they replaced. Even the newly promoted sergeants, however, tended to be more urban than the soldiers under their command.

The general broadening of recruitment practices, which by 1792 drew upon a considerably larger portion of the population than before the Revolution, necessarily affected the social composition of the line army. The men who served in the line army between 1789 and 1793 included many more peasants than had served in the army before the outbreak of the Revolution. The proportion of artisans who enlisted during this time, on the other hand, declined, as did the number of recruits from the middle class.

As with other changes in military personnel that occurred during the Revolution—e.g. the decline in the proportion of professional soldiers, the increase in enlistments of men from western and southern France, and the overall increase in recruits from rural areas —the changes in the social background of the line troops had the general effect of making the line army more representative of the nation. Out of principle and necessity the government of the Revolution exploited the human resources of France more equitably and more extensively than had the Old Regime.

The most notable result of this was the increase in the number of peasants in the line army.[1] In early 1793 peasants constituted approximately one-third of the enlisted personnel in our sample of the line army.[2] Although peasants were still grossly under-represented in the army—compared to their numbers in the total civilian population—this proportion represented an increase of more than 10 per cent over the number of peasants in the ranks of the line army in mid-1789. Most of this increase came from the poorest groups of the peasantry, the agricultural day labourers. Economic necessity was almost certainly an important factor in their decision to enlist. The larger, wealthier peasants, *fermiers* and *cultivateurs*, disdained service in the infantry, where most of the labourers enrolled, and sent their sons into the more prestigious cavalry and artillery regiments.

The proportion of artisans in the line army in 1793, in contrast to that of the peasants, had declined by more than 10 per cent since 1789. Furthermore, artisans from rural communities comprised a majority of this group in 1793. Still, artisans and small shopkeepers made up nearly half of the line troops in this year. The most numerous artisans were, as in 1789, from the most basic trades, clothing, building, textiles, and metal. These artisans together with apprentices and wage-earners, both rural and urban, and the peasants below the class of large farmers constituted well over 90 per cent of the line troops in 1793; and, in a social sense, they formed a 'popular' army.

The proportion of soldiers from the upper classes of society had

[1] The sample used for the social composition of the line troops in 1793 includes all enlisted men serving as of 28 Feb. 1793 whose professions were recorded in the troop registers of the infantry, cavalry, and artillery regiments and light infantry battalions. The sporadic way in which such data were usually recorded gives a random character to this sample, although recent recruits are somewhat over-represented. The total sample constitutes just about 2% of the line army in Feb. 1793, although the cavalry is seriously under-represented. No inspection reports with information on the professions of the soldiers were available for this period. See 'Background of the Soldiers' in Appendix I.

[2] In addition to those men whose civilian occupations were clearly identified as agricultural (e.g. *cultivateur*, *laboureur*, *vigneron*), most of those whose professions were recorded as *journalier*, *manouvrier*, or *sans profession* must be regarded as peasants. Over 80% of such men were in fact from rural areas.

correspondingly declined by 1793. The most striking decrease was in the proportion of troops from the professional middle class, lawyers, doctors, and especially students; the percentage of soldiers from these professions was less than half of what it had been in 1789. This change, however, was due primarily to the fact that soldiers with such a background were being promoted from the ranks in order to fill the numerous officer vacancies which occurred between 1789 and 1793; and it is this phenomenon, rather than a drastic decline in enlistments, which explains the decrease in the number of men from the professional bourgeoisie.[1] Similarly, the proportion of men who listed their occupation simply as 'soldier' also declined by nearly one half between 1789 and 1793. Many of these men too had been promoted to officer during this interval. Members of the commercial middle class, who had never been a very important element in the army, continued to serve in approximately the same proportion as before the Revolution, about 3 per cent of the total number of regulars.

Nobles who served in the ranks of the line army represented an interesting and peculiar, if not very important, element.[2] Of the 400–500 known nobles who served in the line army between 1787 and 1793, all but a handful had disappeared by the latter date. Nobility had been officially abolished by the Revolution and the use of noble title proscribed. In addition, political expediency demanded a discreet silence about such origins. Some few nobles did, however, continue to serve in the ranks of the line army until February 1793 and even after. For example, Jacques-Philippe-Charles Bernard enlisted in the 1st Carabiniers in February 1787, was promoted to sergeant in October 1791, and to sergeant-major in April 1792. He was not discharged 'as a former noble' until 29 April 1794. Jean-Joseph-Gérard de la Garde enlisted in the 11th Cavalry in May 1791 and followed a similarly successful career until he was discharged at the rank of sergeant-major on 2 June 1794, for being a noble.[3] Such

---

[1] Of the men who served *only* between the two sample dates, 30 June 1789 and 28 Feb. 1793, 4% were members of the liberal professions, a percentage only slightly inferior to the proportion of such men in the ranks of the line army on 30 June 1789.

[2] Information on nobles serving in the ranks is based on a sample of all soldiers specifically noted as such in the registers of forty line units.

[3] See the troop registers for these two regiments in A.G., *Contrôles de troupes*. Bernard was numbered 559 in the register of the 1st Carabiniers and De la Garde bore no. 662 in the register of the 11th Cavalry.

examples, however, are of more importance in understanding the mentality of the petty nobility than in analysing the social composition of the army.

All in all, the changes in the personnel of the line army between 1789 and 1793 made this institution more representative of civil society. These changes took place within the existing structure of the army and did not completely transform its composition. Even had the regular army been abolished and then re-created, it would have undoubtedly retained numerous characteristics of the former Royal Army; no efficient military establishment could have existed without these. Nevertheless, the changes which occurred were substantial. The youth and limited experience of a majority of the regular troops in early 1793 made the line army very comparable to the citizen-soldiers of the national volunteers, a fact which helps to explain the successful amalgamation of these two forces in the following months. Not only did the line army become more 'civilian' in composition, but it also became more 'national' between 1789 and 1793. Foreign units were abolished and the proportion of foreign soldiers became almost negligible. At the same time, new physical requirements opened the line army to more Frenchmen, and conscription broadened the regional basis of recruitment. Finally, a substantially larger portion of rural, peasant France was drawn into the army, and thus into a greater participation in national life. Although the line army preserved many of the traditions, practices, and institutions of the eighteenth century, it had also developed many of the characteristics of a national, citizen army and in these respects was distinctively 'modern'.

THE NEW OFFICER CORPS

As the soldiers of the line army became less professional during the early years of the Revolution, the officer corps became more professional. The extensive changes of personnel in the ranks of the army due to the military turmoil during the years 1789–92 and the considerable expansion in the size of the army necessitated by the war had resulted in a large proportion of soldiers who were essentially civilians with limited military experience. To train and lead such troops, an experienced and skilled officer corps was necessary. Both the official policies of the government and the circumstantial developments of the early Revolution contributed to the professionalization of the French officer corps during this period.[1]

The process of professionalization had begun well before the Revolution. The last decades of the Old Regime had witnessed extensive modernization in the organization of the Royal Army; but such policies had always stopped short of any fundamental change in the social structure of the officer corps. The new government of the Revolution, however, was committed to abolishing the standards of a society based on privilege; and it intentionally aimed at more rational, more impersonal criteria for officers. This was part of a general programme to rationalize all the major institutions of French society. In the army the application of these principles led to the professionalization of the officer corps.

Early in the Revolution the National Assembly established the principle of equal opportunity for entry into and advancement within the officer corps. Substantial pay increases, voted in July 1790, made this more realizable by doing away with the necessity for outside financial resources.[2] The revolutionary regime also drastically reduced the number of officers to a figure more consistent with efficient operation, and made education and experience the criteria for admission and promotion. New circumstances, however, soon required the modification of these rational, professional standards. The emigration of most pre-revolutionary officers, especially after the king's flight, and the increasing likelihood of war accelerated and altered the process of professionalization. Existing military educational facilities were totally inadequate for the training of the thousands of officers required; and by late 1791 examinations had to be eliminated. Instead, officer vacancies were increasingly filled by the promotion of talented and experienced N.C.O.s. The

[1] The use of the term 'professionalization' in this study is described in Appendix I, the section entitled 'Professionalization of the Officer Corps'. A more thorough treatment of this problem can be found in my essay on 'The French Revolution and the Professionalization of the Officer Corps', of which this part of the chapter is an abbreviated version.

[2] The connection between increased pay and greater professionalism was made explicit by contemporaries. In an address to the National Assembly in July 1791 one deputy argued that '... better paid officers ... would be more attached to their functions [emplois] ...'. The same representative also argued that the Old Regime had uselessly multiplied officer positions for the privileged, but that this had succeeded only in creating 'a burden for society'. See 'Rapport des commissaires de l'Assemblée Nationale, Envoyés dans les départemens de la Meuse, de la Moselle et des Ardennes; fait par M. de Montesquiou, Député de Paris, le 13 Juillet 1791' Maclure Collection, vol. 832.

criterion of specialized education, as determined by examination, gave way to the more empirical norm of experience.

The outcome of the new policies and standards which developed as results of the principles of the Revolution, the effect of the defection of most of the previous officers, and the impact of the war can best be measured by an investigation of the officer corps of the line army in 1793. As with our examination of the enlisted personnel of the line army, such a study must be a rather broad one, dealing only with the general characteristics of the civilian background and military career of a sample of the officers serving in the line army in early 1793.[1]

In the rather brief period between July 1789 and February 1793 there were significant changes in the age of regimental officers.[2] Almost no colonels in 1793 were younger than 30. Most officers in this rank were between 50 and 60 years old, although about one-third were between 30 and 50. This situation was in marked contrast to the conditions that existed before the Revolution, when young court nobles, most of them in their thirties, nearly monopolized the rank of colonel. Another striking difference is evident at the opposite pole of regimental grades, among the lieutenants. Five out of every eight lieutenants in 1793 were older than 30, and less than one in ten was under 21. This situation too was very different from the Old Regime, when adolescent nobles constituted a large segment of the junior officers.

In the intermediate regimental grades—lieutenant-colonel and captain—the Revolution did not have such an impact on age distribution. Lieutenant-colonels, who in 1793 were often the *de facto* regimental commanders due to the shortage of colonels, were most commonly in their late forties and early fifties, as they had been before 1789. Similarly, the captains of 1793 were mostly between the ages of 35 and 55, just like their pre-Revolutionary counterparts. Both before and after 1789 these ranks contained the men who were making a career of military service.

Over all, the officer corps of 1793 was older than it had been four years earlier. A substantial proportion of officers, especially junior officers, however, were comparatively young. Only a handful of

---

[1] For the bases of the following conclusions, see the section on the 'Composition of the Officer Corps' in Appendix I.

[2] Information on the ages of officers before the Revolution is based primarily on the research of Prof. Charles Wrong who has generously permitted me to use his findings.

officers, about 2 per cent in all, were 60 or older; and these men generally performed administrative duties in regimental depots far behind the front lines.[1] Furthermore, whatever disadvantage there may have been in an older officer corps was more than compensated for by the extensive military experience of almost all line officers in 1793.

Of all the colonels in the sample used for this study, none had less than ten years of service and 80 per cent of them had served twenty-five years or more. Nearly two-thirds of the lieutenant-colonels also had twenty-five years or more of experience, while less than 1 in 20 had served fewer than ten years in the army. Among captains, less than one-tenth had served for fewer than ten years; and most of these were in the infantry where changes in personnel since 1789 had been the greatest. More than half of all the captains had twenty-five years or more of service. Even among the lieutenants, more than a quarter had served in the army for at least twenty-five years. On the other hand, almost 30 per cent of the lieutenants had served less than ten years. In all, more than 80 per cent of the infantry officers had served five years or more; approximately 85 per cent of the cavalry officers had served an equal time; and nearly all (97 per cent) of the artillery officers had five years or more of service. Almost all of the officers with under five years' service were lieutenants.

Factors other than simple length of service affected the military experience of the regimental officers in early 1793. With little variation according to branch, 70 per cent had served some time as enlisted men. There were, however, substantial differences according to rank. Of 37 colonels in the sample for the three major branches, only 5 had any service in the ranks. Almost 40 per cent of the lieutenant-colonels had served at one time as enlisted men; and most of these were officers of fortune who had already been promoted to officers before the Revolution. On the other hand, more than 70 per cent of the captains and lieutenants had previous enlisted service. This stands in marked contrast to the situation less than four years earlier, when only about 10 per cent of all officers were ex-rankers and these officers were effectively barred from advancing beyond the grade of lieutenant. By 1793 the former N.C.O.s of the regular army

---

[1] A typical example of this is Captain Carbonel of the 49th Infantry. He was 65 years old in 1793 and had served in the army for 46 years. Carbonel commanded the depot of his regiment and his primary duty was supervising the training of recruits. See A.G., X[b] 180.

dominated the officer ranks below the grade of lieutenant-colonel. A lieutenant-colonelcy was as high as most of the ex-rankers had reached. Colonel was still a grade dominated by men whose only military service had been in the capacity of officers.

Although most of the men who were regimental officers in 1793 had received one, two, or even three promotions, meteoric rises were very unusual. None of the colonels in this study had been enlisted men in July 1789; almost all of them had been majors or captains at that date and a small number, less than one-tenth, had been lieutenants. Some few soldiers who were sergeants in 1789 had reached the grade of lieutenant-colonel by 1793. More than half of the lieutenant-colonels of 1793 had been captains before the Revolution; and approximately one-third had held the rank of lieutenant. Nearly 45 per cent of the captains of 1789 had been lieutenants in 1789 and an equal number had been sergeants at the same date. Approximately one-tenth of the captains serving in 1793 had held the same rank before the Revolution. A very small number, 1 out of 100, had risen from simple soldier to captain since 1789. A large majority (85 per cent) of the lieutenants of 1793 had been sergeants in 1789. Approximately 7 per cent of the lieutenants of 1793 had been corporals before the Revolution; and one in twenty had served as an ordinary soldier.

The regimental officers in early 1793 had impressive records of combat experience. More than 40 per cent of the infantry officers had participated in military campaigns prior to the Revolution, and almost another 40 per cent had seen combat in the campaign of 1792. Less than one-fifth of the line infantry officers of 1793 had no previous combat experience, and almost all of these were young lieutenants. The proportion of artillery officers with some combat experience in early 1793 was approximately the same, 80 per cent. In the cavalry the proportion of officers with campaign experience was smaller, although nearly two-thirds (63 per cent of them) had combat experience by 1793. Only a quarter of the cavalry officers had served in campaigns prior to the Revolution, since these had been primarily overseas conflicts (e.g. in America, on Corsica) where mostly infantry units had been employed.

Thus, the regimental officers of the line army in 1793 were men with long service and considerable campaign experience; they were, at least by these criteria, professional soldiers. Their age and length of service indicate that few of them, since reaching adulthood, had

much experience of civilian occupations or had known a home outside army garrisons. Most of them had received rapid but limited
promotion since the Revolution; more importantly, the majority,
who had risen from the ranks, knew how restricted their chances for
such promotion had been before 1789. Despite the fact that the
highest grades were still controlled by officers from the old army,
there were clear opportunities for junior officers to attain these
ranks. Although many officers, even among captains and lieutenants,
were in their forties and fifties, there was a substantial minority of
young officers and only 2 per cent of the regimental officers were 60
years of age or older. The officers were battle-hardened veterans; in
spite of their age, they were probably younger than the officers of
other European armies;[1] and they were certainly more familiar with
the situation of the men under their orders.

Besides some markedly similar characteristics in their military
careers, many regimental officers of 1793 also shared a number of
common traits in their civilian backgrounds. A disproportionately
high number of officers came from the frontier regions of northern
and eastern France. More than 38 per cent of the captains and
lieutenants in the three branches came from Flandre and Artois,
Champagne, Lorraine, Alsace, and Franche-Comté, which is over
twice as many as the total population of these provinces would
warrant. This proportion is almost the same as the proportion of
enlisted men in 1789 who came from these regions, and reflects the
large number of captains and lieutenants in 1793 who had been
promoted from the ranks since the Revolution. On the other hand,
slightly less than a quarter of the colonels and lieutenant-colonels
of 1793 came from these same provinces; and a higher percentage of
these superior officers came from southern and western France. In
their regional origins, the colonels and lieutenant-colonels, most of
whom had been officers before 1789, reflected the composition of the
officer corps of the Old Regime.[2]

There was also a marked difference between superior and junior
officers as regards foreign birth. There were almost three times as
many foreigners among the colonels and lieutenant-colonels as
among captains and lieutenants. Even in the former Irish regiments

[1] For example, in 1806 a quarter of all the regimental and battalion commanders in the
Prussian army were older than 60. See Gordon Craig, *The Politics of the Prussian Army,
1640–1945* (Oxford, 1964), p. 26.
[2] The research of Charles Wrong substantiates this conclusion.

of the Royal Army, which maintained the most distinctively foreign character, this change was evident. For example, in the 87th (formerly Dillon) Infantry Regiment in 1793, the colonel, lieutenant-colonel, adjutant-major and all but one of the captains were foreign-born. In contrast, five of the eight lieutenants and only one of the four second-lieutenants were foreigners.[1] Foreign officers who had not resigned or emigrated were kept, but few foreigners were being admitted to French service as officers.

One of the most marked characteristics of the officer corps in 1793 was the urban background of many officers. Of the infantry officers whose birthplaces could be identified as rural or urban, slightly more than half came from cities or towns with over 2,000 inhabitants. 44 per cent of the cavalry officers were from urban centres. And even in the artillery, which was the most rural in composition of the three major branches, 42 per cent of the officers were born in cities or towns. When the domiciles, rather than the birthplaces, of these officers were used as the measure of rural–urban origins, the results were even more remarkable.[2] Slightly over 60 per cent of the infantry officers and over 48 per cent of the artillery officers made their homes in cities or towns with 2,000 or more inhabitants. Approximately a quarter of the infantry officers and an eighth of the artillery officers had their residence in cities of 25,000 or more.

The origins of the regimental officers of 1793 were not only much more urban than those of the general population of France, of whom less than 20 per cent lived in urban centres, they were also considerably more urban than those of the men under their command, of whom c. 30 per cent came from cities or towns. This was due in part to the fact that people from urban areas rallied to the Revolution more completely than country people. More than two-thirds of the officers who had joined the army since 1789 came from cities. Another reason for the disproportionate number of officers from an urban background was that literacy was a prerequisite for officers, and men from urban communities were more likely to possess this requirement.[3] In fact, literacy was one of the primary characteristics

---

[1] See the report on the civil and military status of the officers in this regiment in the spring of 1793 in A.G., X^b 192.

[2] This could not be calculated for cavalry officers because their domiciles were recorded too infrequently.

[3] Literacy had been higher in the urbanized areas of France since the seventeenth century. See Michel Fleury and Pierre Valmary, 'Les progrès de l'instruction élémentaire de Louis XIV à Napoléon III, d'après l'enquête de Louis Maggiolo (1877–1879)', *Population*, XII (Jan.–Mar. 1957), 71–92.

of the officer corps of 1793 and this was intimately related to the civilian background of the officers.

Although its social composition was much broader than in 1789, the officer corps was still dominated by the upper classes of French society in 1793.[1] At least 40 per cent and possibly over half of the colonels and lieutenant-colonels of the line army were former nobles, as were 10–20 per cent of the captains and lieutenants. It is impossible to be more precise than this because a number of officers, more than one-eighth in all, gave vague information about their civilian status, e.g. 'without profession', 'living with parents', 'son of a proprietor', or 'student'. It is certain that some of these were nobles (possibly motivated by political expediency),[2] but in many cases one cannot determine this. What is clear is that the nobles who were still in the army were hardened veterans who had spent much of their life in the service and for whom the Revolution had greatly improved opportunities of advancement. Their continued service was at the same time a recognition of their military ability and a gauge of their attachment to a military career.

These nobles shared the officer corps with the higher classes of non-noble society. Middle-class 'notables'—members of the liberal professions, bourgeois living on their incomes, government officials, and businessmen—accounted for c. 40 per cent of the field-grade officers and 30 per cent of the company-grade officers; the liberal professions alone contributed one-fifth of all regimental officers. Excluded from a successful military career before 1789, these men could now gain advancement through their skill and experience because the Revolution had destroyed the feudal concept of and requirements for an officer. The lower middle class of small merchants and manufacturers, master-artisans, clerks, and large farmers comprised a negligible segment of the colonels and lieutenant-

---

[1] Of the 2,246 regimental officers studied, the civilian professions of 1,602 were recorded. Since in 90% of the cases where this information was recorded the officers were in the infantry, no distinction by branch can be made. In 1793 over 70% of the regimental officer corps was composed of infantry officers.

[2] E.g. Captain du Perron of the 94th Infantry and Captain Stipplin of the 77th Infantry both indicated that they had no civilian profession; both were commissioned while still teenagers in the mid-1780s when this was virtually impossible for non-nobles. See the reports on these two officers in A.G., X^b 195 and 189 respectively. Captain Viart of the 14th Cavalry specifically denied that he was a noble, although he had served as a royal page, a position reserved exclusively for the nobility. See A.G., X^b 198 and A.G., *Contrôles des officiers, Révolution et Empire*, the register for the 14th Cavalry (later the 23rd Dragoons).

colonels but constituted about 12 per cent of the captains and lieutenants.

The popular or lower classes—artisans and shopkeepers, apprentices, wage-earners, and small peasants—provided about 5 per cent of the field-grade officers and 33 per cent of those of company grade. The poorer elements of these groups—day labourers, domestic servants, agricultural workers—were especially under-represented, comprising less than 3 per cent of the colonels and lieutenant-colonels and only slightly more than 4 per cent of the captains and lieutenants. Most officers from popular social groups were former tradesmen or members of the more substantial peasantry, the *laboureurs*.

The vast majority of the officers, therefore, came from social groups that were generally literate. In addition, most of these men had previously served as sergeants in the Royal Army and consequently had been required to be able to read and write in order to achieve this rank. Literacy, then, was a hallmark of the officer corps. Of all the officers studied, only fourteen—four infantry captains and ten infantry lieutenants—were definitely illiterate.[1] In one typical case, the 104th Infantry Regiment, it was not until mid-1793 that the first officers who could not sign their names were appointed to the regiment.[2] Yet in all of France during the period 1786–90 only 47 per cent of the male population could sign their names.[3]

Literacy was essential for an efficient officer corps at a time when the size of armies reached hundreds of thousands but the means of communications were still basically those of previous centuries. In the beginning of the Revolution the government had attempted to establish more bureaucratic standards for officers by requiring examinations. Circumstances, however, forced the government to dispense with these and rely on the more pragmatic criteria of literacy and experience. The effects of this can be seen in the educational background of the regimental officers of 1793. Of the colonels in our sample, approximately 19 per cent had received either military schooling or cadet training; and nearly a quarter of the lieutenant-colonels had such specialized preparation. In contrast, only one-ninth of the captains and a mere 2 per cent of the lieu-

---

[1] In almost half the cases there was no indication of literacy or illiteracy. However, in 1,142 cases the ability to read and/or write was indicated.

[2] Scott and Bertaud, 'Le 104ᵉ Régiment', pp. 10–11.

[3] Fleury and Valmary, 'Les progrès de l'instruction', pp. 84–9.

tenants had attended a military school or undergone cadet training; and most of these were nobles whose only service had been as officers. The new regime reluctantly abandoned the requirement of specialized instruction but continued to insist on general education as a fundamental qualification for its officers.

On the basis of the preceding data, we can attempt a general description of the regimental officer corps of the line army on the eve of its disestablishment. The superior officers came from the nobility and upper bourgeoisie. All had extensive military service and a significant minority had received specialized military education. Junior officers were more heterogeneous and included nobles, members of the middle classes, and representatives of popular groups. Most had substantial military service, generally acquired in the ranks, and almost all had at least a rudimentary education. A large majority of all these officers, particularly those promoted from the ranks, had reached the limit of advancement within the army by 1789, but the Revolution had provided them with unexpected promotions. As a group they constituted the most professional officer corps in Europe.

There were striking similarities, as well as important differences, between the regimental officers of the line army and the general officers who commanded them.[1] One distinctive characteristic of the group of general officers was their professionalism. Like their subordinate officers, the generals of 1793 conformed to many standards which can best be described as professional.

The French generals in early 1793 were older than the colonels and lieutenant-colonels of the same period, as one might expect. More than two-thirds of the lieutenant-generals were older than 50.[2] On the other hand, approximately one-seventh of them were 40 years old or younger. The youngest lieutenant-general was the Duc de Chartres, Louis XVI's nephew and the future Louis-Philippe, King of the French; he was only 19 years old in February 1793 and held his high rank on the basis of his family's position. It might be noted, however, that this young man had served admirably in the two greatest victories of the renovated French army, at Valmy and

---

[1] Unless indicated otherwise, the data on all general officers serving as of 28 Feb. 1793 is drawn from Georges Six, *Dictionnaire biographique des généraux et amiraux français de la Révolution et de l'Empire (1792–1814)*, 2 vols. (Paris, 1934).

[2] Generals-in-chief and commanders of armies are included among the lieutenant-generals, since this was their official rank whatever their command.

Jemappes in September and November 1792. Although slightly younger than the lieutenant-generals, the major-generals of 1793 were older than the regimental commanders serving at the same time.[1] Almost 40 per cent of them were 50 or younger; but only Grouchy, who was the brother-in-law of Condorcet and later became a marshal of Napoleon, was less than 30.

The military experience of these generals was considerable. Only 4 per cent of all generals in 1793 had served less than fifteen years; and among those with less service than this were the Duc de Chartres, Santerre, an important Parisian revolutionary, and Miaczynski, a Polish émigré. Almost four-fifths of the generals had twenty-five years or more of military service. Although they had served in the army for somewhat less time than the lieutenant-generals, the major-generals were also old military men, of whom less than a quarter had served for fewer than twenty-five years.

Only a few of the generals had served previously in the ranks. Among the lieutenant-generals in early 1793, only two, Berruyer and Diettmann, had served in a grade below that of officer; and Diettmann's service as a soldier had been in the Gendarmes, part of the royal household troops with considerably more prestige than the line units. Service in the ranks was more common among the major-generals; a dozen of them, about 9 per cent of the total, had served some time as enlisted men. Length of service in the ranks varied from one year to twenty-six years. Jacques Thouvenot had served as a soldier in the regiment of Picardie Infantry in 1769–70; but it was his experience as a royal surveyor that earned him a commission and rapid promotion from 1787 on.[2] On the other hand, Joseph Gilot had come up laboriously through the ranks and had already served more than twenty-six years when he became a second-lieutenant in 1776.[3] In fact, these two examples represent well the combination of skill and experience found among the generals of 1793.

A majority of the sixty-four lieutenant-generals had already achieved general officer rank by mid-1789; five of them were lieutenant-generals and thirty-two were major-generals when

---

[1] Provisional major-generals are here treated in the same category as those whose grades had been confirmed. They were in fact fulfilling the duties of this rank, and all but two of them were confirmed in their rank by May 1793.

[2] Six, *Dictionnaire biographique*, II. 499.

[3] Ibid., I. 502.

the Revolution began. Thirteen officers who had been colonels and nine who had been lieutenant-colonels in 1789 had been promoted to lieutenant-general by the end of February 1793. Two officers had even risen from the rank of major to lieutenant-general during this brief period. Three of the lieutenant-generals of 1793 had not been in military service at the outbreak of the Revolution.

Some of the officers serving as major-generals in early 1793 had received extraordinary promotions since 1789. Of the 131 major-generals of 1793, only fourteen had held the same rank in mid-1789. On the other hand, seventeen colonels and thirty-nine lieutenant-colonels of 1789 had become major-generals by February 1793. Even more remarkable, twenty-three who were captains when the Revolution began had reached the rank of major-general in less than four years. One officer—Thouvenot the royal surveyor mentioned above—had risen from lieutenant to general during the same period. Thirteen of the major-generals of 1793 were not on active duty in mid-1789, although all but one of them, Santerre, an obvious political appointee, had previous military service.

As among the regimental officers of 1793, only a minority of the general officers at the same date had received a special military education. Thirteen of the sixty-four lieutenant-generals (about one-fifth), and thirty-one of the 131 major-generals (nearly one-quarter) had either attended a military school or received cadet training. The pressures created by the emigration of the former officers and the foreign war made it impossible to demand such specialized training of general officers.

Although the educational background of the generals may have been, on the whole, inadequate, their military experience certainly compensated for this deficiency. At least three-quarters of the lieutenant-generals and about two-thirds of the major-generals of 1793 had been in combat prior to the outbreak of the war in April 1792.[1] Furthermore, after the campaign of 1792 only about a dozen general officers had not yet served in combat.

Thus, by the character as well as the length of their service, most of the generals of 1793, like their subordinate officers, could be classified as professional military men. Their experience, had, naturally, come with age; yet, they were not excessively old. More than a third of them were 50 years of age or younger, and more than

---

[1] These are minimum percentages since only *explicit* references by Six to combat experience have been taken into consideration.

70 per cent were 60 or less.[1] Among the major-generals, more than three-quarters had received two or more promotions since 1789. More than one-fifth of the generals had received a specialized, military education. In 1789 general officer rank had been explicitly reserved for nobles who had the influence and wealth to be presented at court; by 1793 the career expectations of officers were limited primarily by experience and ability.

In their regional origins the generals in 1793 were in many ways similar to the colonels and lieutenant-colonels of the same date. The same proportion (approximately a quarter) of both groups came from the frontier provinces of the north and east. Officers of foreign birth constituted about 10 per cent of both the generals and the regimental commanders. On the other hand, fewer generals came from the south and west than did colonels and lieutenant-colonels. More than twice as many generals came from the Parisian region, Île-de-France, as did regimental commanders; and 10 per cent of the generals of 1793 came from the city of Paris itself. This, in part, reflects the differences within the officer corps of the Old Regime. Many of the colonels and lieutenant-colonels of 1793 were members of the provincial nobility who had been effectively barred from the highest regimental grades before the Revolution. In contrast, over 40 per cent of the generals of 1793 had held a rank of colonel or higher in 1789 and represented, generally, the aristocratic élite, the court nobility. These nobles seldom devoted their energies to their estates, but rather gravitated to large cities, particularly Paris, where they found society, education, and royal favour.

Of all the generals whose place of birth could be identified as rural or urban, nearly 60 per cent came from urban centres and over a quarter were born in cities whose population exceeded 25,000 inhabitants. Information on the domicile of the generals was not available, but it is most likely that an even higher proportion of generals had their residence in towns and cities. Although the proportion of generals from urban areas is comparable to that of regimental officers, the social origins of the generals are quite distinctive.

There was, apparently, a greater homogeneity in the social background of the generals than among other echelons of the officer corps. Georges Six calculated that of 202 generals serving on 1 January

---

[1] Of 142 generals in the Prussian army in 1806, 62 (43·6%) were over 60 years old. See Craig, *Politics of the Prussian Army*, p. 26.

1793, 139, or *c.* 69 per cent, were nobles;[1] and this proportion did not change significantly in the following two months. From the information provided in the same author's biographical dictionary, however, it is impossible to be very precise about the social origins of the generals serving at the end of February 1793. What is clear is that nobles continued to dominate the general officer ranks at least as late as this stage of the Revolution.

This substantial majority of nobles, however, can blur the diversity which existed among the general officers. Of the sixty-four lieutenant-generals of 1793, fifty held the rank of colonel or higher in 1789. Although it is not evident in every individual case, most of these officers were members of the court aristocracy. Of the 131 major-generals of 1793, only thirty-one had been colonels or major-generals before the Revolution. From the data available and what can be reconstructed, the following conclusions can be drawn. Approximately 7 out of 10 generals in early 1793 were nobles; but this proportion was somewhat higher, probably about 80 per cent, among the lieutenant-generals. Furthermore, the court aristocracy continued to dominate the rank of lieutenant-general. On the other hand, the predominant social group among major-generals was the provincial nobility; and these nobles, who had been lieutenant-colonels, majors, and captains in 1789, owed their advancement to the new standards imposed by the Revolution.

On the basis of the social origins of the generals of 1793, especially of the lieutenant-generals, it might appear that in these grades social status still counted more than professional ability. To assume this, however, would be to ignore the historical situation in which the professionalization of the officer corps took place. To promote a mass of company officers to regimental commands in less than four years is unusual but not unthinkable, since these officers continued to perform their functions in the same branch, or even the same regiment, although on a higher administrative level. To replace all general officers within less than four years and in the face of a major war would have been to court disaster. Indeed a concern for military efficiency necessitated the maintenance of at least a core of officers with previous experience at the higher echelons. To adopt new social prejudices in place of the old would have been equally detrimental to military professionalization.

Furthermore, an exaggerated emphasis on the similar social back-

[1] Six, *Généraux de la Révolution*, p. 25.

ground of general officers before and after the Revolution ignores the dramatic changes that had taken place. Of the more than 200 marshals and lieutenant-generals in the French army in mid-1789, only five remained in February 1793. Of the more than 900 brigadier- and major-generals before the Revolution, only forty-six remained three years and eight months later.[1] There had been a large influx of provincial nobles into the general officer ranks; and their devotion to military service, whatever the motivation, can hardly be questioned. There was a sizeable minority of non-nobles who were serving as generals by 1793.[2] Finally, it is impossible to find fault with the military credentials of most of the nobles who were generals in 1793; almost all of them were officers who had long and distinguished service and who were, from all the evidence, devoted to a military career. Despite different social origins and various career-patterns, the term which would be almost universally applicable to the generals of 1793—as to the officer corps as a whole—is 'professional soldiers'.

In spite of a disastrous commencement, the campaign of 1792 eventually proved that the line army had sufficiently recovered from the problems besetting it; the regular troops, together with the volunteers, succeeded in defending France from foreign invaders. The most serious of the line army's problems, insubordination, had been, in large measure, resolved; and the restoration of discipline after three years of disorder reflected the greater cohesion between officers and men, necessitated by combat and encouraged by major changes in officer personnel. The difficulties experienced by the army during the winter of 1792–3 were, for the most part, caused by circumstances outside and beyond the control of the military.

By the beginning of 1793 the line army was a vigorous institution, although not all of its problems had been solved. But by this time, practical and ideological, military and political considerations dictated the amalgamation of the line troops with the levies of

---

[1] For the number of general officers in the French army before the Revolution, see Duruy, *L'Armée royale*, pp. 83–4.

[2] It is impossible to describe adequately the social background of the commoners who were generals on 28 Feb. 1793. Six's biographical dictionary provides explicit information on only fifteen such officers. Seven of these were from families connected with military service, sons either of officers or of officials of the Ministry of War. Three were sons of civilian officials under the monarchy. Two were from the professional middle class, the son of a lawyer and the son of a doctor. And three were from the popular classes, a shoemaker, a brewer, and a glazier.

volunteers. To some extent, this merger represented official recognition of the great changes that had taken place in the composition of the regular army since 1789. The drastic decline in strength suffered in 1789 and 1790, due to wide-scale desertion and insubordination, and the growing danger of foreign war had led the authorities to establish more rational and efficient methods of recruitment in 1791 and 1792. These policies further benefited from popular enthusiasm for the defence of France and the Revolution against foreign enemies. As a result, by 1793 the composition of the line army was considerably more civilian and more national than it had been before the Revolution. An increase in the number of civilians under arms had been common in all the wars of the eighteenth century when the French army was rapidly expanded in size. The wholesale departure of tens of thousands of soldiers during the early Revolution, however, greatly accentuated this trend. Consequently, the soldiers of the line regiments were more easily combined with the citizen-soldiers of the volunteer battalions. In this respect, the Amalgam completed a process that had been going on in the line army since 1789.

On the other hand, while the number of professional soldiers had declined dramatically in less than four years, the old soldiers who did remain provided the fundamental element of experience in the new, amalgamated forces. Of even greater importance was the contribution of the cadres of the line army to the Amalgam. The officers of the regular army supplied the military professionalism essential to the functioning of the new citizen army. Although a substantial majority of the pre-revolutionary officer corps had left the army by 1793, the noble officers who stayed were devoted to their military career. Despite the drastic changes initiated in the first few years of the Revolution, the 'semi-professional' orientation of these officers, which had developed in the last two decades of the Old Regime, prevailed over their social attitudes. Alongside these military nobles served the officers of common origin, promoted from the ranks. For them the Revolution provided advancement which their personal and professional ambitions sought and to which their ability and experience entitled them, but which had been denied them before 1789.

The line army at the time of its disestablishment was an institution that had been fundamentally altered by the events of the early Revolution. Yet, it had not been simply the passive object of official policies and revolutionary developments. The actions of the personnel of the line army had helped to determine its fate and even played an active, sometimes critical, role in determining the course of the Revolution itself.

CONCLUSION

THE RESPONSE of the Royal Army to the French Revolution indicates the critical but complex relationships between a standing army and a society in a revolutionary upheaval. Because it was the primary agency for the maintenance of order in the country as a whole, the reaction of the line army could seriously affect the course of the Revolution. The significance of the military's role was clearly and dramatically revealed at the very beginning of the Revolution when thousands of regular troops were summoned to the capital as a prelude to dismissing the Estates General and nipping rebellion in the bud. The troops were not employed against the disorganized and poorly armed Parisians because their officers, most of whom knew and cared little about their men, lost confidence in their ability to command obedience. Although the accuracy of this evaluation before 14 July is open to serious doubt, after that date discipline did indeed collapse.

This breakdown of discipline was not complete; most regular units continued to perform customary police functions obediently. However, when confronted by the unprecedented situation of political conflicts in which opposing groups claimed to represent legitimate authority, the troops could, and frequently did, make their own decisions as to which party had the greater claim on their loyalty. In such circumstances civilian officials, on both national and local levels, lost the power to control events. Attempts by contending civilian factions to win the allegiance of different elements within the army further contributed to the disintegration of established civil and military authority.

The line army, despite its unique organization and functions, reflected the divisions that existed in society as a whole. Social and professional distinctions strictly separated soldiers from officers; and tradition and training reinforced the subordination of the former to the latter. The Revolution, with its promise of reforming society and abolishing past inequities, led soldiers to seek immediate redress of their long-standing grievances; and the immunity with which early acts of insubordination were treated encouraged further military disobedience. Formal and informal civilian support provided sanctions for such behaviour. Thus emboldened, soldiers and N.C.O.s more and more frequently acted on their own initiative, as personal, professional, and political motivations increased their hostility towards officers. The officer corps of the Old Regime, for its own, contrary motives, opposed the soldiers, thereby intensifying the conflict and establishing within the army a microcosm of the Revolution. In both cases the old élite was ultimately forced to give way; and the soldiers gradually gained control over the internal operations of the army.

The new regime, dominated by bourgeois politicians whose aim was moderate revolution, found itself in a quandary, unable to achieve both discipline and political loyalty at all military echelons. Fearing both radicalism and counter-revolution, national and local authorities responded to insubordination with ambivalent policies. In the end, the government's role in resolving the internal divisions of the army was largely a passive one. In contrast to its impotency in dealing with the bitter split between officers and men, the central government's accomplishments in reorganizing and restructuring the army were substantial. In order to solve specific difficulties and to implement principles, the revolutionary assemblies carried out a major programme of military reform which often paralleled the more general changes taking place in France. The conscription of citizens into the armed forces, for example, was a natural corollary of national sovereignty, just as a professional officer corps was a necessary consequence of the principle of careers open to talent. The over-all result of these policies was the creation of a military establishment that is clearly recognizable as a modern army.

In early 1793 the line army lost its identity as a distinct institution, although its former personnel continued to play a crucial role in the defence and propagation of the Revolution. The relationship between the army and the Revolution, however, had already been drastically altered by the outbreak of foreign war. While the war improved discipline and cohesion within the army, it reduced and eventually eliminated the army's contact with revolutionary developments. Henceforth, when the military intervened in internal affairs—in 1795 to save the Convention, in 1797 to rescue the Directory, and in 1799 to establish the Consulate—it acted as an 'outside' force called upon by civil politicians who were incompetent to deal with the conflicts unleashed by the Revolution. The intimate interaction between conditions in the line army and the course of the early Revolution, which had profoundly affected both, had come to an end.

NOTES ON SOURCES AND METHODS

CHANGES IN STRENGTH

The most fundamental and comprehensive source on the enlisted men of the line army during the period under discussion is the *contrôles de troupes* described in the Bibliography. Although strength and inspection reports are available for many of the units during this period, these sources were often constructed to make actual figures tally with authorized numbers. Also, the information given in such documents on the types of losses and gains is rather general and no dates are provided to indicate when in a twelve-month period changes occurred. Despite the fact that entries in the *contrôles*, or troop registers, are sometimes inaccurate and occasionally erroneous, they are, on the whole, a much more specific and dependable source on changing patterns of strength.

To determine variations in strength during the period from January 1787 to February 1793 a sample of approximately a quarter of the line units that served throughout this time was selected at random. This sample included 23 of 89 infantry regiments, 3 of 12 light infantry battalions, 15 of 60 cavalry regiments, and 2 of 7 artillery regiments. An investigation of all gains and losses, including the reasons for these changes, served as the basis for the conclusions about the strength of the line army, except for the Swiss regiments in French service.

The estimates for the eleven Swiss regiments that served in the line army are based upon annual inspection reports in series X^g of the Archives de la Guerre because no *contrôles* were available for these units which were dismissed in 1792.

BACKGROUND OF THE SOLDIERS

The most basic and detailed source of information on the background of all the enlisted personnel, the troop registers, provides only elementary data: date and place of birth, height, the companies in which the men served, dates of enlistments and promotions, the reasons why the soldiers were dropped from the unit register, and, occasionally, civilian occupations. Simply to record this information for all of the more than 300,000 men who served as soldiers and N.C.O.s in the line army between 1787 and 1793 would be an overwhelming task, the results of which would not justify such a labour and expense. Therefore, a sample of the enlisted personnel on active duty on two dates, in 1789 and 1793, was made in order to determine the composition of the line army and the changes that occurred in this composition during the early Revolution.

For a general view of the enlisted men in the Royal Army a sample of all the troops on duty as of 30 June 1789 was taken. Because of daily fluctuations in personnel a specific date had to be selected. The date chosen was close to the traditional 14 July and provided an accurate picture of the line troops on the eve of the Revolution. The terminal date, 28 February 1793, was within a week of the official disestablishment of the line army as a distinct institution. The results would have been essentially the same for any date in the first four to six months of that year.

Because of the manner in which the soldiers are listed in the registers, according to length of service in the unit, a sample was taken of 3 out of every successive 100 men in half of the infantry and cavalry regiments and in all of the light infantry battalions and artillery regiments. The men about whom the data were recorded and the specific infantry and cavalry regiments sampled were selected by the use of a random numbers table. This sample provided the age, length of service, regional origins, height, and rural–urban origins of the soldiers and N.C.O.s in 1789 and in 1793, a total of 2,280 and 2,858 men respectively.

Once again, the enlisted men in the eleven Swiss regiments (and one Liégeois regiment) had to be excepted from this sample. These regiments, discharged from French service in 1792, apparently retained their *contrôles* which are not available in the Archives de la Guerre. Wherever possible this lacuna has been filled by inspection reports in series X^g and X^b (for the Liégeois). These reports are, however, subject to the criticisms made in the following two paragraphs.

Besides the troop registers, another source of information on the background of the soldiers of the line army is the reports of annual inspections which took place in late summer or early autumn. These reports, for some years, contain summaries on the composition of the units inspected: the height, length of service, campaign experience, provincial or national origins, and professions of the enlisted men in the unit. They provide a compilation of data easy to use for all the men in a given unit. This source, however, has some severe limitations in comparison with the troop registers. The reports are available for only a fraction of the units. Although complete for specific units, they can be misleading for a study of the army as a whole, or even of a given branch. For example, complete inspection reports for 1788 or 1789 are available for eighteen of the ninety-one French and non-Swiss foreign regiments of infantry. In contrast, full inspection reports are available for six of the eleven Swiss regiments. Thus, although the reports provide data on well over 25,000 men, the Swiss regiments, which were recruited and organized in a peculiar way, are grossly over-represented. Similarly, among mounted troops there are complete inspection reports for only two of eighteen dragoon regiments, but for three of six hussar regiments which were recruited largely among foreigners.

There are other, substantive difficulties with this source besides the tendency to misrepresent certain types of units. The reports contain no information on the ages of soldiers. The data in them cannot be broken down according to rank. And there are no complete reports for any of the artillery regiments. Moreover, sometimes the categories used in the reports are not mutually exclusive (e.g. two categories on length of service are 4–8 years and 4 years or less) and are often too broad to be very useful. In the breakdown of personnel according to profession only fourteen occupations are listed, primarily those of greatest interest to the army (such as baker, saddlemaker, tailor); and the vast majority of the soldiers fall into two large but amorphous groups labelled 'Ploughmen, pioneers and other workers in the countryside' and 'Inhabitants of cities, workers in luxury trades and artists'. While the inspection reports provide information on a much larger number of men than do the samples drawn from the *contrôles*, the results must be treated much more carefully.

Although the troop registers contain information on the age, birth-place, height, and service record of almost every soldier, civilian occupation is noted only irregularly; only a small number of unit registers record this information, but they do so for a large number of men in these units. Consequently, the random samples selected to provide a general view of the line soldiers in 1789 and in 1793 cannot furnish acceptable evidence about the social origins of the men in the ranks. What has been done in this study is to record this information—the simple indication of profession—wherever it is noted (in 1,510 cases in 1789 and 3,537 in 1793) and trust that the randomness with which this characteristic was entered in the registers is sufficient to provide a fairly reliable sample. The inspection reports with their very limited number of very broad categories are little help in alleviating this problem; and the only possible checks are comparisons between the data for the two sample dates and with the findings of Corvisier for 1763.

INCIDENCE OF INSUBORDINATION

In order to determine how widespread insubordination was in any given year, it was necessary to compile a sample of units whose history could be traced during the early Revolution, from 1788 to 1793. Such an investigation had to proceed by unit since it is virtually impossible to determine with any precision the number of individuals involved in such activity. With the exception of a few leaders, the participants in this illegal be-haviour are largely passive and are, understandably, reluctant to identify themselves individually, at least until the success of the insubordinate movement is assured. Even in detailed studies, such as William Baldwin's intensive investigation of the mutineers at Nancy in 1790, it remains impossible to determine the total number of active participants.

Since the more dramatic incidents of insubordination are often well known and accounts of them are usually available in a number of sources, they tend to distract attention from the less striking examples and from those units in which discipline was maintained. Therefore, for the purposes of this study a sample of units was examined throughout the entire period under discussion. As far as possible these units were selected at random, but at the same time two other essential criteria were required: reasonably complete records for every year from 1788 to 1793, and a degree of representation of each arm or branch that was roughly proportional to its importance in the line army as a whole.

Although these last two criteria may have injected some bias, the sample's size should minimize this. In all, *c.* 40 per cent of the units in the line army between 1788 and 1793 were studied. These included 41 infantry regiments, of which 10 were foreign regiments (7 Swiss and 3 German); 4 light infantry battalions; 25 cavalry regiments (1 of Carabiniers, 9 of heavy cavalry, 7 of dragoons, 5 of chasseurs, 3 of hussars); and 3 artillery regiments. In addition, this sample was supplemented by data available for other units in a given year. For example, while the sample for insubordination in 1790 includes the 73 units indicated above, information on a further 31 regiments was also utilized.

The sources which provide the information on all these units are far too numerous to be cited in every individual case. They include almost all of the works on the army during the Revolution that are listed in the Bibliography. The most commonly used sources, however, are in the Archives de la Guerre: the *contrôles de troupes* for all units of infantry, light infantry, cavalry, and artillery during the period 1788–93; X^b 13–106 and 162–202; X^c 30–83 and 90–251; X^d 3, 7, 12, 16, 21, 25, 30, and 33; X^g 87–92; *Historiques des Régiments d'Infanterie*, cartons 1–70; *Historiques des Bataillons de Chasseurs*, cartons 81–83; *Historiques des Régiments de Cavalerie*, cartons 94–127; *Historiques des Régiments d'Artillerie*, cartons 133–9. In the Archives nationales, D xv⁵, dossier 45 was also useful.

POLICE FUNCTIONS OF THE ARMY

The line army in eighteenth-century France was continually used in a police role. Its purpose in this capacity, however, was often accomplished by the mere presence of troops which could serve to maintain or restore order. This was perhaps the most common form of police activity by the army and usually the one most desirable to the authorities. But it is often impossible to analyse or evaluate the role of the army in these situations because the troops were not actually employed.

Only those instances in which line units or detachments were expressly called upon to keep order by threatening or perpetrating violence can be analysed in this study. Unfortunately, not all such examples between 1787 and 1793 can be treated. Besides the extremely large number of such cases, the sources for them are diverse and scattered, many (perhaps a majority) of them buried in the vast mass of local archival material. The sample selected to evaluate the incidence of insubordination provides substantial evidence about the police functions of the regular army, but it is somewhat biased by the origin of the sources. Insubordination was of greatest concern to the military authorities, and most of the sources on it originated with them. The employment of troops as police concerned both military and civil authorities, but it was the latter who were most interested in and primarily responsible for such measures. Hence, it is in the records of civilian officials, often local officers, that the most complete sources on the use of troops as police exist. The most fruitful sources for this study were in the Archives nationales: BB^{30} 87 and 161; F^7 3659$^{1-3}$, 3679^1, 3682^{21}, 3683^5, 3686^1; F^9 40, 41 and 44–6; and H^{1453}. In the Archives départementales the following provided valuable data on the police functions of the army: Ille-et-Vilaine C 4701, Nord C 3645, Bouches-du-Rhône L 3245, and Bas-Rhin 1L 1439. Similarly useful were B^{1*} 208 and 209 in the Archives de la Guerre. Other primary and secondary sources, where pertinent, are cited in the text.

An exhaustive treatment of the police role of the line army is impossible within the limits of this more general study. Instead, conclusions are based upon the examination of 233 instances of soldiers serving in a police capacity (6 in 1788, 83 in 1789, 64 in 1790, 56 in 1791, and 24 in 1792). Without a study devoted solely to this problem or without a comprehensive record of all such cases from which a representative sample could be taken, the conclusions reached on the basis of these examples must be considered tentative and subject to revision in the light of subsequent research. Despite these reservations, I believe that the evidence presented here helps to clarify the role of the line army in the Revolution and I hope that it might encourage further study of this very important subject.

PROFESSIONALIZATION OF THE OFFICER CORPS

Definitions of and criteria for professionalization are still very much in dispute, despite—or perhaps because of—the considerable attention devoted to this phenomenon recently. Samuel Huntington has devoted important sections of his influential work, *The Soldier and the State* (New York, 1957), to this problem and lists what he considers the essential characteristics of professionalization in the military or any profession: expertise, responsibility, and corporateness (pp. 8–10). Except for the first criterion, these characteristics are internalized values difficult to measure or even determine in historical circumstances. Despite this difficulty,

Huntington does not hesitate to locate the beginning of officer professionalism in Prussia in 1808 (pp. 30–1).

Without necessarily contesting the validity of Huntington's criteria of responsibility and corporateness, but despairing of finding conclusive evidence of these characteristics (in the sense in which he uses them), I have relied upon certain structural characteristics of the officer corps by which professionalization can be measured. These include new standards for commissions and promotions, a new emphasis on the purpose of the officer corps, new composition, and a new definition of a military career. These criteria are primarily empirical and eclectic; however, Max Weber's description and analysis of bureaucratization have provided a general theoretical framework which, although not explicitly followed, has greatly influenced my approach. See the section on 'Bureaucracy' in H. H. Gerth and C. Wright Mills, eds., *From Max Weber: Essays in Sociology* (New York, 1958), pp. 196–244.

The new standards for a commission and promotion were professional standards. Before 1789 social status and wealth were the primary means of entering and advancing in the officer corps. Early in the Revolution new criteria were established, based on the principle of careers open to talent. Talent, or ability, was measured by professional standards of education (determined at first by examination and later simply by literacy) and experience or length of service.

The aim of the officer corps became more purely professional than ever before in the past. Military efficiency had always been the aim of armies; but other considerations, notably social and financial, had been allowed to interfere with it. The governments of the early Revolution, faced with a hostile Europe, made efficiency the explicit requirement for its officers. This, in turn, made the officers concentrate on this professional aim to the exclusion of other considerations.

The establishment of professional standards and goals necessarily affected the composition of the officer corps. Their effects were compounded by the fact that by early 1793 approximately three-quarters of the pre-revolutionary officers had left the French army in reaction to the political and social policies of the new regime. This exodus, combined with the pressure of war, necessitated an almost complete renewal of the personnel of the officer corps. The new officers and those recently appointed to new positions and grades conformed to the new professional requirements. By 1793 the officer corps was composed almost exclusively of men whose adult life had been spent entirely in the army. In short, these officers were professional soldiers.

The professional character of the new standards, goals, and composition of the officer corps necessitated a change in attitude towards a military career. In the Old Regime the performance of military duties was regarded by most officers as a service, not a full-time occupation. The inadequate pay which officers received made it difficult for them to support themselves without income from outside sources. The Revolution not only required a more complete dedication to military duties, but also provided a salary sufficient to permit such a concentration of energies. In this way, military service was transformed into a professional career.

These characteristics—new standards, aim, composition, and attitude towards career—were intimately related and together constituted the professionalization of the French officer corps.

COMPOSITION OF THE OFFICER CORPS

In the spring of 1793 reports on the civil and military status of the officers in line regiments were prepared in the units for the National Convention. Although I was unable to find such reports for all officers, the Archives de la Guerre has preserved them for a sufficiently large number for valid conclusions to be drawn about the regular officer corps as a whole.

From A.G., X^b 162–98 I have used reports on 1,771 infantry officers (27 colonels, 58 lieutenant-colonels, 564 captains, and 1,122 lieutenants and second-lieutenants) in 50 regiments. Among the data recorded for these men were date and place of birth, residence, civilian profession, and a synopsis of the military career of each officer. Although the authorized strength was 60 officers per infantry regiment, the reports indicate that the average officer strength was *c*. 50 per regiment. This sample, therefore, represents slightly more than one-third of the line infantry officers in February 1793. Unfortunately, there were no reports available on the 406 officers authorized in the fourteen battalions of light infantry.

Much less complete information was available for the officers of line cavalry regiments at this date. Series X^c in the Archives de la Guerre did not contain reports on cavalry officers comparable to those in X^b for the infantry. Some data, which did not usually include civilian professions, were available for cavalry officers in A.G., *Contrôles des Officiers, Révolution et Empire* (uncoded). These registers, kept by regiment, were begun in 1788 and continued through the Empire; but they were not well maintained and they concentrate almost entirely upon the officers' military achievements. However, those cavalry regiments serving in the Army of the West in the summer of 1794 were required to send reports, which included information on the civilian background of officers, to the government; and these reports are contained in this same series. By extracting from them information on men who were serving as cavalry officers in early 1793, I have been able to acquire some further data on the social background of cavalry officers. In all, complete or partial information on 366 cavalry officers (9 colonels, 20 lieutenant-colonels, 96 captains, and 241 lieutenants and second-lieutenants) in 13 regiments was thus obtained. This number constitutes about one-sixth of the total officer strength in this branch in February 1793.

Most difficult to obtain was full information on artillery officers. Incomplete copies of the reports prepared for the Convention in spring 1793 can be found in A.G., X^d 3, 7, 12, and 16. This information was supplemented by gleaning the names and units of other artillery officers from correspondence in X^d and then checking for data on these officers in A.G., *Classement général alphabétique: Officiers, 1791–1847*. The latter series is a huge collection of nearly 4,000 cartons, which contains assorted papers on various officers who served in the regular army during a 57-year period. Not all the officers during this time have any papers here, and these are often of little value. In short, this series was a very unsatisfactory and tedious means of supplementing the reports in X^d. In all I compiled data for 109 artillery officers (1 colonel, 7 lieutenant-colonels, 53 captains, and 48 lieutenants and second-lieutenants) in four regiments —approximately 15 per cent of the total officer strength of the eight artillery regiments.

Information on general officers (who are treated separately in the text) was most readily obtainable in the excellent work of Georges Six, *Dictionnaire biographique des généraux et amiraux français de la Révolution et de l'Empire (1792–1814)*, 2 vols. (Paris, 1934). According to this source, as of 28 February 1793 there were 195 general officers serving in the French army. Sixty-four were lieutenant-generals; 118 were *maréchaux de camp* or major-generals; and thirteen were provisional major-generals, all but two of whom were confirmed in that rank by 15 May 1793. All of these generals have been included in this study.

General staff officers, adjutants-general, and aides-de-camp below the rank of general have not been included in this study due to lack of data. In early 1793 there were *c.* 200 of these. Likewise excluded are the engineer officers who numbered *c.* 300 (see Picq, *Législation militaire*, pp. 127–8 and 136).

In order to avoid an excessive number of categories, some officer grades have been grouped together in the text. All lieutenants have been put into a single category. Similarly, captains, whether captains-in-second or captains commanding, are treated as one group. This simplification can be justified on the grounds that all lieutenants or captains, whatever their precise rank, formed identifiable and similar echelons in the military hierarchy.

Finally, a brief note on ranks is in order. The grade of major had been suppressed on 1 January 1791. On 21 February 1793 the title *chef de bataillon* (*chef d'escadron* in the cavalry) replaced the designation of lieutenant-colonel and *chef de brigade* replaced that of colonel. The old, more familiar titles, however, are used here. The rank of *brigadier* (brigadier-general) was eliminated.

DESIGNATIONS OF LINE UNITS, 1787–93

LINE INFANTRY

Old Regime	1791	Amalgam[1]	
Colonel Général	1st Regiment	1st Battalion < 1st Demi-Brigade	
		2nd Battalion < 2nd	,,
Picardie	2nd Regt.	1st Bn.	< 3rd ,,
		2nd Bn.	< 4th ,,
Piémont	3rd Regt.	1st Bn.	< 5th ,,
		2nd Bn.	< 6th ,,
Provence	4th Regt.	1st Bn.	< not amalgamated
		2nd Bn.	< not amalgamated
Navarre	5th Regt.	1st Bn.	< 9th Demi-Brigade
		2nd Bn.	< 10th ,,
Armagnac	6th Regt.	1st Bn.	< not amalgamated
		2nd Bn.	< 12th Demi-Brigade
Champagne	7th Regt.	1st Bn.	< 13th ,,
		2nd Bn.	< 14th ,,
Austrasie	8th Regt.	1st Bn.	< 15th ,,
		2nd Bn.	< 16th ,,
Normandie	9th Regt.	1st Bn.	< 17th ,,
		2nd Bn.	< not amalgamated
Neustrie	10th Regt.	1st Bn.	< 19th Demi-Brigade
		2nd Bn.	< 20th ,,
La Marine	11th Regt.	1st Bn.	< 21st ,,
		2nd Bn.	< 22nd ,,
Auxerrois	12th Regt.	1st Bn.	< 23rd ,,
		2nd Bn.	< 24th ,,
Bourbonnais	13th Regt.	1st Bn.	< 25th ,,
		2nd Bn.	< 26th ,,
Forez	14th Regt.	1st Bn.	< 27th ,,
		2nd Bn.	< 28th ,,
Béarn	15th Regt.	1st Bn.	< 29th ,,
		2nd Bn.	< 30th ,,
Agenois	16th Regt.	1st Bn.	< 31st ,,
		2nd Bn.	< not amalgamated

[1] The list of demi-brigades into which the battalions of regular infantry were incorporated is drawn from Rousset, *Les Volontaires*, pp. 356–71. Those units not amalgamated continued to exist and operate outside the new organization until 1796 when the infantry was again reorganized at which time almost all of them were incorporated into new demi-brigades; see pp. 372–99 in Rousset.

Old Regime	*1791*	*Amalgam*	
Auvergne	17th Regt.	1st Bn.	< 33rd Demi-Brigade
		2nd Bn.	< 34th "
Royal Auvergne	18th Regt.	1st Bn.	< 35th "
		2nd Bn.	< 36th "
Flandre	19th Regt.	1st Bn.	< not amalgamated
		2nd Bn.	< 38th Demi-Brigade
Cambrésis	20th Regt.	1st Bn.	< 39th "
		2nd Bn.	< 40th "
Guyenne	21st Regt.	1st Bn.	< 41st "
		2nd Bn.	< 42nd "
Viennois	22nd Regt.	1st Bn.	< 43rd "
		2nd Bn.	< 44th "
Royal	23rd Regt.	1st Bn.	< 45th "
		2nd Bn.	< 46th "
Brie	24th Regt.	1st Bn.	< 47th "
		2nd Bn.	< 48th "
Poitou	25th Regt.	1st Bn.	< 49th "
		2nd Bn.	< 50th "
Bresse	26th Regt.	1st Bn.	< 51st "
		2nd Bn.	< 52nd "
Lyonnais	27th Regt.	1st Bn.	< 53rd "
		2nd Bn.	< 54th "
Maine	28th Regt.	1st Bn.	< 55th "
		2nd Bn.	< 56th "
Dauphin	29th Regt.	1st Bn.	< not amalgamated
		2nd Bn.	< not amalgamated
Perche	30th Regt.	1st Bn.	< 59th Demi-Brigade
		2nd Bn.	< 60th "
Aunis	31st Regt.	1st Bn.	< 61st "
		2nd Bn.	< not amalgamated
Bassigny	32nd Regt.	1st Bn.	< not amalgamated
		2nd Bn.	< not amalgamated
Touraine	33rd Regt.	1st Bn.	< 65th Demi-Brigade
		2nd Bn.	< 66th "
Angoulême	34th Regt.	1st Bn.	< 67th "
		2nd Bn.	< 68th "
Aquitaine	35th Regt.	1st Bn.	< 69th "
		2nd Bn.	< 70th "
Anjou	36th Regt.	1st Bn.	< 71st "
		2nd Bn.	< 72nd "
Maréchal de Turenne	37th Regt.	1st Bn.	< 73rd "
		2nd Bn.	< 74th "
Dauphiné	38th Regt.	1st Bn.	< 75th "
		2nd Bn.	< 76th "
Île de France	39th Regt.	1st Bn.	< not amalgamated
		2nd Bn.	< not amalgamated

Old Regime	*1791*	*Amalgam*	
Soissonnais	40th Regt.	1st Bn.	< 79th Demi-Brigade
		2nd Bn.	< 80th ,,
La Reine	41st Regt.	1st Bn.	< not amalgamated
		2nd Bn.	< not amalgamated
Limousin	42nd Regt.	1st Bn.	< 83rd Demi-Brigade
		2nd Bn.	< 84th ,,
Royal Vaisseaux	43rd Regt.	1st Bn.	< 85th ,,
		2nd Bn.	< 86th ,,
Orléans	44th Regt.	1st Bn.	< 87th ,,
		2nd Bn.	< not amalgamated
La Couronne	45th Regt.	1st Bn.	< 89th Demi-Brigade
		2nd Bn.	< 90th ,,
Bretagne	46th Regt.	1st Bn.	< 91st ,,
		2nd Bn.	< 92nd ,,
Lorraine	47th Regt.	1st Bn.	< 93rd ,,
		2nd Bn.	< 94th ,,
Artois	48th Regt.	1st Bn.	< 95th ,,
		2nd Bn.	< not amalgamated
Vintimille	49th Regt.	1st Bn.	< 97th Demi-Brigade
		2nd Bn.	< not amalgamated
Hainaut	50th Regt.	1st Bn.	< 99th Demi-Brigade
		2nd Bn.	< 100th ,,
La Sarre	51st Regt.	1st Bn.	< 101st ,,
		2nd Bn.	< 102nd ,,
La Fère	52nd Regt.	1st Bn.	< 103rd ,,
		2nd Bn.	< 104th ,,
Alsace (German)	53rd Regt.	1st Bn.	< 105th ,,
		2nd Bn.	< not amalgamated
Royal Roussillon	54th Regt.	1st Bn.	< 107th Demi-Brigade
		2nd Bn.	< 108th ,,
Condé	55th Regt.	1st Bn.	< 109th ,,
		2nd Bn.	< 110th ,,
Bourbon	56th Regt.	1st Bn.	< 111th ,,
		2nd Bn.	< 112th ,,
Beauvaisis	57th Regt.	1st Bn.	< 113th ,,
		2nd Bn.	< 114th ,,
Rouergue	58th Regt.	1st Bn.	< not amalgamated
		2nd Bn.	< 116th Demi-Brigade
Bourgogne	59th Regt.	1st Bn.	< 117th ,,
		2nd Bn.	< 118th ,,
Royal Marine	60th Regt.	1st Bn.	< not amalgamated
		2nd Bn.	< not amalgamated
Vermandois	61st Regt.	1st Bn.	< 121st Demi-Brigade
		2nd Bn.	< 122nd ,,
Salm-Salm (German)	62nd Regt.	1st Bn.	< 123rd ,,
		2nd Bn.	< not amalgamated

Old Regime	*1791*	*Amalgam*	
Ernest (Swiss)	63rd Regt.	dismissed 1792	
Salis-Samade (Swiss)	64th Regt.	dismissed 1792	
Sonnenberg (Swiss)	65th Regt.	dismissed 1792	
Castella (Swiss)	66th Regt.	dismissed 1792	
Lanquedoc	67th Regt.	1st Bn.	< not amalgamated
		2nd Bn.	< not amalgamated
Beauce	68th Regt.	1st Bn.	< 127th Demi-Brigade
		2nd Bn.	< 128th „
Vigier (Swiss)	69th Regt.	dismissed 1792	
Médoc	70th Regt.	1st Bn.	< 129th Demi-Brigade
		2nd Bn.	< 130th „
Vivarais	71st Regt.	1st Bn.	< 131st „
		2nd Bn.	< 132nd „
Vexin	72nd Regt.	1st Bn.	< not amalgamated
		2nd Bn.	< 134th Demi-Brigade
Royal Comtois	73rd Regt.	1st Bn.	< not amalgamated
		2nd Bn.	< not amalgamated
Beaujolais	74th Regt.	1st Bn.	< not amalgamated
		2nd Bn.	< 138th Demi-Brigade
Monsieur	75th Regt.	1st Bn.	< 139th „
		2nd Bn.	< 140th „
Châteauvieux (Swiss)	76th Regt.	dismissed 1792	
La Marck (German)	77th Regt.	1st Bn.	< 141st Demi-Brigade
		2nd Bn.	< 142nd „
Penthièvre	78th Regt.	1st Bn.	< 143rd „
		2nd Bn.	< 144th „
Boulonnais	79th Regt.	1st Bn.	< 145th „
		2nd Bn.	< 146th „
Angoumois	80th Regt.	1st Bn.	< 147th „
		2nd Bn.	< 148th „
Conti	81st Regt.	1st Bn.	< 149th „
		2nd Bn.	< 150th „
Saintonge	82nd Regt.	1st Bn.	< not amalgamated
		2nd Bn.	< 152nd Demi-Brigade
Foix	83rd Regt.	1st Bn.	< not amalgamated
		2nd Bn.	< 154th Demi-Brigade
Rohan	84th Regt.	1st Bn.	< not amalgamated
		2nd Bn.	< not amalgamated
Diesbach (Swiss)	85th Regt.	dismissed 1792	
Courten (Swiss)	86th Regt.	dismissed 1792	
Dillon (Irish)	87th Regt.	1st Bn.	< 157th Demi-Brigade
		2nd Bn.	< not amalgamated
Berwick (Irish)	88th Regt.	1st Bn.	< 159th Demi-Brigade
		2nd Bn.	< not amalgamated
Royal Suédois (German)	89th Regt.	1st Bn.	< 161st Demi-Brigade
		2nd Bn.	< 162nd „

Old Regime	1791	Amalgam	
Chartres	90th Regt.	1st Bn.	< 163rd „
		2nd Bn.	< 164th „
Barrois	91st Regt.	1st Bn.	< 165th „
		2nd Bn.	< 166th „
Walsh (Irish)	92nd Regt.	1st Bn.	< not amalgamated
		2nd Bn.	< not amalagmated
Enghien	93rd Regt.	1st Bn.	< 169th Demi-Brigade
		2nd Bn.	< 170th „
Royal Hesse-Darmstadt	94th Regt.	1st Bn.	< 171st „
(German)		2nd Bn.	< 172nd „
Salis-Grisons (Swiss)	95th Regt.	dismissed 1792	
Nassau (German)	96th Regt.	1st Bn.	< 173rd Demi-Brigade
		2nd Bn.	< 174th „
Steiner (Swiss)	97th Regt.	dismissed 1792	
Bouillon (German)	98th Regt.	1st Bn.	< 175th Demi-Brigade
		2nd Bn.	< 176th „
Royal Deux-Ponts (German)	99th Regt.	1st Bn.	< 177th „
		2nd Bn.	< 178th „
Reinach (Swiss)	100th Regt.	dismissed 1792	
Royal Liégeois (Liégeois)	101st Regt.	dismissed 1792	
	102nd Regt.	1st Bn.	< 179th Demi-Brigade
	(created 1791)	2nd Bn.	< 180th „
	103rd Regt.	1st Bn.	< 181st „
	(created 1791)	2nd Bn.	< 182nd „
	104th Regt.	1st Bn.	< 183rd „
	(created 1791)	2nd Bn.	< 184th „
Du Roi	dismissed	1st Bn.	< 185th „
	1790; re-	2nd Bn.	< 186th „
	created as		
	105th Regt.		
Du Cap (colonial)	106th Regt.	1st Bn.	< not amalgamated
	(1792)	2nd Bn.	< not amalgamated
Pondichéry (colonial)	107th Regt.	1st Bn.	< not amalgamated
	(1792)	2nd Bn.	< not amalgamated
Isle-de-France (colonial)	108th Regt.	1st Bn.	< not amalgamated
	(1792)	2nd Bn.	< not amalgamated
Martinique and Guadeloupe	109th Regt.	1st Bn.	< 193rd Demi-Brigade
(colonial)	(1792)	2nd Bn.	< 194th „
Port-au-Prince (colonial)	110th Regt.	1st Bn.	< not amalgamated
	(1792)	2nd Bn.	< 196th Demi-Brigade

LIGHT INFANTRY

Old Regime	1791	Amalgam
Chasseurs Royaux de Provence	1st Battalion	1st Light Demi-Brigade

Old Regime	1791	Amalgam	
Chasseurs Royaux de Dauphiné	2nd Bn.	2nd ,,	,,
Chasseurs Royaux Corses	3rd Bn.	3rd ,,	,,
Chasseurs Corses	4th Bn.	4th ,,	,,
Chasseurs Cantabres	5th Bn.	5th ,,	,,
Chasseurs Bretons	6th Bn.	6th ,,	,,
Chasseurs d'Auvergne	7th Bn.	7th ,,	,,
Chasseurs des Vosges	8th Bn.	8th ,,	,,
Chasseurs des Cévennes	9th Bn.	9th ,,	,,
Chasseurs du Gévaudan	10th Bn.	10th ,,	,,
Chasseurs des Ardennes	11th Bn.	11th ,,	,,
Chasseurs du Roussillon	12th Bn.	12th ,,	,,
	13th Bn. (created 1791)	13th ,,	,,
	14th Bn. (created 1791)	14th ,,	,,

CAVALRY

Old Regime	1791	Comments	
Carabiniers			
Corps of Monsieur Carabiniers	1st Carabiniers		
	2nd ,,		
Heavy Cavalry			
Colonel Général	1st Cavalry		
Royal	2nd ,,		
Commissaire Général	3rd ,,		
La Reine	4th ,,		
Royal Pologne	5th ,,		
Du Roi	6th ,,		
Royal Étranger	7th ,,		
Cuirassiers du Roi	8th ,,		
Artois	9th ,,		
Royal Cravattes	10th ,,		
Royal Roussillon	11th ,,		
Dauphin	12th ,,		
Orléans	13th ,,		
Royal Piémont	14th ,,		
Royal Allemand	15th ,,	emigrated 1792	
Royal Lorraine	16th ,,	15th Cavalry 1792	
Royal Bourgogne	17th ,,	16th ,,	,,
Berry	18th ,,	17th ,,	,,
Royal Normandie	19th ,,	18th ,,	,,
Royal Champagne	20th ,,	19th ,,	,,
Royal Picardie	21st ,,	20th ,,	,,
Royal Navarre	22nd ,,	21st ,,	,,

Old Regime	1791		Comments		
Royal Guyenne	23rd	,,	22nd	,,	,,
Mestre de Camp Général	24th	,,	23rd	,,	,,
	24th	,,	created 1793	,,	

Dragoons

Royal	1st Dragoons	
Condé	2nd	,,
Bourbon	3rd	,,
Conti	4th	,,
Colonel Général	5th	,,
La Reine	6th	,,
Dauphin	7th	,,
Penthièvre	8th	,,
Lorraine	9th	,,
Mestre de Camp Général	10th	,,
Angoulême	11th	,,
Artois	12th	,,
Monsieur	13th	,,
Chartres	14th	,,
Noailles	15th	,,
Orléans	16th	,,
Schomberg	17th	,,
Du Roi	18th	,,

Chasseurs

Alsace	1st Chasseurs		
Evêchés	2nd	,,	
Flandre	3rd	,,	
Franche-Comté	4th	,,	
Hainaut	5th	,,	
Languedoc	6th	,,	
Picardie	7th	,,	
Guyenne	8th	,,	
Lorraine	9th	,,	
Bretagne	10th	,,	
Normandie	11th	,,	
Champagne	12th	,,	
	13th	,,	created 1792

Hussars

Berchény	1st Hussars		
Chamborant	2nd	,,	
Esterhazy	3rd	,,	
Saxe	4th	,,	emigrated 1792
Colonel Général	5th	,,	4th Hussars 1792
Lauzun	6th	,,	5th Hussars 1792
	6th	,,	created 1792
	7th	,,	created 1792

ARTILLERY

Old Regime	1791		Comments
La Fère	1st	Artillery	
Metz	2nd	,,	
Besançon	3rd	,,	
Grenoble	4th	,,	
Strasbourg	5th	,,	
Auxonne	6th	,,	
Toul	7th	,,	
Artillerie des Colonies	8th	,,	incorporated into line army 1792

BIBLIOGRAPHY

ARCHIVAL SOURCES

Archives de la Guerre

B¹* 208 and 209. Correspondence of General Biron, Dec. 1790–Sept. 1791.

B¹³ 56–69. *Justice militaire. Jugements. Ancien régime.* Not to be confused with another series coded B¹³ entitled *Correspondance militaire générale* (*1791–1804*). This series contains verdicts and sentences passed on military crimes and, infrequently, transcripts of trials. The cartons indicated cover the period 1787–92.

Xᵇ 13–106 and 162–202. This series contains inspection reports, strength reports, proposals for promotion, reports on officers, and miscellaneous correspondence. Arranged by units in numerical order, cartons 13–106 and 162–98 are for line infantry regiments; cartons 199–202 for light infantry battalions. Cartons 13–106 cover the period from *c.* 1705 (the date of the regiments' formation) until 1790; and cartons 162–202 cover the subsequent period up to the date of the units' amalgamation with volunteer units.

Xᶜ 30–83 and 90–251. This series is the counterpart of Xᵇ for regiments of Carabiniers, Cavalry, Dragoons, Chasseurs, and Hussars. Cartons 30–83 cover the period from the regiments' formation until 1790; and cartons 90–251 are for the period 1791–1815.

Xᵈ 3, 7, 12, 15, 16, 21, 25, 30, 33 and 40. Comparable to the previous two series, but for artillery units.

Xᵍ 87–92. This series is on the Swiss regiments in French service that were disbanded in 1792. It contains inspection and strength reports, requests for promotions and replacements, and other assorted documents.

Xʷ 48, 51, 64, 73, 74, and 92. Although this series is devoted to the battalions of National Volunteers, the cartons indicated also contain information on the line army. Organized by department.

YA 305, 309, 420, 437, 440, and 447. *Documents d'intérêt collectif ou général.*

YB 494–528. *Contrôles des Officiers.* These cartons concern the officers of Swiss regiments; but they also contain information on soldiers in some of these units. Data on officers include name, date and place of birth, and an outline of their military careers, e.g. promotions, campaigns, decorations.

Y 14ᶜ 1–158. *Contrôles de Troupes. Régiments d'Infanterie, 1786–An III.*

This series provided the basic source of data on enlisted men in line infantry regiments. This information includes name, names of parents, date and place of birth, height, company in the regiment, dates of enlistments, promotions and demotions, and the reason why each man was dropped from the register. Sometimes other information, e.g. physical description, civilian occupation, and religion, is included. Organized by regiment in numerical order.

Contrôles de Troupes. Bataillons d'Infanterie Légère, 1788–An III. This series is uncoded and uncatalogued; it is presently shelved with the registers for the battalions of National Volunteers. It contains the same type of information as the previous series. Organized by battalion in numerical order.

Contrôles de Troupes. Régiments de Carabiniers, Cuirassiers, Cavalerie, Chevaux Légers et Dragons, Chasseurs à Cheval, et Hussards, 1786–1815. Uncoded and uncatalogued, this series contains the same kind of data as the infantry *contrôles*. Organized by regiment in numerical order.

Contrôles de Troupes. Régiments d'Artillerie à pied, 1786–1815. This series is also uncoded and uncatalogued. Organized by regiment in numerical order.

Contrôles de Troupes. Garde Nationale (Parisienne) Soldée. Registers exist for three—the 3rd, 4th, and 5th—of the six divisions of this force. The registers cover the period from 1789 to 1791, when the men of these divisions were incorporated into regular infantry units. This series is uncoded and uncatalogued. It can be found shelved among the *contrôles* of the battalions of National Volunteers.

Contrôles des Officiers. Révolution et Empire. This uncoded series is organized by branch and by regiment. It begins in 1788, except for units formed after that date. The data on officers are far less complete than those for enlisted men; and, generally, the registers are less carefully kept.

Classement général alphabétique. Officiers, 1791–1847. This huge series of 3,997 cartons contains available information on individual officers, filed alphabetically according to the officers' names. The data on each officer are of very uneven quality and quantity; and not all officers are listed.

Historiques des Régiments d'Infanterie, 1–70. This series contains published and manuscript histories of line infantry regiments, most of which date from the period 1871–1914. Although they are of very unequal quality, these histories form the most complete collection of such information available. The series is organized by regiment in numerical order. The histories of the 76th–89th Infantry Regiments also contain information on the first fourteen battalions of light infantry.

Historiques des Régiments de Cavalerie, 94–127. This series is comparable to the preceding one. Cartons 94–9 are on Cuirassier, or Cavalry,

Regiments; cartons 100–12 are on Dragoon Regiments; cartons 113–21 are for Chasseur Regiments; and cartons 122–7 contain information on Hussar Regiments.

Historiques des Régiments d'Artillerie, 133–9. The counterpart of the previous two series for the artillery. Organized by regiments in numerical order.

Mémoires historiques et reconnaissances, 1751, 1770, 1774, and 1777.

Ordonnances militaires. A useful, but unindexed, collection of military legislation, arranged in chronological order.

Registre de délibérations du comité de la Brigade de Cavalerie assemblée à Strasbourg, le 12 aoust 1789. Uncoded and uncatalogued, this is a photocopy of a manuscript whose source is not identified.

Archives nationales

AB xix 702, Plaquette 10. *Ministère de la Guerre. Correspondances militaires.*

119 AP. *Papiers du Vicomte de Mirabeau (1785–1792).*

BB³⁰ 87 (*Émeutes*) and 161 (*Enquêtes et poursuites contre le baron de Besenval pour sa conduite lors de la prise de la Bastille*).

D^{iv bis}, Dossier 47. *États de Population.*

D^{xv} 2–5. *Comité militaire, 1789–1795.*

F⁷. *Police Générale.* 3659^{1–3} (Bouches-du-Rhône, 1790–An III); 3679¹ (Ille-et-Vilaine, 1790–An V); 3679³ (Isère, 1789–1820); 3682¹² (Meurthe, 1790–1825); 3682²¹ (Moselle, 1789–An VI); 3683⁵ (Nord, 1790—Nivôse An IV); 3686¹ (Bas-Rhin, 1789–An VI); 3688¹ (Seine, 1789–92).

F⁹. *Affaires militaires.* 39–47 (*Service de la troupe à l'intérieur*); 55 (*Justice militaire, 1790–1850*); 65 (*Casernement et couchage, 1789–1821*); and 129 (*Logement des gens de guerre, 1791–1849*).

H¹⁴⁵³. *Pièces et correspondances relatives aux troubles et émeutes (dossier transmis par M. de Saint-Priest); Correspondances diverses adressées à Necker, 1789–1790.*

Y 9999 and 13,818. These cartons contain documents on trials at the Châtelet in mid-1789.

Archives départmentales

Bouches-du-Rhône L. *Administration de 1789 à l'an VIII.* 289 (*Troubles d'Arles, 1790–1791*); 423bis (*Procédure contre les officiers du régiment de Lyonnais,, 1790–1791*); 2,054 (*Société des antipolitiques d'Aix. Affaires militaires, 1791–1793*); 3,245 (*Affaire du régiment de Lyonnais. Information contre divers officiers de ce régiment tenant garnison à Salon et à Aix, 1790–1791*).

Ille-et-Vilaine C. *Administration provinciale.* 1113 (*Jugements rendus par les Conseils de guerre assemblés, 1756–1789*); 1115 (*Jugements rendus par les Conseils de guerre assemblés, 1784–1789*); and 4701 (*Affaires militaires. Étapes et fourages, 1748–1790*).

Isère L. *Administration de 1789 à l'an VIII.* 56 and 68.

Nord C. *Administration provinciale.* 3645 (*Armée. Régiment d'Esterhazy. Correspondance, journal, 1785–91*). L. *Administration de 1789 à l'an VIII.* 5783 (*Délibérations du directoire du district de Bergues*); 5788 (*Délibérations du directoire du district de Bergues*); 6760 (*Régiments suisses licenciés. Prestation de serment des recrues incorporées, 1792*); 8546 (*Recrutement. Engagements volontaires dans les troupes de ligne, 1792*); 8582 (*Police et discipline militaires, 1790–an III*).

Bas-Rhin 38J. Collection Fernand-J. Heitz. 178 (*Intégration du 53e régiment d'infanterie d'Alsace—jusqu'alors compris sur l'état de l'infanterie allemande—dans l'infanterie française dont il potera désormais l'uniforme. Décret de l'Assemblée nationale du 12 juillet 1791*); 179 (*Adresse d'hommage et de dévouement de la Société des amis de la Constitution et des militaires de la garnison de Sélestat envers le général Luckner, commandant de 5e et 6e divisions, Sélestat, 30 décembre 1791*); 180 (*Supplique adressée par les chasseurs à cheval du 7e régiment au général Luckner, commandant les 5e et 6e divisions, pour réintégrer leur ancienne garnison de Hagenau, 1791*). L. *Administration de 1789 à l'an VIII.* 1439 (*Police et discipline militaire, troubles, insurrections, désordres, vols dans les régions, espions; lois, instructions et correspondance générale; état civil de militaires: dossiers individuels; distinctions militaires, 1790–an VIII*); 1446(*Justice militaire, tribunaux, maisons d'arrêt militaires, 1790–an VIII*).

Bibliothèque nationale

Manuscrits français (*Ancien supplément français*). 7002 (*Documents militaires, 1791–1815*); 7004 (*Documents divers sur les affaires militaires, la Légion d'honneur, les finances, les journaux, la Révolution à Paris, à Strasbourg, etc., 1790–1812*); 13713 (*Journal des évenements survenus à Paris du 2 avril au 8 octobre 1789; analyse des comptes rendus des séances de l'Assemblée nationale, etc., par un clerc de procureur au Châtelet.*

Maclure Collection of French Revolutionary Materials

(Univ. of Pennsylvania). Vols. 831, 832, 842, 848, 861, 874, 967, 983, 992, 1009, 1018, 1128, 1129, and 1130. Part of a very useful collection of materials ordered published by the Revolutionary Assemblies.

MEMOIRS, CORRESPONDENCE, DIARIES

BESENVAL, PIERRE VICTOR, BARON DE. *Mémoires du Baron de Besenval.* 2 vols. Paris, 1821.

BOUILLÉ, FRANÇOIS-CLAUDE-AMOUR, MARQUIS DE. *Mémoires du Marquis de Bouillé.* Paris, 1821.

COLIN, JEAN. *La Tactique et la discipline dans les armées de la Révolution:*

Correspondance du Général Schauenbourg du 4 avril au 2 août 1793. Paris, 1902.

COMEAU DE CHARRY, SÉBASTIEN-JOSEPH, BARON DE. *Souvenirs des guerres d'Allemagne pendant la Révolution et l'Empire.* Paris, 1900.

CHUQUET, ARTHUR. *Lettres de 1792.* Paris, 1911.

DUMOURIEZ, CHARLES-FRANÇOIS-DUPERIER. *Mémoires du Général Dumouriez.* 2 vols. Paris, 1848.

LAFAYETTE, MARQUIS DE. *Mémoires, correspondance, et manuscrits du Général Lafayette, publiés par sa famille.* 2 vols. Brussels, 1837.

LAHURE, LOUIS-JOSEPH, BARON. *Souvenirs de la vie militaire du lieutenant-général Baron L.-J. Lahure, 1787–1815.* Paris, 1895.

MANGEREL, MAXIME. *Le capitaine Gerbaud, 1773–1799.* Paris, 1910.

[MARIELLE, COMMANDANT]. 'Souvenirs de campagne d'un soldat du régiment de Limousin (1741–1748).' *Carnet de la Sabretache,* X (1902), 668–90 and 737–62.

MAUTORT, CHEVALIER DE. *Mémoires du chevalier de Mautort, Capitaine au régiment d'Austrasie, Chevalier de l'Ordre royal et militaire de Saint-Louis (1752–1802).* Paris, 1895.

MIOT DE MELITO, COMTE. *Mémoires du Comte Miot de Melito.* 3 vols. Paris, 1858.

MONEY, JOHN. *The History of the Campaign of 1792, between the Armies of France under Generals Dumourier, Valence, etc. and the Allies under the Duke of Brunswick; with an Account of What Passed in the Thuilleries on the 10th of August.* London, 1794.

MORRIS, GOUVERNEUR. *Journal de Gouverneur Morris, Ministre plénipotentiaire des États-Unis en France de 1792 à 1794, pendant les années 1789, 1790, 1791 et 1792.* Translated by E. Pariset. Paris, 1901.

PETITFRÈRE, CLAUDE. *Le Général Dupuy et sa correspondance (1792–1798).* Paris, 1962.

PINGAUD, LÉONCE. *L'Invasion austro-prussienne (1792–1794): Documents publiés pour la Société d'histoire contemporaine.* Paris, 1895.

PION DES LOCHES, ANTIONE-AUGUSTIN-FLAVIEN. *Mes campagnes, 1792–1815.* Paris, 1889.

SIMON, CLAUDE. *Correspondance de Claude Simon, Lieutenant de Grenadiers du régiment de Walsh (no. 92) aux armées du Nord, des Ardennes et de Sambre-et-Meuse, 1792–1793.* Grenoble, 1899.

THE FRENCH ARMY UNDER THE OLD RÉGIME

BABEAU, ALBERT. *La Vie militaire sous l'ancien régime.* Vol. I: *Les Soldats* and Vol. II: *Les Officiers.* Paris, 1889 and 1890.

BACQUET, CAPITAINE. *L'Infanterie au XVIII⁰ siècle: L'Organisation.* Paris, 1907.

BIEN, DAVID D. 'La Réaction aristocratique avant 1789: l'exemple de l'armée.' *Annales, Economies, Sociétés, Civilisations*, XXIX (1974), 23–48 and 505–34.

BUTTET, HENRI-JOSEPH DE. 'La Dépense du soldat en 1772.' *Actes du quatre-vingt-dixième congrès des sociétés savantes*, vol I. Paris, 1966.

CHALMIN, P. 'La Désintégration de l'armée royale en France à la fin du XVIIIᵉ siècle.' *Revue historique de l'armée*, 1964, No. 1, pp. 75–90.

CHALMIN, PIERRE. 'La Formation des officiers des armes savantes sous l'ancien régime.' *Actes du soixante-seizième congrès des sociétés savantes: Rennes, 1951*. Paris, 1951.

CHARTIER, ROGER. 'Un recrutement scolaire au XVIIIᵉ siècle: L'École royale du Génie de Mézières.' *Revue d'histoire moderne et contemporaine*, XX (1973), 353–75.

CHUQUET, ARTHUR. 'Roture et noblesse dans l'armée royale.' *Séances et travaux de l'Académie des sciences morales et politiques*, CLXXV (Jan.–June 1911), 204–42.

COLIN, J. *L'Infanterie au XVIIIᵉ siècle: La Tactique*. Paris, 1907.

CORVISIER, ANDRÉ. *L'Armée française de la fin du XVIIᵉ siècle au ministère de Choiseul: Le Soldat*. 2 vols. Paris, 1964.

—— 'Hiérarchie militaire et hiérarchie sociale à la veille de la Révolution.' *Revue internationale d'histoire militaire*, XXX (1970), 77–91.

—— 'Un officier normand de Louis XV: Le Lieutenant-colonel Jean-François Le Parsonnier du Landey d'après sa correspondance (1714–1785).' *Annales de Normandie*, IX (1959), 191–216.

DEJOB, CHARLES. 'Le Soldat dans la littérature française au XVIIIᵉ siècle.' *Revue politique et litteraire: Revue bleue*, 4th Series, XII (7 Oct. 1899), 449–58.

DESBRIÈRE, ÉDOUARD and SAUTAI, MAURICE. *La Cavalerie de 1740 à 1789*. Paris, 1906.

DURUY, ALBERT. *L'Armée royale en 1789*. Paris, 1888.

GROUVEL, VICOMTE. 'Le Régiment suisse de Waldner au service de la France (1673–1792).' *Vert et Rouge*, I (1945), 28–32.

HENNET, LÉON. *Les Compagnies de cadets-gentilshommes et les écoles militaires*. Paris, 1889.

—— *Les Milices et les troupes provinciales*. Paris, 1884.

KENNETT, LEE. *The French Armies in the Seven Years' War: A Study in Military Organization and Administration*. Durham, N.C., 1967.

LACOLLE, NOËL. *Les Gardes françaises: Leur histoire, 1563–1789*. Paris and Limoges, 1901.

LATREILLE, ALBERT. *L'Armée et la nation à la fin de l'ancien régime: Les Derniers Ministres de la guerre de la monarchie*. Paris, 1914.

LAULAN, ROBERT. 'Pourquoi et comment on entrait à l'École royale et militaire de Paris.' *Revue d'histoire moderne et contemporaine*, IV (1957), 141–50.

LÉONARD, ÉMILE. *L'Armée et ses problèmes au XVIIIᵉ siècle*. Paris, 1958.

Lettre à M. le Comte de * * *, *ancien capitaine au Régiment D* * * *, *sur l'obéissance que les Militaires doivent aux Commandemens du Prince.* n.p., n.d.

MENTION, LÉON. *L'Armée de l'ancien régime.* Paris, [1900].

NAVEREAU, ANDRÉ EUGÈNE. *Le Logement et les ustensibles des gens de guerre de 1439 à 1789.* Poitiers, 1924.

NAVEREAU, GÉNÉRAL. 'Les Lignes d'étape.' *Revue historique de l'armée*, 1962, No. 2, pp. 19–29.

O'CALLAGHAN, JOHN CORNELIUS. *History of the Irish Brigades in the Service of France, from the Revolution in Great Britain and Ireland under James II to the Revolution in France under Louis XVI.* New York, 1885.

PICARD, ERNEST and JOUAN, LOUIS. *L'Artillerie française au XVIIIᵉ siècle.* Paris, 1906.

QUIMBY, ROBERT S. *The Background of Napoleonic Warfare: The Theory of Military Tactics in Eighteenth-Century France.* New York, 1957.

ROSS, STEVEN T. 'The Development of the Combat Division in 18th Century French Armies.' *French Historical Studies*, IV (Spring 1965), 84–94.

SALERIAN-SAUGY, GHOUGAS. *Les Conseils de guerre judiciares en France sous l'ancien régime.* Bourges, 1925.

SARS, ROBERT. *Le Recrutement de l'armée permanente sous l'ancien régime*, Paris, 1920.

SIX, GEORGES. 'Fallait-il quatre quartiers de noblesse pour être officier à la fin de l'ancien régime?' *Revue d'histoire moderne*, IV (1929), 47–56.

TUETEY, LOUIS. *Les Officiers sous l'ancien régime.* Paris, 1908.

WILKINSON, SPENSER. *The French Army before Napoleon.* Oxford, 1915.

THE FRENCH ARMY DURING THE REVOLUTION

Avis aux Grenadiers et soldats du Tiers-État par un ancien Camarade du Régiment des Gardes Françoises. n.p., [1789].

BALDWIN, WILLIAM CLINTON. 'The Beginnings of the Revolution and the Mutiny of the Royal Garrison in Nancy: *L'Affaire de Nancy*, 1790.' Unpublished Ph.D dissertation, Univ. of Michigan, 1973.

BEAUREPAIRE, EUGÈNE DE. 'L'Assassinat du Major de Belsunce (Caen, 12 août 1789).' *Revue de la Révolution*, III (Jan.–June 1884), 409–29 and IV (July–Dec. 1884), 26–47.

BÉGIN, ÉMILE. 'Une insurrection à Metz en 1790.' *Le Pays lorrain et le pays messin*, VI (1909), 707–10.

BERTAUD, JEAN-PAUL. 'Aperçus sur l'insoumission et la désertion à l'époque révolutionnaire: Étude de sources.' *Bulletin d'histoire économique et sociale de la Révolution française: Année 1969.* Paris, 1970.

—— 'Les Armées de l'an II: Administration militaire et combattants.' *Revue historique de l'armée*, 1969, No. 2, pp. 41–9.

—— 'Notes sur le premier amalgame (février 1793–janvier 1794).' *Revue d'histoire moderne et contemporaine*, XX (1973) 72–83.

—— 'Le Recrutement et l'avancement des officiers de la Révolution.' *Annales historiques de la Révolution française*, XLIV (1972), 513–36.

—— *Valmy: La Démocratie en armes.* Paris, 1970.

—— 'Voies nouvelles pour l'histoire militaire de la Révolution.' *Annales historiques de la Révolution française*, XLVII (1975), 66–94.

BOULOISEAU, MARC. 'Deux relations de l'arrestation du roi à Varennes.' *Annales historiques de la Révolution française*, XLIV (1972), 438–55.

—— 'Une source ignorée de l'histoire de la Contre-Révolution: *Les Archives françaises*: Le Royal-Allemand-Cavalerie en juillet 1789.' *Actes du quatre-vingt-douzième congrès national des sociétés savantes: Strasbourg et Colmar 1967. Section d'histoire moderne et contemporaine*, vol. III. Paris, 1970.

BOURDEAU, GEORGES. 'L'Affaire de Nancy—31 août 1790.' *Annales de l'Est*, XII (1898), 280–92.

BUTTET, HENRY-JOSEPH DE. 'Le Comité de la brigade de cavalerie en garnison à Strasbourg (août 1789).' *Actes du quatre-vingt-douzième congrès national des sociétés savantes: Strasbourg et Colmar 1967. Section d'histoire moderne et contemporaine*, vol. III. Paris, 1970.

—— 'La Mission de Monsieur de la Chapelle, Maréchal de camp commandant les troupes envoyées à Lyon pour le rétablissement des barrières et ses rapports avec la municipalité (septembre 1790 à janvier 1791).' *Actes du quatre-vingt-neuvième congrès national des sociétés savantes: Lyon 1964. Section d'histoire moderne et contemporaine*, tome 2, vol. I. Paris, 1965.

CAHAN, L. and GUYOT, R. *L'Oeuvre législative de la Révolution.* Paris, 1913.

CANTAL, PIERRE. *Études sur l'armée révolutionnaire.* Paris, [1907].

CARDENAL, LIEUTENANT DE. *Recrutement de l'armée en Périgord pendant la période révolutionnaire (1789–1800).* Perigueux, 1911.

CARON, PIERRE. *La Défense nationale de 1792 à 1795.* Paris, 1912.

—— 'La Tentative de contre-révolution de juin-juillet 1789.' *Revue d'histoire moderne*, VIII (1906–7), 5–34 and 649–78.

CHALMIN, LIEUTENANT-COLONEL. 'La Guerre "révolutionnaire" sous la Législative et la Convention.' *Revue historique de l'armée*, 1958, No. 3, pp. 39–52.

CHAMBORANT DE PERISSAT. *L'Armée de la Révolution: Ses généraux et ses soldats, 1789–1871.* Paris, 1875.

CHARAVAY, ÉTIENNE. *Les Grades militaires sous la Révolution.* Paris, 1894.

CHASSIN, CHARLES-LOUIS. *L'Armée et la Révolution.* Paris, 1867.

CHILLY, LUCIEN DE. *Le Premier Ministre constitutionnel de la guerre, La Tour du Pin: Les Origines de l'armée nouvelle sous la Constituante.* Paris, 1909.

CHOPPIN, HENRI. *Les Insurrections militaires en 1790.* Paris, 1903.
—— *Notes sur l'organisation de l'armée pendant la Révolution, 4 août 1789–8 brumaire an IV.* Paris, 1873.
CHUQUET, ARTHUR. *Les Guerres de la Révolution.* Vol. I: *La Première Invasion prussienne (11 août–2 septembre 1792)*; vol. II: *Valmy*; vol. III: *La Retraite de Brunswick*; vol. IV: *Jemappes et la conquête de la Belgique*; and vol. V: *La Trahison de Dumouriez.* Paris, 1886–91.
CLERGET, CHARLES. *Tableaux des armées françaises pendant les guerres de la Révolution.* Paris, 1905.
DÉPREZ, EUGÈNE. *Les Volontaires nationaux (1791–1793).* Paris, 1908.
DESBRIÈRE, ÉDOUARD and SAUTAI, MAURICE. *La Cavalerie pendant la Révolution, du 14 juillet 1789 au 26 juin 1794.* 2 vols. Paris, 1907 and 1908.
DES POMMELLES, CHEVALIER. *Mémoire sur le mode de formation et de recrutement de l'armée auxiliaire.* Paris, 1790.
DRUÈNE, LIEUTENANT-COLONEL. 'Régiments parisiens: Des Gardes-Françaises à la Garde imperiale.' *Revue historique de l'armée,* 1952, No. 1, pp. 25–37.
DUFAY, PIERRE. *Les Sociétés populaires et l'armée (1791–1794).* Paris, 1913.
DUMONT, G. *Études sur l'armée pendant la Révolution. Première série: 1791. Bataillons de volontaires nationaux.* 2 vols. Paris and Limoges, 1914.
DURIEUX, JOSEPH. *Gardes françaises du 14 juillet.* Paris, 1933.
—— *Les Vainqueurs de la Bastille.* Paris, 1911.
État des officiers de tous grades déserteurs ou émigrés classés par régiment. Paris, 1793.
GODECHOT, JACQUES, ed. 'Quatre lettres sur les journées des 11–23 juillet et 5–6 octobre 1789.' *Annales historiques de la Révolution française.* XLII (1970), 646–56.
GODECHOT, JACQUES. *The Taking of the Bastille: July 14th, 1789.* Translated by Jean Stewart. London, 1970.
GOTTSCHALK, LOUIS and MADDOX, MARGARET. *Lafayette in the French Revolution, Through the October Days.* Chicago, 1969.
GOURNAY, B. C., ed. *Journal militaire,* vols. I–VI. Paris, 1790–93.
HARTMANN, L. *Les Officiers de l'armée royale et la Révolution.* Paris, 1910.
HAUTERIVE, ERNEST D'. *L'Armée sous la Révolution, 1789–94.* Paris, 1894.
HENNET, LÉON, ed. *État militaire de France pour l'anneé 1793.* Paris, 1903.
JOUSSAIN, ANDRÉ, 'Méfiance dans l'armée sous la Révolution.' *Les Libertés françaises,* XXVII–XXX (Feb.–May 1958), 28–35, 33–41, 33–42, and 61–7.
JUNG, THÉODORE. *L'Armée et la Révolution: Dubois-Crancé (Edmond-Alexis-Louis), mousquetaire, constituant, conventionnel, général de division, ministre de la Guerre (1747–1814).* 2 vols. Paris, 1884.
LABARRE DE RAILLICOURT, D. *Généraux et amiraux de la Révolution et de*

l'Empire: Complément aux dictionnaires de G. Six et D. Labarre de Raillicourt. Paris, 1966.

LACHOUQUE, HENRY. *Aux armes, citoyens! Les Soldats de la Révolution*. Paris, 1969.

LAUERMA, MATTI. *L'Artillerie de campagne française pendant les guerres de la Révolution*. Helsinki, 1956.

LEGRAND, CHEF DE BATAILLON. *La Justice militaire et la discipline à l'Armée du Rhin et à l'Armée du Rhin-et-Moselle (1792–1796)*. Paris, 1909.

LEGRAND, ROBERT. *Le Recrutement des armées et les désertions (1791–1815): Aspects de la Révolution en Picardie*. Abbeville, 1957.

LEVERRIER, JULES. *La Naissance de l'armée nationale 1789–1794*. Paris, 1939.

LEVY-SCHNEIDER, LÉON. 'L'Armée et la Convention.' *L'Oeuvre sociale de la Révolution française*. Edited by Émile Faguet. Paris, [1901].

—— *Les Soldats de la Révolution*. Trévoux, 1917.

LOMBARÈS, MICHEL DE. 'Varennes ou la fin d'un régime (21 juin 1791).' *Revue historique de l'armée*, 1960, Nos. 3 and 4, pp. 33–56 and 45–62; and 1961, No. 1, pp. 23–36.

MARTIN, MARC. 'Journaux d'armées au temps de la Convention.' *Annales historiques de la Révolution française*, XLIV (1972), 567–605.

MATHIEZ, ALBERT. *La Victoire en l'an II*. Paris, 1916.

MÉRILYS, JEAN, 'La Propagande révolutionnaire dans l'armée en 1789.' *La Revue hebdomadaire* (22 May 1937), pp. 478–91.

MEYNIER, ALBERT. 'Quelques précisions nouvelles sur les levées et pertes militaires en France sous la Révolution et le Premier Empire (1793–1815).' *Bulletin de la Société d'histoire moderne*, Neuvième série, VI (Jan. 1938). 3–8.

MICHELET, JULES. *Les Soldats de la Révolution*. Paris, 1878.

MICHON, GEORGES. *La Justice militaire sous la Révolution*. Paris, 1922.

MOUILLARD, BERNARD. *Le Recrutement de l'armée révolutionnaire dans le Puy-de-Dôme*. Clermont-Ferrand, 1926.

PHIPPS, RAMSAY W. *The Armies of the First French Republic and the Rise of the Marshals of Napoleon*. 5 vols. London, 1926–39.

PICARD, LOUIS. *La Cavalerie dans les guerres de la Révolution et de l'Empire*. 2 vols. Saumur, 1895–6.

PICQ, ANTOINE. *La Législation militaire de l'époque révolutionnaire: Introduction à l'étude de la législation militaire actuelle*. Paris, 1931.

PINASSEAU, JEAN. *L'Émigration militaire: Campagne de 1792*. 2 parts. Paris, 1957 and 1964.

POISSON, CHARLES. *L'Armée et la Garde Nationale*. 4 vols. Paris, 1858–62.

—— *Les Fournisseurs aux armées sous la Révolution française: Le Directoire des achats (1792–1793): J. Bidermann, Cousin, Marx-Berr*. Paris, 1932.

QUARRÉ-REYBOURBON, LOUIS-FRANÇOIS. *Souvenirs Béthunois: Un Épisode de la Révolution à Béthune*. Lille, 1886.

REINHARD, MARCEL. *L'Armée et la Révolution pendant la Convention*. 2 Fascicules. Paris, n.d.

—— *L'Armée et la Révolution*. 2 Fascicules. [Paris], n.d.

—— 'Nostalgie et service militaire pendant la Révolution.' *Annales historiques de la Révolution française*, XXX (1958), 1–15.

Relation de ce qui s'est passé à Rennes en Bretagne, lors de la nouvelle du renvoi de M. Necker. [Paris], n.d.

Relation de ce qui s'est passé au Régiment de Royal-Cavalerie du 27 juin jusqu'au 11 juillet 1790 : Les Sous-officiers et cavaliers de Royal, aussi amis de l'honneur de la Liberté qu'attachés à leur état, aux Citoyens de Strasbourg et aux garnisons. Strasbourg, 1790.

ROSS, STEVEN T. *Quest for Victory : French Military Strategy, 1792–1799*. New York, 1973.

ROUSSET, CAMILLE. *Les Volontaires, 1791–1794*. Paris, 1892.

SABATIÉ, A. C. *La Justice pendant la Révolution : Le Tribunal révolutionnaire de Paris*. Paris, 1912.

SAGNIER, GEORGES. *La Désertion dans le Pas-de-Calais de 1792 à 1802*. Blangermont, 1965.

SCOTT, SAMUEL F. 'The French Revolution and the Professionalization of the French Officer Corps, 1789–1793.' *On Military Ideology*. Edited by Morris Janowitz and Jacques van Doorn. Rotterdam, 1971.

—— 'Les Officiers de l'infanterie de ligne à la veille de l'Amalgame.' *Annales historiques de la Révolution française*, XL (1968), 455–71.

—— 'Problems of Law and Order During 1790, the "Peaceful" Year of the French Revolution.' *American Historical Review*, LXXX (1975), 859–88.

—— 'The Regeneration of the Line Army during the French Revolution.' *Journal of Modern History*, XLII (Sept. 1970), 307–30.

—— 'Les soldats de l'armée de ligne en 1793.' *Annales historiques de la Révolution française*, XLIV (1972), 493–512.

SCOTT, SAMUEL and BERTAUD, JEAN-PAUL. 'Le 104ᵉ Régiment de ligne: Gardes françaises et gardes nationaux parisiens aux armées de la Révolution (1792–1793).' *Études de la région parisienne*, Nouvelle Série, No. 12 (Oct. 1966), pp. 5–12.

SÉREAU, R. 'La Révolution vue de Strasbourg.' *Revue historique de l'armée*, 1947, No. 4, pp. 91–106 and 1948, No. 1, pp. 55–63.

SERVICE HISTORIQUE DE L'ARMÉE. 'Aux armées de la Révolution: Organisation, discipline, justice militaire.' *Revue historique de l'armée*, 1957, No. 1, pp. 91–92.

SIX, GEORGES. *Dictionnaire biographique des généraux et amiraux français de la Révolution et de l'Empire (1792–1814)*. 2 vols. Paris, 1934.

—— *Les Généraux de la Révolution et de l'Empire*. Paris, 1947.

SOANEN, H. 'La Franc-Maconnerie et l'Armée pendant la Révolution.' *Annales historiques de la Révolution française*, V. (1928), 530–40.

SOBOUL, ALBERT. *L'Armée nationale sous la Révolution (1789–1794)*. Paris, 1945.

—— *Les Soldats de l'an II*. Paris, 1959.

TINTOU, JULES. *Soldats limousins de la Révolution et de l'Empire*. Tulle, 1967.

VIALLA, S. *Marseille révolutionnaire : L'Armée-nation (1789–1793)*. Paris, 1910.

INDEX*

* Army units are listed under Old Regime names; for their numerical correspondence, see Appendix II.

National Assembly, 44, 46, 58, 70, 74, 82, 83, 85, 89, 97, 112, 124, 128, 140, 145; and the Royal Comtois affair, 27; and venality, 28; in July 1789, 52–3, 57; soldiers' support for 70–1, 96, 152; attempts to control army, 72, 73, 101, 103, 104, 106, 107, 125, 151, 167; approval of *fédérations*, 86, 150; and Vicomte de Mirabeau, 88; fear of mutiny, 87, 90, 91, 102, 152, 160; repression of Nancy revolt, 94–5, 152; troops' defiance toward, 100; and military reforms, 153–7, 161, 191; recruitment policies, 155–9, 163

National Guard, 77, 117, 124, 125, 126, 127, 129, 149, 150, 157, 161, 165, 170, 177, 180, 184; of Aix-en-Provence, 137; of Amiens, 149; of Apt, 110; of Arles, 146; of Bergues, 131; of Caen, 72; of Clermont-en-Argonne, 104; of Colmar, 129; of Douai, 84, 131; of Dunkerque, 132; of Franche-Comté, 149; of Hesdin, 86; of Lille, 84–5; of Lyon, 142–4; of Marseille, 139–41; of Montauban, 149; of Nancy, 93, 95–6; of Orléans, 149; of Paris, 67–9, 72–3, 75–6, 92, 117, 158; of Perpignan, 87–8; of Saint-Malo, 130; of Sainte-Menehould, 104; of Saumur, 130; of Schilligheim, 148; of Strasbourg, 148; of Toulouse, 149; of Tours, 99; of Uzès, 101; of Varennes, 105; of Versailles, 53, 75

Necker, Jacques, 53, 70, 71, 80
Neuf-Brisach, 170
Nevers, 127
Nice, 173, 176
Nicolon (merchant of Douai), 131–2
Nîmes, 100–02, 112, 113, 128, 143, 161
Nivernais (province), 136
Nobles serving in ranks, 3, 16, 18, 189–90
Normandie (province), 10, 21, 63, 86
Normandie (11th) Chasseurs, 85
Normandie (9th) Infantry, 150
Noue, General de, 93, 94–5

Oath: of August 1789, 73, 75, 151; of 11 June 1791, 103; after flight to Varennes, 106–07, 109, 119, 160; of August 1792, 117
October days, 69, 74–6

Officers of fortune, 6, 20, 23, 30, 32, 33, 60, 65, 72, 76, 83, 109, 112–14, 138, 193, 200
104th Infantry, 158, 198
102nd Infantry, 158
103rd Infantry, 158
Orléanais (province), 63
Orléans, 149
Orléans, Duc d', 55
Orléans (13th) Cavalry, 38
Orléans (16th) Dragoons, 47, 70, 79 n., 126

Pache, Minister of War, 176
Palais Royal, 53, 54, 55, 61
Parlements, 46, 47, 48
Pay, 31, 43–4, 55, 56, 67, 69, 89, 151, 152, 154, 157, 158, 159, 162, 163, 165, 179, 181, 191, 215
Peasants in army, 16, 17–18, 33, 158 n., 187, 188, 190, 198
Penthièvre (78th) Infantry, 38, 47, 114, 132
Perpignan, 37, 87–8, 96, 108
Phalsbourg, 107, 112, 161
Philippeville, 41
Picardie (province), 9, 50, 63, 130, 137
Picardie (7th) Chasseurs, 163
Picardie (2nd) Infantry, 89–90, 200
Poitiers, 134
Poitou (province), 11, 50, 185 n.
Poitou (25th) Infantry, 89, 129
Police role of army, 3, 46–59, 78–80, 125–136, 144, 147, 155, 167, 168, 207, 212–213
Political conflicts, 46–8, 79, 96–7, 124–5, 126, 128, 132, 135–6, 136–49, 167, 176, 207
Pont-à-Mousson, 49
Pont-de-Somme-Vesle, 104, 105
Popular societies, political clubs, 98, 99, 101, 124, 137, 138, 142, 147, 153, 159, 176; *see also* Jacobins, soldiers' committees
Pouilly (officer of fortune in Vexin Infantry), 114
Professionalism: of soldiers, 8, 9, 19, 111, 180, 183, 187, 190, 205; of officers, 21, 24, 26, 29, 103, 120, 168–70, 190–5, 199, 201, 203–4, 205, 208, 213–15
Promotion, 8–9, 21, 25, 29, 56, 112, 120, 151, 153–4, 157, 158, 160, 161, 180–1, 184, 191, 194, 195, 199, 200–01, 202, 209